D0209174

Praise for the book
Women Who Were Sexually Abused as Children

"In this deeply compassionate, timely, and immensely practical text, Teresa Gil explores adulthood experiences of mothering by women sexually abused as children, drawing on interviews, clinical experiences, and research to document vulnerabilities. More important, she identifies resiliency resources and ways to nurture these within and outside clinical settings, permitting women to care for themselves and their children in transformative ways. Informative for clinicians and accessible for the public, Gil's book should be read widely as a guide for recognizing the harms of this too common adversity, appreciating the healing power of our enduring capacity to love, and acting on policies for prevention."
>—**Ester R. Shapiro, associate professor, Department of Psychology, University of Massachusetts, Boston**

"I've been wanting to read this book for my entire career: now it is finally available. I recommend it for mothers but also therapists, healthcare workers, people who work in social service systems that serve families, and families of those who have survived sexual abuse as children. It radiates hope."
>—**Leslie Ann Costello, PhD, founder, WomanCare Psychological Services, Fredericton, New Brunswick, Canada**

"It's clear from her new book that Teresa Gil is on a very important mission: how to help mothers who were sexually abused as children rise above their painful past so that they and their children can go on to lead meaningful and productive lives. Through her many years of experience treating mothers who were sexually abused as children, Teresa has grown keenly aware of their resilience and courage, and the human capacity to grow stronger in the face of adversity."
>—**Mark Katz, author of *Children Who Fail at School but Succeed at Life* and *On Playing a Poor Hand Well***

"In this era of heightened awareness of sexual abuse against women, one group of women has up to now received too little attention. Psychotherapist Teresa Gil redresses this in her important book, which focuses on women who were sexually abused as children and then went on to become mothers. After twenty-five years as a clinical psychotherapist working with such women, she lifts the veil of silence and shame that kept them isolated and alone. By telling their stories, highlighting their struggles, and examining the factors that support resiliency in them and emotional health in their children, her book offers hope and practical help for these women, their family and friends who act as allies, and professionals in the field who work with this group of mothers and their children."

—Sally Wendkos Olds, award-winning author

"Gil has written a book that breaks the silence endured by many mothers who are also survivors of sexual abuse, normalizes their experiences, offers the potential of healing their shame, and provides a sense of hope for the future. With heartfelt compassion and clarity, Dr. Gil brilliantly combines theory and practical information for therapists with interviews and stories that clients can learn from and/or relate to their own life situations."

—Hope Langner, director of coach training, CTI

"Gil's book is the first to look specifically at the effects of childhood sexual abuse on mothering. The challenges that arise at different stages of development, single-parenting, learning new skills to make mothering easier, developing support systems—especially when families are not supportive, and preventing another generation of abused children are all addressed in this important and timely book."

—Mia Morosoff, LCSW

"For practitioners and survivors, this book brings awareness to the often unrecognized effects that sexual abuse survivors may experience when mothering. The narratives demonstrate the broad spectrum of reactions and normalize these experiences for survivors. However, the book also highlights the mind-body connections and the ways to foster resiliencies to help women heal. This is a must-read for every mothering survivor and every clinician who works with these women."

**—Nicole Arduini-Van Hoose, MEd, LMHC, assistant professor,
Hudson Valley Community College**

"In her writing, Gil unravels the pain and fear of women victimized by childhood sexual assault. While powerful stories of trauma serve as the backdrop, it is the process of healing and breaking the silence of abuse that resonates throughout the book, highlighting the protective factors that promote resiliency and serve to stop the cycle of intergenerational abuse. The book brings to light the struggles and challenges of women striving to take back their agency, coming to terms with the potential long lasting implications of abuse. It is an insightful read for anyone affected by the trauma of assault as well as for practitioners in their efforts to support women."

—Todd M. Wysocki, PhD, Reframing Leadership Consulting

WOMEN WHO WERE SEXUALLY ABUSED AS CHILDREN

Mothering, Resilience, and Protecting the Next Generation

Teresa Gil

ROWMAN & LITTLEFIELD
Lanham • Boulder • New York • London

Published by Rowman & Littlefield
An imprint of The Rowman & Littlefield Publishing Group, Inc.
4501 Forbes Boulevard, Suite 200, Lanham, Maryland 20706
https://rowman.com

Unit A, Whitacre Mews, 26-34 Stannary Street, London SE11 4AB,
United Kingdom

British Library Cataloguing in Publication Information Available

Library of Congress Cataloging-in-Publication Data
Names: Gil, Teresa, 1958– author.
Title: Women who were sexually abused as children : mothering, resilience,
    and protecting the next generation / Teresa Gil.
Description: Lanham : Rowman & Littlefield, [2018] | Includes bibliographical
    references and index.
Identifiers: LCCN 2018008429 (print) | LCCN 2018009438 (ebook) | ISBN
    9781538101780 (electronic) | ISBN 9781538101773 (cloth : alk. paper)
Subjects: LCSH: Adult child sexual abuse victims. | Sexually abused girls. |
    Motherhood. | Child sexual abuse—Prevention.
Classification: LCC RC569.5.A28 (ebook) | LCC RC569.5.A28 G55 2018
    (print) | DDC 616.85/8369—dc23
LC record available at https://lccn.loc.gov/2018008429

∞ ™ The paper used in this publication meets the minimum requirements of
American National Standard for Information Sciences Permanence of Paper
for Printed Library Materials, ANSI/NISO Z39.48-1992.

Printed in the United States of America

This book is dedicated to my mother and father, Hannah Mabel Egan and Joseph Gaetano Gil, who came to this country as immigrants and fostered resiliency in their nine children by offering limitless love, encouragement, and unwavering support.

CONTENTS

Acknowledgments   xi

Introduction   1

1   Defining Child Sexual Abuse and the Factors that Impact Resiliency and Recovery   5

2   The Long-Term Impact of Child Sexual Abuse   21

3   Transcending Adversity and Overcoming Abuse: Risk Factors, Protective Factors, and Resiliency   49

4   Mothering: Challenges and Risks   71

5   Mothering: Sustaining Resiliency   93

6   The Therapeutic Relationship and Its Importance to Resiliency and Healing   113

7   A Legacy of Trauma: Mechanisms for Intergenerational Abuse   133

8   Implications for Treatment and Policy: Strengthening Resiliency   159

Notes   183

Bibliography   195

Index   201

About the Author   205

ACKNOWLEDGMENTS

I want to thank my life partner, Rolf Haerem, for supporting me in all my educational, professional, and personal pursuits and interests. He has been patient and loyal, without complaint (most of the time), willingly offering consistent encouragement and commitment. I would like to acknowledge and offer my gratitude and deep thanks to Mia Morosoff. She is both brilliant and generous, and has been a reliable and dependable friend and colleague throughout this process. I want to offer my appreciation to James LaBate for his assistance and steady encouragement, and to extend my gratitude to Suzanne Staszak-Silva for her invaluable guidance and expertise in all phases of the book. I also want to give thanks to Abbi Coffin, and special recognition to William Cook for his time, advice, and direction.

I offer my deep gratitude to the women who participated in the interviews. They were willing to discuss the difficulties and triumphs they have experienced in their mothering so that their stories may help others.

I thank my colleagues at Hudson Valley Community College (HVCC) for their friendship, humor, and encouragement. It is also with deep appreciation that I mention HVCC administrators who offered me a sabbatical and the resources to continue my academic and professional interests.

INTRODUCTION

During casual conversations with my hairdresser, doctor, and people I meet at social gatherings, invariably I am asked what I do for a living. I say that I am a therapist and that I work with women who have been abused as children. The answer always provokes a pause, then a drastic change in mood. Even among colleagues in the counseling field, my answer induces a comment along the lines of "What a difficult group of clients to work with!" or a question about how I am able to "cope with that difficult population." On the contrary, I find working with women who have been victims of abuse, and primarily sexual abuse, to be both humbling and rewarding.

Indeed, their stories are filled with physical acts of abuse forced upon vulnerable children, and therapy sessions are spent untangling the psychological and emotional violence and manipulation they have endured. Yet I will always remain awed by my clients' abilities to maintain a sense of humor and to be compassionate and caring toward others while they courageously grapple with the difficult and painful issues that arise in the therapeutic process. Working with women who have experienced child sexual abuse has its challenges, but their tenacity and strength as they face their past wounds and present challenges, their desire to change, and their hope for a better life for themselves and their children impress and inspire me.

This book unravels the veil of silence and captures the experiences of mothers who were sexually abused as children. The first step in both supporting mothers and disrupting the cycle of intergenerational abuse is to break the silence that keeps these mothers isolated and alone in their mothering challenges and successes. The experiences of mothering for this group of women need to be told in order to promote and encourage discourse. This book represents my commitment to making a contribution and to facilitating change for this large but poorly understood and disenfranchised group. I hope to cast a light on the therapeutic needs, concerns, and struggles of mothers who have survived childhood sexual abuse, and to provide direction for the professionals who support these remarkable women.

To begin, in chapter 1, I present the definition of child sexual abuse, including both covert and overt behaviors that constitute abuse, and explore the characteristics of abuse and the experiences that promote resiliency and recovery. Chapter 2 details the long-term effects of abuse, including mental health issues such as depression, anxiety, eating disorders, feelings of low self-worth, and a sense of being damaged. Some survivors may use drugs and alcohol as a form of self-medication in order to endure and manage their emotional pain and recurring memories. Chapter 3 explores the concepts of risk factors, protective factors, and resiliency in childhood. Chapter 4 examines the challenges and risks mothers who experienced child sexual abuse (CSA) struggle with as they try to love and care for their own children.

Chapter 5 more closely explores the protective factors in mothers' lives that support resiliency and their capacity to mother their children in healthy and appropriate ways. Chapter 6 delves into the importance of the therapeutic relationship in healing the effects of child sexual abuse, while simultaneously offering mothers a model for their mothering. Chapter 7 examines the dynamics that facilitate the intergenerational transmission of abuse and the revictimization of abuse in many aspects of a survivor's life. Chapter 8 examines the protective factors for this population and discusses the significance of incorporating these factors into one's life and/or therapy practice, in order to support resiliency in the lives of mothers and their children. I include a discussion of the importance of employing alternative mind/body therapies, and recommend public policies to address the obstacles that interfere with and undermine a mother's ability to care for her children.

Women Who Were Sexually Abused as Children: Mothering, Resilience, and Protecting the Next Generation presents interviews with brave women who were generous enough to participate in my study and to share their stories. It also synthesizes the related scholarly literature, and includes my twenty-five years of experience as a psychotherapist working with women survivors of child sexual abuse. In order to protect the identities of the mothers, names and identifying information have been changed; however, their struggles and concerns are real, and the case studies are composites of interviews with the mothers who experienced child sexual abuse, and my therapy practice.

Researchers have examined the long-term consequences of childhood sexual abuse on the survivor's physiological, psychological, and social functioning. In contrast, there is less information on how the ramifications of child sexual abuse may impact the survivor in mothering her own children. In order to gain an understanding into the subjective experiences of this vulnerable population, I conducted a qualitative study. Interviews were the primary method used to collect in-depth information into the shared mothering experiences of this group. The women I interviewed have self-identified as experiencing childhood sexual abuse, and are parenting, or have parented, children. Interviewing mothers who are presently parenting children provided information on the present challenges these women are dealing with. However, interviewing women who have grown children provided information that was insightful and thoughtful as they recollected their past mothering experiences.

A qualitative study utilizing interviews was used as a means to gain an understanding of the dynamics and complex effects that childhood sexual abuse may have on later adult mothering. Interviews allowed for an in-depth exploration of mothers' thoughts, ideas, feelings, and experiences and gave them the ability to frame the salient issues relevant to their mothering and early experiences of abuse. This method of inquiry offers insight into these women's subjective experiences on a sensitive and clinically relevant topic. The literature on CSA survivors and their mothering and the interviews with mothers have been woven throughout the experiences that my clients discuss in our sessions.

This book provides a voice to a special group of mothers who, up to this point, have gone unheard. It is important to know what helps individuals to survive negative life experiences; these are the protective factors that we can all include in our lives and promote in the lives of our loved ones. Professionals working with individuals and families can foster protective factors in the lives of their vulnerable clients to buffer trauma and support resiliency, ensuring that those at risk can move forward, build competency, and live more fulfilling lives.

The book is also written for these mothers who have experienced child sexual abuse and offers them the opportunity to break their silence, share their struggles, and give voice to their experiences, pains, and triumphs. Just as important as expressing the pain and struggles of one's past and present experiences is learning what helped mothers with histories of abuse to cope with and, eventually, overcome obstacles. Breaking the silence, ending the fear and shame that exists for many survivors, and building hope starts with telling one's story. By sharing common experiences, women can begin to transform shame into pride, and silence into strength.

I

DEFINING CHILD SEXUAL ABUSE AND THE FACTORS THAT IMPACT RESILIENCY AND RECOVERY

In my psychotherapy practice, I work with adult women recovering from child sexual abuse (CSA). Many of these women are mothers seeking therapy out of a desire to protect their children from the abuses they themselves have experienced. My clients describe having difficulties caring for and meeting the needs of their children, and although they want to mother in more loving and appropriate ways, they express feelings of inadequacy in their mothering. They speak of an inability to feel spontaneous, to laugh and play, and to show affection to their children, and they grieve that their past experiences are impacting their ability to be effective mothers.

I also work with women who have made a conscious decision not to become mothers. Even though many of these women have stated that they love children, they have vowed not to have any. They say they do not believe they are emotionally capable of being "a good mother," and that having a child would be a selfish act. They speak of being terrified of "messing up" or "screwing up" their children, and are fearful of passing down their pain to the next generation. They do not want to bring children into the world only to have them experience the same hurts they experienced when young. Finally, they express the fear that they may not be able to protect their children from abuse or keep them safe. This group of women mourn not having children and deeply feel the loss of not having a mothering experience during their lifetime. To reconcile these feelings and find contentment, some of these women develop close relationships with their nieces and nephews, become Big Sisters, and/or support their friends in their mothering.

My clients chose to go to therapy because they were struggling from the consequences and symptoms associated with the long-term impact of abuse. They believed that their past had followed them into their current lives and was negatively impacting their ability to function in their families, friendships, and work environments. The women wanted to break negative behaviors, thought patterns, and defenses that at one time had helped them to manage the dysfunction and violence they experienced as children but no longer worked for them as adults. Clients stated they felt the existence of emotional barriers that reduced their capacity to be loved and to express love in healthy ways. They felt overwhelmed and did not know how to set healthy boundaries, seeing themselves vacillating between being overly rigid and/or overly permissive with others. Even more important, they did not know how to protect themselves or their children. Some women talked about feeling numb or "zombie-like." Many felt they were minimally functioning, and struggled with fulfilling their own basic needs for food, clothing, and shelter. Some women expressed feeling dead inside and unable to feel joy, to laugh or smile, or to feel positive for long enough to penetrate their numbed existence and to give life meaning.

For a child, feeling numb is a defense, used to cope with dysfunctional dynamics at home. Going emotionally numb helps to screen out the yelling, hurtful comments, scenes of domestic violence, and abuse and/or manage the experiences associated with poverty. Yet, for an adult, continuing to use defense mechanisms such as numbness, denial, and dissociation is unhealthy and interferes with day-to-day functioning.

On the first night of one sexual abuse survivors' group, a woman said that her goal for therapy was to "feel something—to feel anything." She did not care if it was sadness or fear or anger; she just wanted to feel. She was tired of her numbness, which she felt separated her from others and from the world. One mother in the group said her numbed state was impacting her ability to care for her children. She was unable to play, laugh, join in games, and be spontaneous, or to hug and kiss her children without images of her own abuse coming to the surface.

Nora's Story

Similarly, another mother, Nora, said that she went through horrific abuse in childhood but was somehow able to suppress her memories long enough to make it to adulthood, find a husband with whom to share her life, and have children. Now, after all these years, the memories of her child abuse were surfacing as she mothered her children. She was terrified and angry. While bathing or changing her children's diapers, she would reexperience distressing and traumatic events from her past abuse. To manage the surfacing memories and keep the flashbacks at bay, she shut down and began acting and mothering in a mechanical manner. As a result, she was unable to be spontaneous and loving.

Nora was able to feed her children, make sure they did their homework, clean their clothes, and provide for their physical needs and wants. She was, however, unable to attend to their emotional needs. Nora understood and appreciated the fact that she was able to provide her children with much more than she had ever had as a child, but she also wanted to feel emotionally connected to them. She wanted to play with her children and to cuddle on the couch while watching television or reading them stories. She stated that she "yearns" for a nurturing connection with her children, while her emotional inability to have those experiences left her feeling "trapped and tied." It is interesting to note that as treatment continued, Nora revealed that part of her experience of sexual abuse consisted of being "trapped and tied." It makes sense that it would be the metaphor that she uses to describe her experiences of mothering.

Nora literally and figuratively wanted to be freed from her past. In therapy, Nora repeatedly commented about being angry that she is in therapy and is forced to deal with her childhood experiences. She had worked hard to make her life look different from her life as a child, and she wanted to leave her past behind her. The external possessions in Nora's adult life are very different from her childhood. She has a home in a middle-class neighborhood, a car, a college education, a good job, and a loving husband. Her education, clothing, job, and possessions are the symbols she used to prove to herself and to the world that she was functioning well, a testimony that she had left behind the traumas of her childhood and created something better for herself and her children. What Nora had not acquired was the opportunity to do the emotional work to heal her past. She had worked arduously to afford the external trimmings of a middle-class life which she felt helped hide from others her internal struggles and acted as a shield to protect her from her past. However, status and possessions were not able to heal her inability to feel or to offer any sustained pleasure or happiness in her life.

Nora was angry that she had to go through the experiences of abuse twice—once in childhood, and then, having to revisit it again in therapy. She said that her perpetrator "never had to suffer." Still, Nora recognized that she needed to look back in order to "free and untie" herself from the past. She wanted more for herself and her children, and she was willing to claim her past so that she could move forward emotionally.

As a therapist, I asked myself the question: "What helps some mothers to be so courageous that they are willing to enter therapy and revisit their painful childhoods in order to mother their children in loving ways?" I was impressed with the strength of character my clients exhibited, and saw their desire to create a more meaningful mother–child relationship as the ultimate exemplar and testimony of a mother's love and resiliency.

This book examines the short- and long-term negative impacts of early sexual abuse on a woman's mothering experiences, but more importantly, it explores the protective factors in these women's lives that helped them to overcome the traumas of the past.

How do these women define good mothering? What are the models they use for good mothering? What experiences promoted their positive mothering capacities? What has enabled them to forge ahead through the healing process, despite the hardships, surfacing memories, thoughts of suicide, and fears of relapsing back to alcohol and drug abuse?

It is important to identify what are known as "protective factors" that help individuals to survive negative life experiences. Once identified, protective factors can be included in our own lives and the lives of the people for whom we care. Professionals working with vulnerable individuals and families can foster protective factors, and in doing so, can buffer trauma, support resiliency, and help to ensure that those at risk will be able to move forward and engage in satisfying lives.

Too often, books and articles about survivors of abuse focus on the negative consequences survivors experience because of their early trauma. The long list of consequences includes problems with alcohol and drug abuse, depression, anxiety, low self-esteem, difficulty maintaining close and intimate relationships, post-traumatic stress disorder, and eating disorders, including anorexia, bulimia, and compulsive overeating. While it is critical that women give voice to their negative experiences and the consequences of their child sexual abuse, it is equally important to pay attention to the factors that have helped these children (now grown women and mothers) overcome their traumatic pasts and strive toward developing self-acceptance, creating healthy relationships with others, and living more fully.

Therapy offers a safe place for mothers who have experienced CSA to explore obstacles they face in mothering and examine the protective factors that support their resilient capacities. Protective factors strengthen a mother's ability to break the intergenerational cycle of abuse and offer her children something significantly different from what she has experienced in her own childhood. By discovering the specific factors that both interfere with and promote mothering capacities in women who experienced child sexual abuse, and identifying the factors that help to protect or shield them from negative experiences, helping professionals and mothers who have experienced child sexual abuse will be in a stronger position to bolster resiliency.

DEFINITION OF SEXUAL ABUSE

Therapists, doctors, and lawyers all use different definitions of child sexual abuse. Therapists who have direct contact with clients use a definition of CSA that includes both overt and covert categories of sexual abuse. Overt abuse is blatant and obvious, and it includes physical contact such as sexualized kissing, touching, fondling, and rape. Covert abuse is more hidden and veiled but has similar psychological and emotional impacts. Covert abuse includes exhibitionism, sexual staring and sexually intrusive commenting about a young child's body and physical appearance, and watching sexually explicit movies or reading sexually explicit magazines with a child.[1]

In therapy, the therapist and the survivor need to address the hurts that have arisen in both overt and covert abuses. Using a broader definition allows the therapist to work with survivors on the wider range of therapeutic issues that many sexual abuse survivors contend with in therapy. Thus, therapists use a definition of CSA which includes both contact and non-contact sexual experiences in which the victim is younger than eighteen and the perpetrator is older than the victim, and/or is sexually more sophisticated. More often than not the perpetrator knows the victim, is in a position of authority or in a caretaker role, and uses the power inherent in his or her role to coerce and manipulate.[2]

The legal system uses a narrow definition of sexual abuse that focuses primarily on overt sexual abuse—physically explicit sexual contact. The much narrower definition used by the legal system is intended to name the behaviors that are considered clearly illegal in order to effectively convict and punish perpetrators. Narrow definitions of abuse are confined to overt physical sexual abuse and ignore the emotional and psychological consequences of covert sexual abuse.

Broad definitions of CSA increase the perceived rates of abuse, while narrower definitions decrease the rates. The most common statistic used to indicate prevalence is that approximately one out of four girls, or 25 percent of all women, have had at least one CSA experience before the age of eighteen.[3] According to the US Census Bureau, more than eighty-five million mothers reside in the United States.[4] If we use the most common statistic regarding sexual abuse rates nationally—one in four—then approximately twenty-one million mothers in the United States have been sexually abused.

Madison's Story

As a therapist, I deal with the emotional and social/relational aspects of my clients' lives, so we discuss both overt and covert sexual abuse in counseling sessions, as both have devastating and long-lasting emotional impacts.

As a child, Madison did not experience overt sexual abuse. However, she did experience covert abuse, which caused intense and chronic psychological and emotional pain that negatively impacted her sense of self-worth and her ability to feel safe in the world. Madison grew up with her father and two brothers, who continually commented on her physical appearance and maturing body. When she walked through the house, it was common for them to make fun of the small size of her breasts, to comment on how her buttocks swayed when she walked, and to taunt her by telling her she was fat and that no man would be attracted to her. Her father and brothers would routinely walk into her room while she was dressing and into the bathroom while she was taking a shower. The constant barrage of comments about her body and intrusive entries into her bedroom and bathroom invaded Madison's privacy and made her feel unsafe in her home. She avoided being at home in the evenings and she kept her bedroom door locked.

The constant derogatory remarks made Madison feel ugly and unworthy, which led to her being unable to set limits and defend herself against abuse by others outside the family. In Madison's world, to be noticed was dangerous and made one a target for verbal abuse and ridicule, so Madison worked hard at being unseen in and outside her home. Her belief manifested in the way she presented her physical self to the world. She was overweight, she wore oversize clothes to hide her body, and she kept her head and shoulders down when she walked. She said her main goal was to get safely from one place to the next, and she felt that being as invisible as possible was the way to accomplish this.

Over time, Madison was able to verbalize that even though her abuse was never physical, she always lived in fear of being raped. The fear of a possible event creates a physiological and psychological stress response in the body. This stress response can impact brain chemistry, immune function, and overall health. The fear of what could happen added to Madison's sense of vulnerability at home and had both immediate and long-term consequences on her emotional and physical well-being. The impact of chronic fear and stress on the body will be explored in more depth in chapter 8.

THE IMPACT OF CHILD SEXUAL ABUSE

Early traumatic events in the lives of children can take a tremendous toll on their current and long-term mental and physical health. However, responses to traumatic events vary from person to person. Although the effects are often incapacitating, not all trauma survivors experience long-term negative outcomes that impair their ability to function well.

Trauma does not necessarily cause the emergence of adverse effects. Some people who experience trauma are able to function fairly well. Child sexual abuse, in particular, can have devastating consequences on its victims, but not all survivors will develop the symptoms associated with abuse. Why do some sexual abuse victims suffer from long-term consequences and others do not? To answer this question, it is important to identify the factors that act as buffers or protectors from the adverse effects of child sexual abuse.

Whether or not a child will develop negative long-term consequences of sexual abuse depends on a number of factors. These include the age of the child when the abuse started, the frequency and severity of the abuse, her relationship to the perpetrator, and the adults' reactions to the child's disclosure of the abuse.[5] Critical to understanding the impact of the abuse on the victim is learning how the adults in the child's life managed and responded to the child's divulgence of the abuse. Each of these factors is addressed below.

Age of Child

The age when the trauma occurred is important, because children who experience trauma in their younger years seem to be more vulnerable. I have found that the younger a child is at the time of the abuse, the more likely she will blame herself for it. Young children are not able to separate the abuse experience from their self-identity. My clients who were abused under the age of seven had internalized the blame and had not been able to separate the abuse experience from their sense of who they are; that is, "What happened to me is bad; therefore, I am bad." This reaction of internalized blame remained with them until adulthood. They blame themselves for the abuse and express deep and ingrained feelings of inferiority, believing they were "dirty" and "different" from other people.

On the other hand, clients who were older when the abuse occurred seem to have been able to externalize the abuse, to separate the abuse from their self-identity. They were able to attribute the blame to the perpetrator rather than to themselves. Thus, the child understood that the perpetrator was bad and they were not. This distinction is critical: Internal versus external attribution of blame is a major variable in the resiliency of sexual abuse survivors. Women who blame themselves for the abuse had more debilitating symptoms that interfered with their recovery process.[6] Women who are capable of externalizing blame to the perpetrator are found to have better coping skills and fewer psychological and emotional symptoms than survivors who internalized blame and held themselves responsible for the abuse.[7]

I found that the women who were abused before the age of seven spent a longer time in therapy and had more difficulty with self-soothing. They had a deep intrinsic sense of being bad that was difficult to shift. I remember one client saying that she intellectually knew she had been just a little girl at the time of the abuse, and that it was not her fault. She was even able to feel empathy for others who were abused as children, and she was aware that the other women in the group were not to blame, for they had been children, too, and their abuse was not their fault. However, she was not able to afford that same compassion to herself. She felt deeply ashamed and believed that her "inner badness" had caused the abuser to choose her.

The child victim of sexual abuse is not developmentally able to comprehend or emotionally manage the sexual experiences imposed on her. Developmentally inappropriate activity can harm the victim by distorting the cognitive schemas associated with sex. Many survivors may reenact their abuse by displaying sexual aggressiveness toward peers, and/or may act out by being sexually promiscuous. Children who have experienced premature sex may reenact their traumatic experience/s, which may place them at danger for additional revictimization.[8]

Frequency and Severity

The length of time during which the abuse occurred also plays a role in the consequences of CSA. A single occurrence often does not have the same impact as abuse that occurs over a period of time. It is not surprising that abuse that lasted several years might have a more profound effect than abuse that was a one-time occurrence. Similarly, if the abuse was violent, it generally has a more devastating impact than abuse that did not include violence. Many professionals in the field try to assess the severity of the abuse and the use of force and aggression in order to understand the impact of the sexual abuse on the child. However, child sexual abuse does not always have visible signs, such as bruises or bleeding. Instead, CSA is often hidden, and takes its toll on the psychological and emotional aspects of a child's well-being.

Although there is merit to analyzing frequency and severity as a way of understanding the short- and long-term impacts of abuse on the child, it is important to view the act from a child's perspective. Roland Summit states the child victim is expected to "forcibly resist, to cry for help, and to attempt to escape the intrusion. By that standard, almost every child fails. The normal reaction is to 'play possum'; that is, to feign sleep, to shift position, and to pull up the covers. Small creatures simply do not call on force to deal with overwhelming threat. When there is no place to run, they have no choice but to try and hide. Children generally learn to cope silently with terrors in the night."[9] That the perpetrator is often known to the child and has created a positive and trusting alliance only adds to the child's degree of psychological and emotional betrayal, manipulation, and exploitation.

Many abusers conveniently claim that the lack of resistance from the child is a sign of consenting to the abuse. Perpetrators will say the sexual contact was not abusive because there were no visible physical signs associated with the abuse, such as bruising or bleeding. However, not all abuse victims experience physical signs of abuse, and the symptoms for many children are emotional and psychological; these include anxiety, depression, aggressive behaviors, problems with sleeping, and nightmares. It is not unusual for perpetrators to defend their actions and deny that they exploited or were hurtful to the child. In Nora's experience, for example, her perpetrator claimed that he loved and cared for her and that she enjoyed the experiences, as evidenced by the fact that she did not ask him to stop.

Relationship to the Perpetrator

Another key factor in assessing the impact of abuse is the relationship between the perpetrator and the child. Child sexual abuse changes a child's view of the world. Children's experiences of early sexualization usually lead to feelings of having been betrayed by the people who were supposed to care for and protect them; whether the perpetrator is a parent, stepparent, grandparent, uncle, sibling, neighbor, teacher, or stranger affects the degree of betrayal a child experiences. At the core of the trauma is the subsequent lack of trust that victims have in those around them.[10]

Women who report physical force during their abuse and whose perpetrator is a family member experience greater mental health concerns, including depression, anxiety, and sleep problems. They are also more likely to be revictimized in adolescence and adulthood than those women whose perpetrators were not family members, and when the abuse did not involve physical force.[11]

In the field, it is generally acknowledged that if the child has a close relationship to the perpetrator, such as a family member, the possibility of the child revealing the abuse is significantly decreased. The degree of closeness is also relevant to the severity of effects on the child, because when a close and trusted relationship is violated, the degree of betrayal and confusion is increased. It is also important to look at what the perpetrator said to the child to compel her to keep the "secret." Sometimes the perpetrator threatens the child's physical safety or threatens to hurt someone or something that is important to the child. One client said her stepfather threatened to hurt her cat, frequently holding the animal over the hot woodstove and threatening to kill it by throwing it in the fire. Another perpetrator told my client that if she revealed the abuse, he would be taken away to jail, her mother would be alone with no money, and the family would be homeless. In order to keep herself and/or her loved ones safe, my client was forced to endure subsequent sexual encounters.

During one group session, Indigo told the other women that she was confused by the sexual abuse she experienced by her stepfather. Unlike the other members of the group, she did not fight the abuse or hate her abuser, even later in her life. She went on to explain how when she was young she received very little emotionally, and barely had enough food and other possessions, like clothes and toys. Her mother was uninvolved, and she never knew her father, who left before she was born. When Indigo was six, her mother married and she felt her life changed for the better. Her stepfather made her breakfast in the morning and packed her school lunches. He took her to buy clothes and toys. When she wanted to learn to play an instrument, he rented her a violin so she could participate in the school orchestra. He paid for her school trips, bought her school pictures, took her for car rides, and spent time with her. He was the only one who showed her kindness, and she would have been alone and isolated without him. The stepfather made her feel special and important. When asked what helped her survive her childhood experiences, Indigo surprised the other women in the group when she answered, "My stepfather, Jack."

It is important to remember that, no matter what the circumstances, the child is never responsible for the abuse. Child sexual abuse is wrong because it is a sexual act that is imposed on a child who lacks the emotional and intellectual maturity to give "informed" consent.

Sophia's Story

Sophia's abuser was her grandfather. She expressed how she enjoyed going to her grandparents' house because she was doted on and given a lot of attention. No rules existed at her grandparents' house: She could watch what she wanted on television, eat goodies, and get breakfast served in bed. She also loved when her grandparents came to visit her house. Grandpa knew all kinds of magic tricks and could pull money from the back of her head and make coins disappear with a snap of his fingers. However, during one overnight visit at her grandparents' house, her grandfather came into her bed and molested her. It lasted for hours. She remembered turning her body and closing her legs tight to stop him. She remembered thinking about her grandmother and wondering where she was and why she was not protecting her.

The next morning, when Sophia awoke, she had difficulty eating breakfast, making eye contact, and talking with her grandmother and grandfather. Visiting her grandparents used to give her joy, but she never returned to their home after the experience. She said she felt that a part of her had died. When she returned home, everything felt strange, and the stability of her world as she once knew it was shaken. Everything she thought she knew was turned upside down. Sophia wondered whether her grandfather had done those things to her mother (his daughter) when she was younger; and if he had molested her mother when she was a little girl, then why did her mother let her stay overnight at his house? If Grandpa did not molest her mother when she was younger, than why did he pick Sophia now? Was something the matter with her?

Additionally, Sophia wondered whether all men were abusers, and began to avoid her father. Sophia was able to state that, although she had been able to survive her grandfather's abuse, she still maintained distance from her father because she was fearful that he might also hurt her. She felt that the distance and wall she created between her and her father kept her from discovering whether or not he would also abuse her. She told me that if her father had molested her, she "would have died, inside and out." As Sophia's experience illustrates, a child's world changes after abuse. It can create a pattern of withdrawing and isolating from family and friends and from experiencing and exploring the world. As a form of protection, survivors may become defensive and suspicious when others attempt closeness. It makes sense when CSA survivors state that they have difficulty creating and sustaining long-term healthy relationships.

Reactions to the Child's Disclosure of the Abuse

The amount of protection and support that a child receives after disclosure of the abuse is the fourth critical factor in the short- and long-term impacts of CSA. Generally, the less protection a child receives after disclosure of the abuse, the greater the risk of long-term problems. In dysfunctional families, the victim may be blamed for instigating the abuse and/or may be recast as the "perpetrator," for telling the secret and exposing the true perpetrator to punishment. Under these conditions, the act of disclosing the abuse brings the child more fear and betrayal. If Child Protective Services (CPS) becomes involved and removes the child from the home, in unhealthy families, the child may be blamed both for revealing the sexual abuse and for the subsequent disruption of the family.

When Naomi revealed to her mother that her father was abusing her, her mother immediately called the police and CPS. The subsequent arrest of her father made the local news and was featured on television and in the newspapers. As a result, the community isolated Naomi and condemned her. She lost her friends and was ostracized by her classmates at school. She was no longer invited to parties and she was harassed on the school bus. Her peers called her "whore" and "slut," and her teachers and the school administration did nothing to stop the bullying. Eventually, her family moved out of the area and Naomi changed schools. Children do not have the emotional or intellectual capacity to understand or articulate the dynamics of their experi-

ences, and when disclosing the secret makes life worse, children become even more traumatized and vulnerable.

Sometimes, a victim's mother will choose the perpetrator over the
child. I worked with one woman, Angela, who told her mother that her
stepfather, John, was making her "touch his penis until it peed." At first,
her mother protected her and asked the stepfather to leave the house,
and Angela felt safe for the first time in many years. However, within a
few months, Angela's mother was talking to John on the phone, and
then she started meeting him for lunch, and then dinner. Eventually, he
was allowed back into the house. Angela was told that what happened
was her fault, and she needed to stay away from John and not "flirt"
with him. Angela tried to stay away from her stepfather, and she with-
drew from her mother. It was apparent to Angela that she could not
turn to her mother, and she had no one else to go to for protection. At
the same time, it was clear to John that he could continue to abuse
Angela without consequence, and he did.

When the people who are supposed to protect a child fail to do so
and the child is abandoned when she asks for help, it intensifies the
effects of the abuse experiences, deepens the shame, and increases
feelings of alienation, aloneness, and abandonment. The impact of trauma can be diminished when the child has a secure attachment to a
caring adult. Robin Karr-Morse and Meredith Wiley assert that "Just
one key relationship—just one person who is available to the child over
time, who sees the baby as valuable, and who communicates that feeling—can make all the difference in how later stress or trauma affects
that child's future."[12] A non-offending caregiver who is loving, kind, and
supportive is a valuable element in a child's recovery. A parent or caregiver who is understanding and compassionate after the abuse is exposed is a significant factor in a child's ability to avoid the negative
impact of the abuse. Not only will the child avoid compounding negative consequences from revealing the abuse, but a compassionate and
protective response from a supportive adult will greatly assist in the
child's recovery, and encourage resiliency.

CONCLUSION

Every trauma is a story that informs us of the human condition. These stories teach us about our fragility, the impact our behaviors have on others, and the importance of how we treat one another. Abuse in any form diminishes a person's self-worth and the capacity to function in healthy and well-adjusted ways. Many of my clients sought treatment during young adulthood, in their twenties and early thirties. Some of the common developmental tasks of this stage are child rearing, career development, and creating intimate relationships. However, a woman's childhood experiences of abuse can complicate and interfere with the successful completion of these tasks.

These stories exemplify how childhood experiences impact current functioning, and the importance of working through the pain of childhood abuse so that early experiences no longer chain survivors to their past, and they can be free to move forward in creating a better life.

The remainder of the book will look more specifically at how mothers who were victims of child sexual abuse have wrestled with overcoming their childhood experiences and continue to strive to mother their children in healthier and more fulfilling ways.

2

THE LONG-TERM IMPACT OF CHILD SEXUAL ABUSE

Child sexual abuse can take a tremendous toll on the mental and physical health of girls and women, negatively impacting their ability to function in many areas of their lives. Developmentally inappropriate sexual activity can harmfully distort the victim's view of herself and of others. Intrinsic in the act of sexual abuse is both physical and psychological coercion; this coercion occurs "when a child's territory and body space are repeatedly invaded against a child's will."[1] *Complex trauma* is a term used to describe a child's enduring exposure to chronic interpersonal and repetitive abuse and neglect. Many of the symptoms of complex trauma lead to a sense of powerlessness, despair, and turmoil within the victim. Shame, isolation, low self-esteem, depression, post-traumatic stress disorder, anxiety, eating disorders, substance use, borderline personality disorder, complicated grief, and self-harm are some of the long-range effects of CSA on later adult functioning.[2]

The child victim of sexual abuse is not developmentally able to comprehend or emotionally manage the sexual experiences being imposed on her. During the abuse phase, in order to psychologically survive the trauma, defense mechanisms such as denial, fantasy, dissociation, and repression are employed by children to manage their overwhelming feelings of betrayal and confusion.[3] Over long periods of time, these defenses are internalized by the victim and continue to be used as their primary means of maneuvering through difficult and challenging life experiences. Although the defense mechanisms are initially effective at managing the traumatic experiences, as an adult, when trauma is no longer imminent, the defenses and associated behaviors that were once helpful become dysfunctional and can severely hinder healthy functioning and relationships.

Clients have told me that while being abused they would dissociate, leave their bodies, and watch the abuse from the ceiling above. In this way, they were not participants in the abuse but observers of it. By dissociating and cutting off their feelings, victims can be cognitively aware but not directly experience the abuse. Clients have said that while dissociating, their numbed bodies did not experience the pain.

Other clients have reported that they fantasized during the abuse as a way of distracting themselves from the experience. One client said that while her brother molested her, she fantasized she was being tested to see if she was a "real princess." Another client shared that during the abuse, she rehearsed her lines from the school play and visualized herself onstage while the audience cheered her performance.

Another common and effective way that children deal with their trauma is to repress, or forget, all or some of the sexual abuse experience. In one severe case of repression, my client had no memories of the summers she spent with her uncle who sexually abused her from the ages of six to twelve years old. She did, however, have many memories of her home life during that period.

When I facilitate a sexual abuse survivors group, on the first night the group meets, the women introduce themselves and we review group rules. In addition, I ask the question, "How did the sexual abuse impact your life?" Participants are asked to brainstorm words that best describe how they believe the child sexual abuse has affected them. As group members throw out adjectives, I write them down on a chalkboard. The list is always quite long. The words they use to describe their internal experiences flow readily, and the exercise not only brings forth a host of personal insights into the negative ways that child sexual abuse has manifested in their adult lives, but also fosters the sharing of personal stories of pain and vulnerability. Group members begin to connect and bond with one another as they share the words that reflect the issues with which they struggle. For many clients, this is the first time they have had an opportunity to speak about and reveal long-held secrets while in an atmosphere of understanding and acceptance. Below is a list of words and phrases generated by group members that describes and captures the ways in which child sexual abuse has impacted their adult lives:

low self-esteem	unlovable
self-hatred	dirty
disgust	damaged goods
problems with closeness	inadequate
problems with intimacy	feeling imperfect
mistrustful	worry all the time
uncomfortable in their bodies	easily irritated
uncomfortable being visible	problems with setting limits
emotionally needy	unprotected
problems with boundaries	gullible
anxiety	naive
depression	people-pleaser
alcohol addiction	put others first
negative worldview	fearful of authority
drug addiction	intimidated easily
problems with managing anger	insignificant
think the worst of everyone	never feeling good enough
fearful	work hard
pessimistic	socially awkward
worthless	emotionally overreactive
undeserving	flashbacks

SHAME AND ISOLATION

When I was a student attending graduate school, and early on in my career, I was taught the theory and skills necessary for counselors to work with child sexual abuse survivors. I learned that many survivors deal with numerous psychological and emotional concerns, including feelings of low self-esteem, inadequacy, isolation, and shame. However, it was not until I started working with survivors as a therapist and listening to their stories that I was able to comprehend the depth of their pain and struggles. The therapeutic sessions between my clients and myself helped me to move from a theoretical understanding to an emotional appreciation of their challenges. Through the process of listening, I was able to gain a deeper understanding of how child sexual abuse manifests in the lives of survivors and contributes to their painful feelings of social inadequacy, shame, and low self-worth.

Sonja's Story

During one session, I asked my client Sonja the question, "When did you learn you were a survivor of sexual abuse?" She said, "As a little girl, I did not know that what my father was doing was called sexual abuse. I was only a little girl. I was only eight, and the concept of sexual abuse was beyond my intellectual capacity. However, there was an incident when I realized that what was occurring between my father and I was 'bad.' "

She went on to explain that when she was in third grade, she had a best friend named Annie Sullivan. One weekend, Sonja was invited to sleep at Annie's house. It was Sunday morning and Annie, Annie's mother, father, two brothers, and Sonja were gathered around the kitchen table to eat breakfast. Sonja had eaten Sunday breakfast at Annie's house before, and it was always a big event. The kitchen table was decorated with six matching place settings, a tablecloth, and flowers. The smell of brewed coffee mingled with the aroma of warm banana muffins fresh from the oven. Banana muffins were Sonja's favorite. She would cut the muffin in half and smear on butter that melted and seeped into the muffin. She would have her choice of bagels and cream cheese, French toast, or cereal. For Sonja, the smells in the kitchen and being gathered at the table with Annie's family for breakfast was a special occasion.

Sonja's father was a truck driver who was on the road for weeks at a time and rarely home. As she put it, "the road owned him." Sonja's half-sister was fourteen years older, had left home at eighteen, when Sonja was four, and had little contact with Sonja and her parents. As a result, Sonja did not have a relationship with her sister and did not feel close to her. Sonja's mother struggled with depression and was not very attentive or emotionally available. Sonja said that her mother "fed her a lot of frozen microwavable meals." Thus, for Sonja, Sunday brunches at Annie's house were a welcome event. She felt the warmth of the relationships between family members as they easily talked and laughed around the breakfast table. Sonja felt at ease at her best friend Annie's house, and staying overnight gave her a sense of family and normalcy that she did not have in her own home.

One morning, while sitting at the table and eating her banana muffin smothered in butter, Sonja picked up a small piece of black curly hair that was lying on the table and innocently proclaimed that it looked "like pubic hair." Her friend Annie asked what pubic hair was, and my client responded it was "the hair around Daddy's penis."

Recounting the story in our counseling session, Sonja recalled the deathly silence that filled the kitchen. She said that Annie's mother had stopped pouring the orange juice, turned around, stared at her, and in a rage, said that "there would be no more talking." Sonja sat at the table filled with shame, knowing that she had said something wrong, but not understanding what she might have said that would merit the cold stillness in the air. Soon after, Sonja was driven back to her house. When Sonja arrived at home, her mother met her at the door, hit her with a belt, and yelled at her. Her mother let her know that Mrs. Sullivan had called and told her what was said at the table, and that Sonja was never to talk about such things again. Sonja was sent to her room, where she cried and, eventually, fell asleep.

Sonja told me that it was not the beating that made her cry but the realization that what Daddy was doing to her when he came home was not "special," as he had told her, but that it was "bad," and she needed to keep it a secret. She had the sense that "the sexual abuse was not as bad as the consequences of speaking about it." This was the pivotal moment in Sonja's life, the moment when her inner and outer world shattered, and she suddenly found herself alone and unprotected. Sonja's life had changed. She had lost her best friend, she could not go to her mother, and what her father was doing to her was very wrong.

From that moment, Sonja experienced feelings of shame and rejection that impacted all aspects of her life. Sonja walked with her head down, avoided eye contact, and silenced herself for fear of future reprisals. At a young age, Sonja realized that she was alone in the world and had no one to turn to for support. She was left to bear the shameful secret and to continue to endure the sexual abuse from her father. It set the tone for the rest of her life. When Sonja came into counseling with me, she showed symptoms of depression, had poor self-esteem, made little eye contact, and had difficulty expressing herself.

Sonja's story exemplifies how child sexual abuse affects every area of a child's life. At a stage when, developmentally, my client was supposed to be riding bicycles and playing with her friends, she was experiencing sexual activity with her father. She learned that she could not talk about what was happening to her because doing so was offensive, and she would be punished. She quickly made the connection that what Dad was doing was also unacceptable, and feelings of shame and of being different permeated her life. She reacted to these feelings by isolating herself. As an adolescent, Sonja tried to escape her pain by running away from home, using drugs and alcohol, and attempting suicide. At times, when the aloneness and isolation became overwhelming, she would self-harm. She said that when she felt like she was "leaving her body and slipping away," cutting her stomach with a razor helped her to stay connected to her body.

Child sexual abuse affects self-perception and self-esteem, and many survivors express a strong sense of inadequacy, of being different, and of not belonging. The guilt, shame, and lowered self-esteem that plague sexual abuse survivors appear to pervade all aspects of their lives.

DEPRESSION

Major depression is one of the most common mental health concerns of the twenty-first century. It is an incapacitating disorder that restricts a person's physical, social, emotional, and intellectual functioning. The symptoms for major depression need to be present for at least two weeks and must interfere with a person's ability to provide basic self-care, to function socially, and/or to perform work-related responsibilities. The symptoms of depression include loss of interest in activities that used to give one pleasure, decreased energy, and difficulty making decisions and concentrating, and changes in sleep, appetite, and/or weight.[4] Clients diagnosed with major depression also complain that they feel empty and sad and struggle with feelings of worthlessness. They may also have thoughts of suicide.

One client confided that she would spend hours in bed thinking about suicide and wondering how to kill herself while simultaneously feeling distressed about who would take care of her two children and pondering whether she should "take the children with her." She recalls how numb, how cut off from her feelings, she felt. Today, she realizes how frightening that period of time was in her life.

Sleep problems are another symptom associated with depression. Some people experiencing depression report that they are able to fall asleep but not stay asleep; for example, they may sleep for three hours and then get up in the middle of the night and be unable to fall asleep again. One of my clients shared that she would lie in bed for hours struggling with negative thoughts and ruminating about past experiences, while other survivors can sleep for many hours and get up still feeling unrested and incapacitated by low energy levels.

Some people with depression gain weight because they eat simple carbohydrates and fatty "junk" foods. These foods are easy to consume, take little preparation, and offer instant, though short-lived, gratification. On the other extreme, some people with depression may not be able to eat at all, and therefore lose weight quickly. Some do not have the energy to prepare food or the desire to eat. For them, preparation and consumption of food can seem overwhelming. As one client told me, "Even simple things like preparing and eating food feel insurmountable."

Persistent depressive disorder (PDD) has the same symptoms as major depression, but the symptoms are not as extreme and must be present for more than two years.[5] Since the symptoms of PDD are less severe, it often goes undiagnosed. Many of my clients tell me they never knew they were depressed because they did not understand it was not normal to feel drained, unhappy, disconnected, and to experience little pleasure in life. Many never questioned how they were feeling because they were unaware that other ways to feel existed.

One client said she felt like she was wearing concrete blocks on her feet. Every step she took was difficult and she was always exhausted. In the mornings, she would get up, feed her children breakfast, get them onto the school bus, and drive to work. When she arrived at work, she would say good morning to her colleagues, go into her office, and close the door. She ate lunch in her office, struggled through paperwork and work-related telephone calls, and then went home at the end of the day. Absolutely everything she did felt like a difficult chore. She pushed herself to go grocery shopping, prepare meals, do the laundry, clean the house, and help the children with homework, while at the same time trying to have quality interactions with her family.

POST-TRAUMATIC STRESS DISORDER

Post-traumatic stress disorder (PTSD) falls under the category of trauma and stress-related disorders. Symptoms of PTSD can be seen in individuals who have either experienced or witnessed a traumatic event during which they believed that they or another person was at imminent risk of injury or death. The person may have experienced an overwhelming sense of powerlessness and terror in the face of the traumatic incident. Symptoms may first appear months or even years after the event.[6]

Many women who have experienced child sexual abuse also exhibit symptoms of PTSD. These symptoms include agitated and/or exaggerated emotional reactions, exaggerated startle response, restricted emotions and behaviors, difficulty with sleep, disturbing dreams, amnesia (forgetting all or part of the traumatic experience), diminished interest, and avoidance of certain people, places, and/or activities that may act as reminders of the trauma.[7]

A common symptom of PTSD is flashbacks, or the reexperiencing of the past trauma in the present. Flashbacks are often "triggered" by a present-day event. Flashbacks commonly occur in the form of visual memories, but they can develop in a variety of sensory forms. Some clients have body/physical memories, and during flashbacks, they experience the physical pain of the early abuse. Some clients have auditory flashbacks during which they hear aspects of the traumatic experience. Some flashbacks are visual, as well as auditory and physical, so the person will see, hear, and feel the past abuse experience, as if it was happening in the present. Sometimes the memories last a few seconds, sometimes minutes, and for one of my clients who had severe PTSD, flashbacks lasted for hours.

Some people with PTSD may experience *flooding*, which occurs when numerous memories of a trauma occur in succession, one after the other, engulfing and overwhelming the person. As one client said, flooding "is like drowning in a tidal wave of memories." Striving to avoid flashbacks, the distressing memories, and their associated feelings, survivors may restrict their lives in ways that help them to avoid people and situations that could remind them of the trauma.

Survivors may respond to early traumatic sexualization by associating intimacy with negative memories of the abuse, as seen in survivors diagnosed with post-traumatic stress disorder. Some clients have reported that while being sexually intimate with their partners, they experience flashbacks of their abuse. These flashbacks can be triggered by a sound, a smell, or physical touch, resulting in the reemergence of their childhood memories of abuse. Consequently, this interferes with the enjoyment of sex with an intimate partner and leads to avoidance of intimate touch because of the fear that it may trigger painful memories and experiences.[8]

Many of my clients and the women I interviewed with PTSD report that they experience flashbacks of their abuse while mothering and caring for their children. Invariably, these women report that they avoid some of their mothering responsibilities because they are afraid of triggering painful memories. In therapy, Wilhelmina revealed that she experienced flashbacks when she was changing her daughter's diapers because the smell of urine triggered memories of her abuse as a child. Wilhelmina also had difficulty setting limits with her child. When her daughter cried or resisted her mother's guidance, Wilhelmina overidentified with her daughter's normal childhood cries and resistance, as if they were her own childhood pleas, and this incapacitated her and kept her from setting boundaries. While mothering her daughter, Wilhelmina felt she was constantly at risk of reexperiencing the events of her own lonely and violent childhood.

Laura's Story

Laura was able to care for and mother her son until he reached puberty. Laura said:

When my little boy became a young man, I stopped being his moth-er. He is taller than me, six foot, two inches, he has a mustache and hairy legs and chest. He is, at times, belligerent when I make re-quests that he go to bed, take out the garbage, turn off the television, or do his homework. When he stands above me and postures, I fall apart. When he raises his voice and becomes angry or aggressive, I sometimes have flashbacks of my father, and once again, I am the frightened and powerless little girl. I crumble and am not able to set or follow through with limits.

One day I came home early from work, and I caught him and his friend, also sixteen, watching a sexually explicit movie on HBO. I about-faced and went into my bedroom and started trembling un-controllably. I had a flashback of my father. My father would watch sexually explicit movies with my brothers.

My son learned that he could intimidate me in order to get his own way and avoid responsibility. He knows that when he is aggres-sive, I become mute and he gets to do what he wants. I have trouble setting limits, and once again, I cannot protect myself. I could not protect myself as a child against my father, and now, as an adult, I cannot protect myself from another man, who happens to be my son.

I am scared and feel paralyzed, because I am fully aware that, as his mother, it is my job to set limits and to teach and model appropri-ate behavior. I am scared because I know that by not setting limits, I am re-creating my father. I am creating a man who uses power, rage, and intimidation to control another person. The world does not need another man like my father. When we engage in those negative pow-er struggles, I vacillate between seeing my son's face and seeing my father's face. I am living with my father all over again, and I do not know what to do. It is terrifying.

Laura says that she sees images of her abuse while mothering her adolescent son. Usually she can talk herself out of the full memory, but the experiences are still extremely disconcerting. Before her diagnosis of PTSD, Laura thought she was losing her mind and going crazy. Now that she has received the diagnosis and understands the symptoms and causes of PTSD, she can put the images in a context which make her feel less vulnerable. Being diagnosed with PTSD was a positive step for Laura. It helped to name her experiences, and therapy helped her learn the skills necessary to manage and eliminate the symptoms that were interfering with her mothering.

Some of my clients diagnosed with PTSD are hypersensitive and often misread signals from people and their surroundings; triggered by someone's look, comment, tone of voice, or touch, they may become hypervigilant and angry in response to imagined threats. They may respond with a defensive and overly emotional reaction that is out of context in the current situation. People who are in this hyper-aroused state offer little opportunity to reason with them, and it is difficult for others to explain their real intentions. Not only is the person's response inappropriate to the situation, but trying to calm them down often only feeds the mistrust and increases the argumentativeness and hostility. Of course, these hypervigilant reactions have more to do with the past than the present, and the person with PTSD is unknowingly experiencing the present situation through the lens of a past threat.

One client described how PTSD operated in her life. She used the comparison of a piece of lined writing paper with a margin on the side. When she is interacting in the world without symptoms, she is on the main part of the page, and her memories are held in the margin. Under those conditions, she is able to function, take care of her family, and engage in the daily responsibilities of home and work. When a flashback occurs, it is as if the margin line on the paper has become blurred, and the memory can no longer be held at bay. The memories permeate and bleed onto the main page. When this happens, she says, it is nearly impossible to stay in the present and engage effectively in the here and now, and she struggles to manage taking care of her children and responsibilities as the painful memories emerge. During times when she was feeling "fragile and "unprotected," like many clients with PTSD, she had difficulty falling asleep and/or staying asleep. She said she was afraid to go to sleep, and the very idea of sleeping made her frightened and vulnerable because she could not "predict or control the memories that may reveal themselves while dreaming."

ANXIETY DISORDERS

Social phobia, agoraphobia, general anxiety disorder, and panic disorder fall under the umbrella of anxiety disorders. These disorders are grouped together because they share similar symptoms, specifically enduring and strong feelings of fear and anxiety that are incapacitating and that interfere with the person's ability to function day to day. The *Diagnostic Statistical Manual of Mental Disorders*-5 differentiates fear and anxiety: "Fear is the emotional response to real or perceived imminent threat, whereas, anxiety is the anticipation of future threat."[9]

People with anxiety disorders have the potential of having "panic attacks." A panic attack can last up to ten minutes and is manifested as feelings of fear, apprehension, and physical discomfort. Some panic attacks have identifiable triggers, but some come on seemingly out of the blue. Such attacks with no readily identifiable triggers are called *un-cued attacks*.

Mary's Story

One of my clients, Mary, was having dinner with some friends from college whom she had not seen for several years. Suddenly, at the dinner table, she experienced a panic attack. Mary said,

> At first I had a hot flash and started to sweat. I became frightened but tried to ignore what was happening. My chest tightened, my heart started to race, and I felt I was choking and losing my ability to breathe. My fear mounted, and within seconds, my breath shortened, and I started hyperventilating and became dizzy. I thought I was having a heart attack. The waitress called an ambulance, and within a short period of time, the paramedics surrounded me and determined that I was having a panic attack. My friend called my husband, who picked me up at the restaurant and drove me home.

Mary, like many people who have had a panic attack in a public place, found the experience extremely distressing and embarrassing. The panic attack in the restaurant made Mary feel utterly demoralized and vulnerable and caused her profound distress. Mary came to me because she was fearful of going outside her home unless she had a close and trusted friend or her husband with her. Her first panic attack had been seemingly un-cued and had come on quickly without warning. Mary was unclear what had caused the first panic attack, and not knowing made her feel fragile and vulnerable. As a result, she avoided social and public situations that might duplicate the context of the first panic attack. The fear that another panic attack would occur made Mary anxious to the point that she became housebound.

Mary was imprisoned by fear and anxiety stemming from the possibility of having another attack. Her life was turned upside down, and activities that used to bring her pleasure now triggered apprehension and avoidance. She avoided social situations and being in crowds unless she had someone she trusted with her. Mary was able to function fairly well at home and took care of household responsibilities. She cooked and cleaned and was able to care for her children. The house ran smoothly because she ordered food and clothes online to be delivered to the house. However, Mary's anxiety and agoraphobia made it difficult to take care of family responsibilities outside of the home, which caused great disruption in her family's life and put a tremendous burden on her husband and children. She did not go to parent–teacher meetings, school plays, or her children's soccer games. She could not take her children shopping, to the park, or to movies. Even when accompanied by her husband, large social situations were difficult.

One day, Mary did attempt to bring her daughter to a birthday party, but halfway down the driveway, she started to get symptoms of a panic attack. She immediately put the car in park and ran into the house. Unable to take the time to turn off the car, she had left her ten-year-old daughter in the running car in the driveway. It was this incident that brought real concern to her and her husband: She saw that her anxiety was putting her children in danger. When Mary came to see me in my office, her doctor had already diagnosed her with panic disorder and agoraphobia. During our therapy, like many women diagnosed with panic disorder, Mary revealed to me that she had a history of child physical and sexual abuse.

Many of my clients are diagnosed with generalized anxiety disorder and suffer from constant worry and anxiety. People with generalized anxiety disorder experience free-floating anxiety, and worry is a constant presence in many aspects of their daily lives. My clients worry about their family and children, finances, work, the state of the economy, the environment, and world politics. They find managing their anxiety difficult because, they say, the worry feels out of their control. As in other anxiety disorders, the excessive worry and anxiety are also associated with physical symptoms such as difficulties with sleep, irritability, problems with concentration, and fatigue.

EATING DISORDERS: ANOREXIA NERVOSA, BULIMIA NERVOSA, AND COMPULSIVE EATING

Many of my clients struggle with eating disorders, including anorexia nervosa, bulimia nervosa, or compulsive overeating. The common thread in all three disorders is a pattern of disturbed eating behaviors that has a negative impact on physical health and psychological and social well-being. Women diagnosed with eating disorders have a dysfunctional relationship with their bodies, body weight, and food.

Anorexia Nervosa

A core symptom of anorexics is their inability to recognize their emaciating and withering bodies. Their decreased food and liquid intake result in dehydration, fatigue, muscle weakness, dry skin, and heart difficulties. In severe cases, symptoms related to starvation include amenorrhea (the cessation of the menstrual cycle for three months or more) and body lanugo, a fine downy hair that grows on the body.[10] The growth of hair is the body's response to the loss of body weight and the lack of body fat, and acts to compensate and regulate body temperature and keep the body warm.

Clients diagnosed with anorexia nervosa are fearful of gaining weight and have a distorted body image. The actual image in the mirror is of a dangerously thin woman; however, the image that the anorexic sees reflected is of a woman who is overweight.[11] Associated with this distorted visual image are feelings of anger and disgust, as well as a destructive internal voice that pressures the anorexic to lose more weight.

Alicia's Story

Alicia grew up in extreme poverty and severe abuse and neglect. She was sent to school without breakfast, and the free lunch program at school provided her only meal for the day. On weekends, a full meal was not guaranteed. As a young girl, Alicia learned to dissociate from her body as a way to manage the abuse and neglect, and to ward off the pangs of hunger from a lack of food.

During therapy, Alicia told me that the more weight she lost, the more empowered and in control she felt. Alicia shared that when she watched others eat, it made her feel sick: "I watch their mouths move up and down as they chew and the sound of them chewing food makes me want to gag. I can literally feel my throat tighten." She said she felt disgust toward the person who was eating and simultaneously felt empowered that she could manage her impulses to eat, forgoing food and rising above her hunger by not "giving in and feeding it." As a little girl, Alicia learned that her personal power was in her ability to deny her hunger and not succumb to her body's need to eat. Today she realizes that her struggle with anorexia is related to her childhood experiences.

Anorexia means "without appetite"; however, this is inaccurate, because many anorexics do experience hunger and the desire to eat. They spend a great deal of time thinking about and being involved with food. Alicia was able to manage her hunger and ignore the rumbling of her stomach as it growled for food and nourishment as she simultaneously baked cookies and cakes for her family and friends.

When Alicia stood on the scale, she gained great satisfaction from seeing it reflect her weight loss. If the scale showed a weight gain, even a gain of a few ounces, Alicia would experience strong feelings of self-loathing and hatred, and would employ further weight-loss techniques, such as taking laxatives and exercising. Her sense of self and well-being was directly related to the number on the scale. The more weight Alicia lost, the more empowered she felt. Alicia was preoccupied with food, her body image, and losing weight.

Bulimia Nervosa

Bulimia nervosa is also a common eating disorder among women who experience early sexual abuse. Like anorexia, individuals diagnosed with bulimia have issues with body shape, eating, and weight. However, unlike anorexia, the person engaging in bulimic behaviors may realize they have a problem but feel powerless to control the binging and purging episodes. During these episodes, the person will consume a large quantity of food in a short period of time, usually within a two-hour time span. To manage caloric intake and control weight, after the binge, the person will engage in purging behaviors such as vomiting in order to rid themselves of the food they have just ingested.[12] Purging may also include other behaviors that are used to burn calories, such as exercise, diuretics, and laxatives. Bulimia nervosa can be extremely harmful to the body, leading to serious health consequences, such as dehydration, constipation, tooth decay (caused by the stomach acids in the vomit), and damage to the esophagus, heart problems, edema, acid reflux, and death.

Compulsive and Emotional Eating

Compulsive eating is different from binge eating. A binge eater will eat a large quantity of food within a short period of time at least once a week. On the other hand, a compulsive overeater struggles daily with food, using it to fend off emotional issues like stress, anger, and frustration, or to contain feelings of emptiness and loneliness. However, after overeating, the compulsive overeater experiences feelings of defeat, failure, and self-contempt. Many overeaters have negative self-perceptions of their body and physical appearance. A number of my clients deal with weight problems and irrational eating patterns.

Maggie's Story

Maggie was a compulsive overeater. She was also a compulsive buyer of women's magazines that promote extremely restrictive diets that promise the reader quick weight loss. The front page, in bold lettering, proclaims alluring guarantees of quick and easy weight loss: "Lose Ten Pounds in Three Days" and "Lose Thirty Pounds in Thirty Days." Maggie tried many diets that promise to be weight-loss solutions, including low-carb diets, gluten-free diets, the Paleo Diet, detox diets, a twenty-one-day fast, a three-liquid-shakes-a-day diet, and an extremely restrictive 800-calorie-a-day diet.

Maggie would wake up in the morning ready, willing, and with the best intentions to start her diet and begin a new life as a thin person. However, by four o'clock in the afternoon, she would break the diet with what she called "an uncontrollable hunger and need for sugar." Maggie would continue to eat, even after she felt satiated, and many times, she ate to the point of experiencing physical discomfort. She had a chronic internal battle and dialogue about food. However, at the end of the day, she would hate herself for not being strong enough and for surrendering to her cravings. Afterward, she would engage in negative and emotionally draining self-talk.

After a roller-coaster ride of failed attempts at dieting, Maggie gave up her attempts at losing weight and sank into a feeling of deep emptiness and depression that permeated other aspects of her life. She felt doomed in her desire to be thin. Having surrendered to the idea that she would never be successful at dieting, Maggie indulged in simple carbs, fats, and sugary foods to manage her feelings of emptiness and despair she felt due to her failure to control her body, eating, and weight.

Maggie struggled with depression, anxiety, and insecurity in many areas of her life. When life presented challenges and unpleasant emotions surfaced, she would "stuff down" her feelings and comfort herself with sweets and simple carbohydrates. After she indulged, she would feel angry and frustrated. Maggie was in an injurious cycle that she could not break, which included experiencing stress and eating for comfort, followed by feelings of self-loathing.

When Maggie came into my office she was downtrodden. At five-foot-four, she weighed 265 pounds. Maggie had an irrational image of body perfection that she aspired to, and the disparity between the body she desired and her current body caused Maggie a great amount of pain. Her feelings of shame coupled with her failure to control her body weight and compulsive eating led her to avoid social situations with family and friends. Maggie's clothing matched her desires to stay invisible and to go unnoticed: She wore large, baggy men's clothes, extra-large T-shirts, and sweatpants. In her home she had only one twelve-by-twelve-inch mirror located in the bathroom, which was only big enough to see her face and aided in the continuous disconnection from her body.

Being overweight made it problematic for Maggie to engage in daily tasks and made physical activity difficult. Her knees hurt and her breathing was labored. She found it hard to stand or walk for long periods of time. Her physical limitations made it difficult to be fully involved in raising her four-year-old son, Joshua. He wanted to play in the park, go for walks, and ride his bike, but she could not physically keep up with her son's activity level. In order for Maggie to supervise her son, Joshua was forced to stay in the house. Maggie's restricted physical abilities ultimately restricted her son's physical activity, and he shared his mother's sedentary lifestyle. They ate and watched television together. Joshua was also overweight for his height and age.

In order for Maggie to move forward in her life, it was important to examine the core issues around her compulsive overeating. In therapy, we explored when her struggles with weight and compulsive eating began. Maggie revealed that she was sexually abused as a child. She said her body never really felt like it was hers—that it had been stolen from her by her uncle, who raped her when she was six, and continued abusing her until she was twelve.

Maggie recognized that she had begun overeating as a child to self-soothe, and that her compulsive overeating offered pleasure and a feeling of numbness that momentary pacified her anxiety and depression. Maggie's body was in chronic pain. The pain in her knees and back prevented her from engaging in life and from fully participating in the care of her son. Although her eating appeared out of control, it was purposeful and quelled her experiences of emotional pain, which allowed her to avoid and circumvent her internal despair.

Maggie's therapy moved forward and we continued to look at how the past child sexual abuse was impacting her current functioning. Maggie shared that when people looked at her body, she felt they could see that she was a victim; and being overweight, wearing dark and baggy clothing helped her to go unnoticed and made her invisible. Maggie discussed how she felt when she was thinner, and said, "It's funny, but when I was thinner, my body took up *less* space in the world, but I received *more* looks, comments, and attention. When I am overweight, I take up *more* space in the world but I feel protected, less exposed and noticed. As an overweight person I feel like I can maneuver through the world unseen. My weight makes me bigger in physical size but helps me to be invisible, and I am provided protection by being an inferior version of myself."

Maggie continued by saying that when she was thinner and walked past men, she would experience a heightened sense of fear and her body would tighten and become rigid, her eyes and gaze would be fixed on the ground, and she would hold her breath. In order to escape suggestive comments and to avoid the uncomfortable fear reaction it created in her body, Maggie went out of her way to avoid passing groups of men. The extra attention and comments made her feel unsafe, which was a duplication of her childhood, where she was not protected from the barrage of comments about her looks and body, and from the sexual abuse by her uncle.

SUBSTANCE USE DISORDERS

Women and girls who have experienced sexual victimization are at increased risk of later substance use. Many survivors of CSA use alcohol and drugs as a means of alleviating the potent negative feelings related to the trauma.[13] The most common drugs that my clients use to ameliorate their distress are alcohol, tobacco, cannabis, and opiates.

Survivors may use alcohol and drugs as a form of self-medication to lessen emotional pain, reduce surfacing memories of abuse, and manage symptoms related to depression and/or anxiety. It is a coping strategy and acts to temporarily mask the pain associated with victimization. However, substance use as a form of self-medication reduces the pain only temporarily and puts the survivor at high risk of addiction. According to Vincent Felitti, adverse childhood experiences, including child sexual abuse, is the major determinant of substance use and addiction.[14]

In order to be diagnosed with a substance use disorder, clinical impairment needs to be demonstrated in two to four of the following areas: impaired control, social impairment, risky use, and pharmacological indictors as evidenced by tolerance/withdrawal symptoms.[15] *Impaired control* is present when usage of a substance is negatively impacting one's life but efforts to reduce or stop using are futile. The person has physical and/or psychological cravings for the alcohol and/or other drugs, and their life is consumed with acquiring and using the substance. The use of the substance causes impairment in many areas of life, including meeting work- and school-related responsibilities.

Social impairment is evidenced when friends and family connections weaken and important relationships deteriorate. Using substances can lead to a failure to follow through on promises, problems with communicating effectively, and an argumentative relational style that, over time, can erode the strongest of relationships. Many addicts may exhibit risky behaviors, such as driving while intoxicated or engaging in high-risk sexual behavior. Although they are aware that their choices and behaviors are putting them at risk, they are unable to abstain from engaging in substance use.

Tolerance and withdrawal symptoms may be present. *Tolerance* is a result of continued use of a substance. As with all substances, over time, tolerance increases. As the individual becomes more tolerant of the substance, more of the substance is needed to create the same psychopharmacological effect. As tolerance level increases, so does the risk of addiction. *Withdrawal symptoms* are the psychological and/or physical symptoms that occur with the reduction or discontinuation of use. Different substances have different withdrawal symptoms, which can range from psychological need to physical discomfort and pain.

In my practice, I do not focus on exploring the past child sexual abuse with a client who is currently an active user of alcohol and/or other drugs. Instead, I believe the client needs to begin the addiction recovery process first. As a general rule, I do not work on CSA issues until the client has had at least a year of sobriety and/or a strong support system. This helps to protect fragile clients, without resources, from relapsing back into using substances as a response to the powerful emotions and memories that may surface when working on healing from CSA.

BORDERLINE PERSONALITY DISORDER

Borderline personality disorder (BPD) falls under the category of personality disorders and is characterized as a "pattern of instability of interpersonal relationships, self-image, and affects, and marked impulsivity that begins by early adulthood and is present in a variety of contexts."[16] Like other disorders, the symptoms of BPD cause significant distress and impairment in many areas of the person's life and everyday functioning. Individuals diagnosed with BPD have difficulty managing feelings of emptiness and are terrified of being alone. They also complain that they feel empty and damaged and struggle with feelings of worthlessness and shame. Although being isolated from others causes intense discomfort, their uneven moods and inability to regulate strong emotions, such as anger, pushes people away and harms relationships. Their unstable self-image and unpredictable anger reactions make it difficult for them to sustain healthy ongoing connections with others.

Individuals with BPD have a tendency to be hypersensitive to any form of real or perceived rejection or abandonment. Canceling an appointment, being late, or being thought of as inattentive in a conversation may create extreme changes in mood and behavior. Assumed rejection or abandonment are viewed as affronts to the relationship and may result in heightened and inappropriate anger reactions. Individuals with

BPD may also engage in *splitting*, in which initially they idealize a person but then rapidly shift into feeling scornful and condescending toward them. Problems with identity and erratic emotions and behaviors make it challenging for individuals to follow through on goals, such as completing school or employment responsibilities.

Individuals in this population may also engage in impulsive and potentially dangerous behaviors involving alcohol and substance abuse, multiple sex partners, and binge eating. Often used as a coping mechanism, individuals with BPD may engage in patterns of self-injury including cutting, head banging, and picking and/or burning body parts. One client shared that she would spend hours with a razor making small cuts in her fingernail until the entire nail was removed. Suicide threats and attempts are also common, and approximately 8 to 10 percent complete suicide.[17]

TRAUMATIC EXPERIENCES AND ADVERSE HEALTH OUTCOMES

Traumatic experiences have detrimental consequences on the body and have the potential to negatively impact physical health. Chronic stress associated with trauma interferes with physiological homeostasis, diminishes the body's defense systems, and over time lowers immune system functioning, making one susceptible to disease and illness.

Childhood trauma has been linked to gastrointestinal illnesses associated with digestion and include symptoms of abdominal pain, diarrhea, constipation, and irritable bowel syndrome. Survivors of child sexual abuse are also vulnerable to cardiovascular disease, including heart attacks or strokes. Diabetes, respiratory distress, chronic fatigue syndrome, fibromyalgia, and migraine headaches are also common disorders diagnosed in this population.[18] According to Robin Karr-Morse and Meredith Wiley, "When it comes to trauma, physical and emotional are inseparable. What happens to us emotionally happens to us physically, and vice versa. And while stress and trauma are on the same continuum, they are not the same thing. Stress is a normal response to feeling threatened or overwhelmed. Trauma, on the other hand, is toxic stress frozen into place in our brains and bodies, where it reverberates chemically, generating tiny pathological shifts in immune and endocrine functions."[19]

The Centers for Disease Control and Prevention and Kaiser Permanente conducted a longitudinal study comprising 17,377 middle-class adults with an average age of fifty-seven years. The study examined the impact of adverse childhood experiences (ACEs) on physical health and social functioning. They also examined the relationship between ACEs and adult health-risk-taking behaviors.[20] The ACE Study divides adverse childhood experiences into ten categories. Under *Child Abuse* the three categories include emotional abuse, physical abuse, and sexual abuse; under *Child Neglect* the two categories include emotional neglect and physical neglect; and under *Household Challenges* the five categories include a mother treated violently, mental illness, divorce or separation, substance abuse, and an incarcerated family member. Participants were instructed to check the categories that reflected their childhood experiences. Each category equals one point, and based on the number of categories that were checked, the participant could receive a score ranging from 0 to 10.

The results showed that adverse childhood experiences are common. Two-thirds of the participants had an ACE score in two or more categories, and one in six participants had an ACE score in four or more categories. The study revealed that high ACE scores in the first eighteen years of life are linked to poor outcomes in physical and mental health and social functioning. People with high ACE scores were significantly more likely to, as adults, engage in behaviors that placed their health at risk. Specifically, an ACE score of 6 or more decreased one's life expectancy by approximately twenty years compared to those participants with an ACE score of 0, and an ACE score of 7 or more increased suicide attempts by 3,100 percent compared to participants with an ACE score of 0.[21]

One mechanism by which adverse childhood experiences result in long-term health consequences is by engaging in adult health-risk-taking behaviors. These include alcohol and drug abuse, having multiple sex partners, cigarette smoking, and compulsive eating leading to obesity. Adult health-risk-taking behaviors such as these are often an individual's attempt at coping and self-regulating the experiences of emotional pain, anxiety, anger, and/or depression related to unresolved adverse childhood experiences.

Cigarette smoking is associated with emphysema, lung and larynx cancer, and cardiovascular disease, such as heart disease and stroke. There is also a strong link between a high ACE score, child sexual abuse, and obesity. Obesity is linked to multiple poor health outcomes, including high blood pressure, type 2 diabetes, osteoarthritis, and breast, colon, and liver cancers. Since the outcome of physical diseases associated with cigarette smoking and morbid obesity are not manifested for many years, the root causes of the diseases can easily go unnoticed. Felitti illustrates the disconnect between adverse childhood experiences, adult health-risk-taking behaviors, and biomedical disease by using the following example of cigarette smoking:

> Smoking, which is medically and socially viewed as a "problem," may, from the perspective of the user, represent an effective immediate solution that leads to chronic use. Decades later, when this "solution" manifests as emphysema, cardiovascular disease, or malignancy, time and the tendency to ignore psychological issues in the management of organic disease makes improbable any full understanding of the original causes of adult disease.[22]

Participants that received high ACE scores but did not engage in adult health-risk-taking behaviors were still susceptible to disease and negative physical health outcomes. Long-term chronic and unrelieved stress overstimulates the brain and body, weakens the immune system, and poses increased risk for the development of cancers, and autoimmune diseases like multiple sclerosis, rheumatoid arthritis, and lupus.[23]

COMPLICATED GRIEF AND MOURNING

Most CSA survivors experience psychosocial losses resulting from their traumas. These losses include loss of childhood, loss of innocence, loss of faith in God, loss of hope in a higher power, loss of family relationships, loss of self-esteem, loss of personal power, loss of self, and loss of the ability to feel pleasure in life.

In one session, Jessie expressed feeling the deep loss of "who I could have been if I had never been abused." Her sustained abuse impacted her every day of her life. "How would I be different if I was not always in survival mode?" she wondered. Jessie felt that she was never allowed the opportunity to develop her talents and to cultivate her real self. She felt that her true self was left dormant by years of surviving daily mistreatment and sexual abuse.

A number of experts in the field have reframed post-traumatic stress as a form of complicated mourning. Therese Rando maintains that "all elements of post-traumatic stress are manifested in some way in both acute and uncomplicated grief and complicated mourning."[24] The challenges that adult survivors of child sexual abuse experience are hopelessness, depression, anger, confusion, and negative beliefs about self and the world. These are similar to the symptoms seen in individuals who have not progressed in their mourning process and are in a state of chronic or prolonged grief. Robert Kastenbaum coined the term "bereavement overload," which is a good description of the mental health status of survivors of long-term child sexual abuse.

Louisa's Story

My client Louisa had a history of excessive childhood neglect and abuse, and it interfered with her ability to develop a sense of trust in herself and her world. Her basic mistrust in herself and others filtered through all aspects of her life. Louisa came into therapy as a twenty-nine-year-old mother of two preschool-age children. She was experiencing a great deal of emotional pain and was ashamed of her inadequate functioning as a mother and a wife. Through the process of therapy, Louisa became aware of how her childhood experiences were contributing to her present-day self-destructive behaviors, social withdrawal, feelings of despair, and impaired relationships with her children, husband, and extended family. Louisa felt that the distress she was experiencing was related to how restrictive her life had become. The experiences that Louisa described in therapy match the symptoms seen in people who have not moved through their mourning process and are, therefore, experiencing a state of prolonged grief.

In order to treat Louisa, we had to address the sexual abuse and examine the issues related to loss and grieving. Reframing Louisa's experiences in the context of loss resonated with her and appeared to convey and match her internal experiences. Louisa had endured a tremendous number of losses in her life and did not have a safe arena to express and work through the grief of these losses. Louisa mourned that her PTSD symptoms were severely interfering with her ability to care for her children. She expressed intense emotional pain and feelings of grief, remorse, and self-disdain for not being able to protect her children from her own inadequacy as a mother, in particular, to be warm and attentive toward her children.

Child sexual abuse survivors experience tremendous secondary losses in their lives. Due to the veil of secrecy that surrounds CSA, survivors do not feel safe to express and work through their grief and mourn their losses. The severe and numerous losses that survivors experience and a lack of sufficient support systems complicate their attempts to resolve multiple traumas and associated grief responses.

SELF-HARM

Self-harm refers to inflicting injury to one's own body.[25] There is a high incidence of self-mutilation among survivors of CSA, who may resort to inflicting self-harm when memories or feelings of despair and self-loathing emerge. Some of my clients use self-mutilation as a way of managing flashbacks, and see self-harm as an act that can convert emotional pain to physical pain. When a flashback occurs, it can last minutes or even hours, and for some clients, self-mutilation is a way of gaining control of the memory by placing their attention and focus on hurting themselves physically.

When memories of abuse and their corresponding feelings emerged, my client Jessie often resorted to a pattern of self-mutilation as an act to gain control and to decrease the tension and the anxiety associated with the memories that were surfacing. Rather than unwillingly reexperience the traumatic event, Jessie would take control by inflicting pain on herself. For her, self-mutilation was a way of staying in the present and managing the flashbacks, which she says come with "surges of pain." Rather than be overcome and flooded with feelings and memories of an event that was horrific and terrifying, Jessie took control by cutting. Jessie exclaimed, "It's just me and the cutting, and the cutting and me, and nothing else exists." I asked Jessie what would happen if she did not cut. She said she thought she would detach from her body and never be able to find her way back. She believed she would permanently disconnect from reality. Cutting was her attempt to stay sane, and to her, the self-inflicted pain kept her connected to herself.

Self-mutilation can take on many forms. The parts of the body that were involved in the abuse are usually the parts that are targeted for self-mutilation, and many times the self-mutilation is related to the emerging traumatic memory or flashback. One client would take hot baths to clean her genitals and would also cut her breasts and vagina with a razor. Another client with visual memories of abuse would very slowly cut her eyelids, making small and consistent slash marks with a razor to avoid reexperiencing the trauma via a flashback. She was meticulous and took great pride in her ability to hide the marks from her partner and her children. It is important to realize that self-mutilation does not indicate suicidal ideation; rather, it is a measure taken to reaffirm the self and to take control using pain, this time inflicted by the hands of the abused.

CONCLUSION

Women who have experienced sexual trauma as children often feel hopeless, powerless, and angry; they feel unprotected and confused, and hold negative beliefs about themselves and the world. Depression, post-traumatic stress disorder, borderline personality disorder, and anxiety and eating disorders are common diagnoses. Frequently, survivors resort to using alcohol and other drugs as a way of coping with and defending against the symptoms of trauma.

Sonja recounted her anguish surrounding the circumstances of when she innocently revealed the sexual abuse with her father while having breakfast with her friend's family. Laura discussed how her memories of child sexual abuse were prompted and exacerbated when her son reached puberty, was taller than her, and when he actively defied her attempts to discipline him. Louisa and Jessie grieved and mourned over how their child sexual abuse interfered with reaching their potential as adults, and Jessie would self-mutilate and cut her body with a razor when she became overwhelmed with flashbacks related to her early CSA. Wilhelmina was diagnosed with PTSD and experienced flashbacks while caring for her young daughter. Mary experienced anxiety and was agoraphobic, which kept her confined to the house and unable to be available to her children for activities outside the home, including parent–teacher meetings and sports events. Alicia struggled with anorexia nervosa and Maggie battled with compulsive overeating.

Although there are many differences in the stories of these women, the one commonality they share is that they all experienced child sexual abuse, and their abuse is linked to their present pain and limited capacity to function as mothers. Lastly, the ACE study reveals how early childhood experiences of abuse, neglect, and violence lead to problems in adult social functioning and physical disease, including cardiovascular and autoimmune diseases and cancers.

3

TRANSCENDING ADVERSITY AND OVERCOMING ABUSE

Risk Factors, Protective Factors, and Resiliency

Resiliency theory explores why some individuals, despite adverse and distressing life events, are able to adapt and continue to function, while others are not able to overcome similar obstacles and have difficulty coping. To understand why some women overcome the effects of child sexual abuse, it is important to understand three key concepts: risk factors, protective factors, and resiliency. *Risk factors* are negative and adverse life experiences that impede a child's ability to function and increase their vulnerability, such as physical abuse, sexual abuse, and child neglect. *Protective factors* are positive influences in a child's life that help support resiliency and the ability to overcome adversities and obstacles, and include having an easy temperament or a caring person in one's life. *Resiliency* is the ability to adapt and recover from stressful or traumatic life experiences and is affected by both risk factors and protective factors.[1]

Resiliency is a balancing act. If an individual's risk factors and stressful events outnumber the protective factors in their life, the stress can erode their resilient capacities and make them more susceptible to adverse physical, psychological, and/or behavioral outcomes. Conversely, if the individual has more protective factors than risk factors in their life, the person is in a better position to overcome adversity and recover. However, it is inaccurate to think that resilient children are not affected by exposure to negative environments and difficult life events. Children who face stressful events are affected, but resilient individuals have the ability to adjust and continue to move forward in life. In sum, individuals who are resilient are indeed affected by stress, and initially may not be able to function, but they have the capacity to overcome the negative experiences and adapt.

It is important to mention that resiliency is *not* an enduring characteristic or permanent condition, and an individual who once demonstrated high resiliency may not necessarily be able to maintain psychological and behavioral adjustment when faced with continued chronic stressors. That is, over a period of ongoing stress, a person's resiliency and functioning capacities can deteriorate.[2] Susan Fine asserts that "resilience is not a miraculous rescue. It can be a mere thread that wrestles itself to the surface of an otherwise despairing existence."[3]

This chapter will examine risk factors and protective factors in the lives of children and how these factors impact their development. The factors will be arranged into three major domains: individual factors, family factors, and school and community factors. Stories from mothers who were victims of child sexual abuse will be used to illustrate how each domain has impacted their lives.

RISK FACTORS

Risk factors are negative events or stressors in a person's life that can challenge or interfere with healthy physical, psychological, and emotional well-being. Risk factors can be found within the individual, the family, or in the school and community. It is not unusual to find only one risk factor in a person's life, and any single risk factor may increase vulnerability. However, children who experience sexual abuse often experience multiple risk factors, and are also subject to emotional and physical abuse and neglect. This increases their susceptibility to short- and long-term physical, psychological, and behavioral difficulties. Risk factors seem to have a potentiating and compounding effect; that is, each risk factor compromises an individual's ability to maintain a resilient position and increases the potency of harmful outcomes, which places a child in danger of having short- and long-term problems in all spheres of development and adjustment.

A primary risk factor for children growing up in the United States is poverty. Poverty is a major stressor because it can affect all aspects of a child's life, including family, friends, neighborhood, and school. Poverty is a predictor of poor outcomes in physical and psychological health, and increases a child's susceptibility to abuse and exploitation. Children who live in poverty have a higher risk of experiencing neglect and abuse, mental health and behavior problems, academic failure, neighborhood violence, teenage pregnancy, and addiction.[4]

Risk Factors in the Individual

Risk factors interfere with resiliency or one's ability to overcome adversities. Distinctive personal attributes can put children at risk for abuse and poor developmental outcomes. Individual attributes that place a child at risk include being born with a difficult temperament, low intelligence, poor physical health, mental health challenges, and a physical and/or learning disability.[5] Children who are "at risk" have more problems with psychological and behavioral functioning, and experience academic failure and high dropout rates from school. These children also exhibit more difficulties with interpersonal relationships and have a propensity to be involved in high-risk behaviors that may lead to problems with the law, incarceration, addiction, gang involvement, sexual promiscuity, and/or teenage pregnancy.

One key risk factor is a difficult temperament, which is a distinctive biological predisposition that pervades and interferes with many realms of social and emotional functioning. Having a difficult temperament includes having problems with irritability, difficulty making changes, displaying aggressive responses to others, erratic sleep and eating patterns, and difficulty adapting to new situations and changes in one's environment.[6] Children with difficult temperaments engage in impulsive verbal and physical behaviors. Their impulsivity interferes with and limits their ability to deal appropriately with challenging situations. As a result, they have problems getting along with others and obeying authority. Just as important, their limited social competence makes it difficult to elicit support from family, peers, teachers, or other adults who could assist and help them. The lack of external support systems leaves these children isolated and without protection, placing them at higher risk of not being able to adequately function, and of mistreatment by others.

In addition to a difficult temperament, having a physical or intellectual disability and/or mental health problem increases the risks a child will confront, and makes it far more demanding for parents and others to care for the child. Children with difficult temperaments and special needs are at higher risk and more susceptible to child abuse and neglect at the hands of isolated caretakers who lack support, who have marital conflict, and/or who lack the knowledge and ability to care for children with challenging behaviors and special needs. As a result, these parents and family members are under increased stress, which puts the child at a greater risk for being the scapegoat of their parents' frustrations and hostility.

Risk Factors in the Family

Family factors that put a child at risk include being born to teenage parents; being raised by a single parent, divorced parents, or having an incarcerated parent; having a parent or caretaker with an undiagnosed or untreated mental illness, such as depression or bipolar disorder; and/or having a parent or family member with an active addiction to alcohol or other drugs. Experiencing the death of a parent, physical or sexual abuse, neglect, and/or disharmony and conflict in the family are also risk factors that decrease and limit positive outcomes for children.[7] Many of these factors overlap and have compounding negative effects on the child, thereby decreasing their resilient capacities.

Many times parents with active addictions or untreated psychological disorders neglect their children and are unable to offer emotional guidance, physical safety, and/or secure attachment. Although they may be able to provide for basic food, clothing, and shelter, they are disconnected from and emotionally unavailable to their children. Whether it is due to an addiction or mental illness, neglectful or under-involved parents have problems with setting limits and following through on consequences. A lack of structure, predictability, and positive parent involvement makes a child feel unsafe because they do not know what to expect or who to turn to in times of distress, increasing their position of vulnerability. When a parent or parents are unable to provide structure

or healthy boundaries, the child's psychosocial development is ham-
pered.

In fact, the lack of parental supervision of young children makes
them predisposed to sexual abuse and other types of victimization. Unprotected and neglected children become prey for predators. Children
become targets of abuse because they are vulnerable to predators who
look for children who are not monitored or protected by their caregivers. In many cases, perpetrators are known to the child and are either
acquaintances or family members. Interviews with perpetrators reveal
that they can pick their victim in a few seconds. Perpetrators look for
the most vulnerable, and are astute at detecting a defenseless child who
appears to be alone, at risk, and neglected—someone they can control.
Specifically, they look for a child that appears to be outside the group,
who is unkempt, and who appears to be passive or troubled. When
choosing a child to exploit, the perpetrator excels at reading the child's
body posture and facial expressions for weakness and fragility. Child
perpetrators may also "groom" a family or a vulnerable mother by becoming a friend, offering financial and/or emotional support, and developing a trusting relationship, with the purpose of having direct access to
the child, or children, in the household.

At the other extreme, being raised in an authoritarian family is also a
risk factor. Authoritarian parents use aversive measures to dominate
and control their children. They believe in the old adages of "spare the
rod and spoil the child" and "children should be seen and not heard." In
authoritarian families the parent is in charge, makes the rules, and
employs aversive discipline methods such as yelling and physical punishment. The parent expects unquestioning obedience and believes the
child should adhere to their rules. The authoritarian parent is demanding and expects children to work hard, at school and at home. Authoritarian homes tend to have harsh and negative interactions between
parents and children, and there are minimal to no displays of physical
affection or terms of endearment. Children from authoritarian families
tend to have insecure attachments, experience low self-esteem, develop
depression, suicidal ideation, resentment, and aggressive behaviors toward others, and engage in substance use.[8]

Being raised by a young parent or a single parent (usually the mother) is often a risk factor. Single parenting is not inherently a risk factor,
but mothers who have been victims of child sexual abuse face a twofold

risk of economic hardships, and often, a lack of extended family supports. A lack of extended family isolates mothers and puts them and their children at risk. If a young single mother lacks the support of an extended family, she is faced with a multitude of challenges inherent in raising a child, or children, by herself. The majority of women who are raising children on their own are working full-time in low-wage jobs that do not afford them the income to lift themselves out of poverty. Stressors related to low wages include difficulty finding affordable housing in safe neighborhoods, sending their children to academically poor-performing schools, paying for reliable and safe day care and/or after-school care, and fulfilling basic needs like food and clothing.[9]

Often, after a long workday, a mother comes home and may have already exhausted her energies. Nevertheless, she must continue to meet the needs of her children; that is, she must cook meals, clean, do the laundry, and give positive attention to her children. The stressors of caring for children without support systems and/or with strained finances put pressures on a mother that, over time, can erode the stamina and wear down the resilient capacities of any well-intentioned mother.

Divorce is also a risk factor, and a stressful and painful event in the lives of children. Even in homes where abuse and discord were dominant during the marriage and the divorce was long overdue, a child's life is turned upside down. They may have to leave their home, school, friends, and neighborhood. It is not unusual for immature parents to not safeguard their children from the consequences of divorce. Volatile relationships usually end in explosive and stressful separations and divorces. The stress is exacerbated when the divorcing couple needs to resolve matters of child custody, visitation, and financial support. Distressed and angry parents often do not always have the ability to protect and shield the children from the impact of their divorce. It is not unusual for distressed parents to put the children in the middle of their conflicts, to denigrate the other parent in front of the children, and to manipulate visitation as a means of expressing hostility toward the other parent. Depending on visitation arrangements, the father especially may have a diminished connection with the children. Many children display grief responses to their parents' divorce, and may experience depression, anger, anxiety, defiance, rebellion, academic difficulties, and lower grades.[10] Children may have further adjustments to make when a parent starts to date and/or gets remarried.

After a divorce, mothers are usually economically compromised and have a reduced amount of money with which to meet the basic needs of their children and household expenses. Once divorced, a mother's household income will decrease, while the father's usable income increases, even after he pays child support.[11] The income discrepancy post-divorce is because mothers, even in shared custody cases, take on more of the financial burdens associated with raising the children, and because of the wage inequities between men's and women's salaries.

If the primary caretaker is incapable of, or averse to, providing for the child's needs, hopefully other extended family members can offer alternative supports in the care of the child. If the extended family is not involved, and the authorities are aware, children who are in imminent danger of physical and/or sexual abuse are taken out of the home and placed in foster care.

Risk Factors in the Community and School

Impoverished inner-city communities and schools contain numerous factors that put children at risk.[12] Impoverished schools are often associated with overcrowded classrooms, high student–teacher ratios, teachers who are overwhelmed, inadequate academic resources, and lack of funds to provide academic supports for children who need remediation or have special needs. The situation in schools may mirror and exacerbate the familial deprivation and risks a child encounters in the home. Ideally, schools could offer a safe refuge from the damaging effects of sexual, physical, and/or emotional abuse and neglect; however, impoverished schools increase the number of risk factors and compound the negative effects of abuse and neglect that may be occurring at home.

Instead of being an environment where learning can take place, talents can be nurtured, and positive relationships can be created, chaotic and underachieving schools potentiate the problems of risk and vulnerability. Children who do not have a daily routine, who have idle and unstructured time, are more likely to engage in undesirable peer relationships that reinforce high-risk and dangerous behaviors. Children and adolescents who affiliate with peers who use alcohol and/or other drugs and/or engage in criminal behaviors are at higher risk for adjustment difficulties and psychiatric problems. Impoverished communities, particularly in extremely poor and violent neighborhoods, have associated risks for children, such as poor housing, gang affiliation, involvement in violence and crimes, substance use, and revictimization.[13]

Claire's Story

When Claire started therapy, it became clear that she had many unhealed wounds from childhood. Claire's mother, Tanya, was eighteen years old when she had Claire. Claire never knew her father. Although Claire's mother worked, she was not able to make ends meet. They lived in Section Eight housing in an impoverished inner-city development. In order to put food on the table, Claire's mother supplemented her income with food stamps.

Claire's mother, Tanya, had several sporadic relationships with men, but they were not serious or long-term. When Claire was five, her mother met a man named Mark, and they eventually got married. Initially, Mark was kind—when he was sober. Mark was an active alcoholic and abusive when he was drinking. His drinking made him unreliable, and as a result, he did not have steady employment. Claire's mother went to work every day and was the sole financial contributor in the family. Mark stayed at home and cleaned, cooked, and cared for Claire.

While Claire's mother was at work, her stepfather had unsupervised contact with Claire. It was during these times that Mark sexually abused her. To ensure that Claire kept "their secret," Mark threatened to kill Claire, her mother, and himself. Claire was sexually abused by her stepfather from the ages of five to sixteen.

In therapy, Claire shared with me a critical moment in her childhood. She said that she remembers praying and asking God to intervene and stop her stepfather from sexually abusing her. However, the abuse did not stop. She said she prayed constantly. She bargained with God and promised to be a "good girl." Claire continued:

> I vowed to God that I would be "good" and not cause problems. I promised I would study and do well in school, I would be respectful to my mother, and do the chores around the house. However, my prayers went unanswered and the sexual abuse continued. I felt deeply unworthy and defective. I remember thinking, "Not even

God loves me or is willing to protect me." At that moment, hope vanished. I felt completely alone, and the world became a very dark place. I was powerless to stop the abuse, so I succumbed. I had no one to turn to, not even God. I stopped praying and went into a numbed despair. I learned to "take it," and resigned myself to life as I knew it.

During her sixteenth year, Claire dropped out of school and left home to live with her boyfriend, Jimmy, and his parents. When Claire left home, her stepfather left her mother. Her mother blamed Claire for their divorce. Claire and her mother still have a frictional and detached relationship today.

Two years after moving out of her parents' house, at age eighteen (the same age Claire's mother was when she gave birth to Claire), Claire gave birth to her son, Jacob. She proceeded to raise him as a single mother. When Claire was twenty-seven years old, she was stopped by the police and arrested for driving under the influence (DUI). The judge gave her the choice of attending a treatment center or serving a twelve-month jail sentence. Claire chose to go to the treatment center because she thought it was the easy route out of her legal difficulty. The program was comprehensive, and combined medically supervised detox, education on alcohol and substance use, individual and group counseling, and a twelve-step recovery program.

At the time of her arrest, Jacob was nine years old. Jacob went to live with his father while Claire attended the residential treatment program. During her time in rehab, Claire received court papers informing her that Jacob's father was filing for full custody of their son. He alleged that Claire was unstable, irresponsible, and not capable of raising their child. Claire felt that her world had fallen apart. Emotionally weakened by the potential custody battle and the accusations of being an unfit mother, she was afraid she did not have the stamina to simultaneously work on her recovery and worry about losing custody of Jacob. She particularly did not feel she had the ability to fight back without the false strength of alcohol, which had seemingly helped her through challenges and difficult times in the past.

While in residential treatment, Claire started to experience panic attacks and tremendous anxiety, and she was flooded with visual, physical, and emotional memories related to her child abuse. When the memories surfaced, she would dissociate, and for several minutes would lose contact with her surroundings. It became difficult for her to focus on her sobriety until the symptoms of PTSD were managed. Her treatment team, which consisted of a psychiatrist, psychologist, social worker, and psychiatric nurse, worked closely together to create an intervention plan, which included medication to reduce the symptoms of PTSD. After two months, Claire was discharged from rehab. Her aftercare recommendations included that she continue her medication, consult a psychiatrist for a medication evaluation every six months, see an outpatient therapist twice a week, attend daily Alcoholics Anonymous meetings, and pick a sponsor to help her navigate through the challenging and difficult times she would encounter in recovery.

When Claire came to see me, she had just been discharged from the treatment center for alcohol and substance use. She had been diagnosed with alcohol and marijuana addiction and post-traumatic stress disorder. When Claire entered my office, she had been sober for two months. Her psychological well-being and sobriety were still fragile and she was at risk of relapse. When she had stopped using, her PTSD symptoms emerged, and memories of her child sexual abuse surfaced. She had been flooded with strong emotional, physical, and visual memories of the past abuse. During sessions, Claire shared that she began smoking pot and drinking alcohol when she was eleven years old, and her dependence continued into adulthood. During treatment, it became apparent that drinking and substance use was Claire's way of controlling her PTSD and managing the pain associated with her history of child sexual abuse; growing up in poverty, with an uninvolved mother; and the challenges of being a single parent.

Claire stated that her child sexual abuse was the precursor to her alcohol and drug use, which negatively impacted her mothering and interfered with her desire to be emotionally available to her son. Claire said that when she was using, she had felt certain that her drinking and smoking pot did not influence the care of her son, since she drank at night when Jacob was sleeping and when he was visiting his father. However, through a sober lens, she realized, in retrospect, that she had been unavailable to her son, particularly on weekends when she invariably slept in late with a hangover. During these times Jacob would have to make his own breakfast, dress himself, and watch television until she dragged herself out of bed later in the day.

Claire was able to meet her son's physical needs and provide a place to live, food, and clothing, but she was not emotionally engaged with her son, and offered little interaction or reciprocal interchanges. She called Jacob "my little man" because he attended to her needs. However, at age nine, he was too young to be a "man," and too little to take care of his mother when she was experiencing withdrawal symptoms from her addiction.

Claire said,

> I framed everything as "Mommy is not feeling well." In reality, I had a hangover. I would tell Jacob I had a headache so he would leave me alone and watch television. I asked him to be quiet when he got overexcited; I told him to go into the other room and play when he would badger me to get up or go out; and I put him down and called him a baby when he whined when he was bored. I would ask him to make me tea or get Mommy the Aleve out of the medicine cabinet, with a glass of water. I even asked him to make his own food when he was hungry.
>
> I feel so guilty. I didn't know any better. I didn't know how to listen or cuddle or be responsive and attentive. I neglected my son's emotional needs, and in that way I abandoned him. I have so much pain and shame from that time of my life. I did not know how to be an involved and engaged mother because I never had that growing up. I didn't even know I had an addiction. I kept thinking that to be an addict, you had to be like Mark, my stepfather—abusive, unpredictable, and incapable of holding down a job. I was not an angry alcoholic, and I had a job, so I naively thought I was a social drinker, not an alcoholic. I was so wrong.

When a parent abuses alcohol, the child has a higher chance of becoming an alcoholic, and girls who have been sexually abused are at higher risk of becoming alcoholic. Claire had both: an alcoholic stepfather, and she had experienced child sexual abuse. Claire was angry when she was mandated by a judge to either go to a treatment center or spend a year in jail; she felt that the world was against her, and she was enraged that she was being treated unfairly. However, during therapy, she recognized her resistance to recovery was really fear in disguise. She was fearful of the emptiness she would experience without a drink to fill the hollowness. Eventually, Claire recognized that drinking and smoking marijuana were keeping her anger, vulnerability, and her past childhood abuse at bay. When she was not using, Claire felt unprotected and frightened, just like she had felt as a little girl with her stepfather.

Claire learned a valuable lesson during her recovery process in Alcoholics Anonymous, and in therapy. She learned that when she is fearful and hides from her vulnerability, the vulnerability grows and endures. She learned that hiding makes her powerless and stops her from moving forward in life. More importantly, she learned that when she feels vulnerable, it is important to reach out to others and speak about the fragility, because sharing, paradoxically, brings her strength.

PROTECTIVE FACTORS

Protective factors help to support an individual's resiliency or ability to overcome adversity and obstacles. Protective factors are a combination of attributes in the individual, the family, and/or the school and community which act to diminish the negative results of risks.

Protective Factors in the Individual

Children who tend to "defy the odds" have particular characteristics that set them apart from those children who experience more difficulty. These include being born with an easy temperament, being intelligent, having good social skills, and having a sense of humor. Good physical health and being energetic are also critical to resiliency.[14]

Children who have an easy temperament are born with certain innate qualities that support resiliency. An easy temperament includes having predictable and consistent eating and sleeping patterns, adapting easily to new situations and changes in the environment, and presenting a calm, friendly, and outgoing disposition. Having an easy temperament and predictable patterns makes it easier to care for the child and decreases the risks that children with difficult temperaments frequently confront, such as abuse at the hands of frustrated caregivers. Children with easy temperaments are also able to engage with others, are curious, and positively contribute to and participate in their environment.[15]

Intelligent children also tend to be more resilient. Intelligent children do well in school and are able to occupy themselves independently. They are inquisitive, engaged in the learning experience, and often have clearly defined academic and vocational goals. Their intellectual abilities allow them to be reflective, and include possessing the skills to monitor one's own internal well-being under stress, and to refrain from thoughtless and impulsive behaviors. Intelligent and resilient children are good at managing stressful experiences. Their ability to engage in introspection is a necessary skill for gaining insight, reframing negative experiences, and learning from consequences.

Intelligent children often have talents in a particular area, whether it be math, writing, art, music, and/or sports. When their talents and gifts allow the child to shine, they gain positive attention from family, teachers, and peers, and the affirmation they receive builds self-esteem and increases supportive social connections. These connections are, in and of themselves, a protective factor. Resilient children have the ability to gain emotional and physical independence and distance from dysfunctional family dynamics.

Resilient children with easy temperaments and intelligence are also socially competent and have the skills to deal with difficult situations. Their good social skills enable them to manage interpersonal interactions and get along with others, which fosters the creation of sustained and supportive relationships. Resilient children are able to elicit assistance from others and create bonds with nurturing individuals. These external support systems act as emotional buttresses and role models of positive, more life-affirming behaviors than those they may be exposed to at home. Part of their social competence is having a sense of humor, which helps them to reframe negative situations, decrease stress, and change potentially negative outcomes. Resilient children also have positive cognitive coping strategies, such as not dwelling on the past, and being able to attribute blame for the abuse to the perpetrator rather than taking responsibility for it themselves.[16]

Protective Factors in the Family

A child's primary relationships occur in the context of family, and the quality of attachment is critical to development. Families that are loving, warm, kind, supportive, and competent in their caregiving are critical influences on a child's success in life, particularly when the child has experienced sexual and/or physical abuse. According to Bessel van der Kolk, one overcomes trauma when the current attachments you have outweigh the terror of the past.[17] Secure attachment with a primary caregiver—in our society, the primary caregiver is most often the mother—is important for the healthy biopsychosocial development of children, and is vital to their ability to be resilient in the face of adversity. Having a parent (or parents) who offer warmth and comfort, and a family that is cohesive and responsive, is central to a child's resilient capacities.

Family factors that help to promote resiliency include being raised in a home environment where the parent or parents are involved in the child's life and offer the child consistent structure and discipline, and expect the child to engage in developmentally appropriate household and personal-care tasks.[18] Having a daily structure at home helps to provide a sense of safety and predictability to children whose world has been turned upside down and whose sense of trust has been damaged by experiences of sexual abuse.

A caregiver who offers a consistent structure and routine with appropriate limits and expectations helps to reduce conflicts and power struggles between parent and child. Certainty and predictability help a child to feel secure because they know what to expect. When children know when they will go to bed, wake up, eat, go to school, and do their homework, it anchors them in a daily routine and provides a sense of safety. Eventually, children will be able to internalize the daily structure and routine for themselves. This encourages maturity and helps children be more independent and self-motivated, characteristics necessary in developing resiliency.

Fatima's Story

As a child, Fatima grew up in a permissive home where her parents were loving and responsive; however, they did not provide rules or structure. In therapy, Fatima says she realizes that the love she received from her mother and father are the foundation of her abilities and strengths, and their support is directly related to her accomplishments as an adult. Her parents listened to her and her siblings, were spontaneous in their signs of physical and emotional affection, took pride in their children's accomplishments, and worked hard to meet their basic physical needs. Fatima and her siblings knew their parents loved them. They were read bedtime stories every night and were woken up with welcoming smiles. Fatima talked about the importance of her mother and father in her life, even though she realizes they failed in a number of parental responsibilities. Fatima expounds on her childhood and the discrepancies between her parents' love and the areas where they were ineffective in the caring for their children:

> I saw my parents struggle and sacrifice to give their five children what they needed. My mother and father were good parents, but there were areas where they were inadequate. I grew up in a chaotic house with yelling and fighting and sexual abuse. My parents failed to protect me from sexual abuse by an uncle, and they failed to give me and my siblings a home that was emotionally and physically safe from one another. There were five children, and since there were no rules and limits set by my parents, my siblings and I fought, and there were continuous power struggles among us. Of course, the strongest siblings won.
>
> I remember one time I was watching my favorite television show and my older brother came in. He wanted my place on the couch and to watch another show, so he physically picked me up and dropped me on the floor. He then changed the channel to the program he wanted to watch and sat on the couch in the spot I was in. Of course, I protested, but to no avail. I complained to my mother, who listened but did not intervene. She asked me to "keep the peace," and find something else to do.
>
> We were poor, and my siblings and I did not always have food on the table; it was always a struggle with money. As a child I knew not to even ask for big items like a bicycle or an expensive outfit. Knowing that I had less than others made me feel less than others. I think feeling less than others and my mother's message of "keeping the peace" are major factors in why I did not tell my parents about the sexual abuse. I felt that because my uncle chose me to abuse, there was something inherently inferior about me. Even as an adult, I continue to have an underlying feeling that I am not allowed to speak up or set limits when I am being taken advantage of or treated unfairly. I am not assertive and I do not protect myself. I have learned to take abuse and keep silent. Since my mother did not protect me, and I am not good at protecting myself, I get terrified that I may not be able to protect my daughter. I have noticed that

there are times in my life where my lack of assertiveness renders me powerless to protect myself. One of the major reasons I am in therapy is to learn to be assertive and to set limits with others, so I can offer a sense of safety and protection for my daughter.

When I ask my clients, "What helped you survive the child sexual abuse?" they consistently answer that there was one person who loved and cared for them. Usually the person was a mother, grandmother, sister, brother, aunt, friend, neighbor, or teacher—the person who took interest in them and guided and cared for them, without the danger of taking advantage, exploiting, or using them. Having access to a supportive person who offers acceptance and acts as a positive role model supports a child's ability to overcome adversity. A strong and positive relationship with a significant and supportive adult increases their sense of self-worth and offers healthy role models to identify with.

Lia responded to the question "What helped you survive the child sexual abuse?" this way:

> My aunt saved me. My aunt lived in California and I lived in New York, but once a year for my birthday my aunt bought me a plane ticket to stay a week with her in California. We would go out and celebrate my birthday every day of the week. My aunt took a week off from work and the two of us spent time together. It was the only time I felt safe and I could put my guard down. I did not have to worry about my father getting drunk and hitting me, or my brother coming into my bed at night when he came home from college to visit on weekends. However, when I was older, I came to recognize that my brother was not coming home to visit the family on weekends, as we always framed it; he was coming home to sexually abuse me.
>
> My aunt took me out to eat at restaurants; we went shopping, and she bought me new clothes. We went to museums, and we watched movies together at night. In the darkness of my childhood, and during the physical and sexual abuse, I would lie in my bed and dream of her. I knew she was out there and that she loved me. She was the light in the darkness that kept me alive and sane. Even though she wasn't there for me every day, she saved me. I knew she loved me. I knew that in time I would eventually be able to see her again.

Grandmothers are also important resources that help to distance the child from the dysfunctional family patterns in their homes. Hannah's grandmother played an important role in her life. When she was younger her grandmother was nurturing and attentive, and spent quality time with her. Hannah stated:

> My grandmother was very giving and loving. I didn't get to spend a whole lot of time with her, but the time I did get to spend with her made a difference. Just the little things, like when we'd go over to visit, she would cook special things for us; she would just be with us, talk to us and give us attention. Those little things make a difference. I don't think I've ever heard my grandmother raise her voice. She was very soft-spoken and generous.

Protective Factors in the Community and School

Persons external to the family are also critical resources, offering emotional support and guidance during one's formative years, acting as confidants, and functioning as role models in life. Having a positive significant relationship with a person external to the family, such as a friend, teacher, mentor, or religious leader, is important in promoting resiliency.[19] Many times abused children create relationships outside the family, and these close relationships compensate for the lack of caring and supportive connections within the family. Having a positive relationship with a significant person is critical in mitigating the long-term effects of child sexual abuse and other adverse experiences. Supportive friends promote a strong self-concept, contribute to self-efficacy, and decrease the impact of the effects of child sexual abuse.

Teachers, mentors, peers, and those who take an interest in the child and offer guidance help to compensate for familial deprivation and the risks that a child may encounter. The women I interviewed said that friends, neighbors, teachers, and mentors were critical resources when they were young, and served as protective factors that helped to ameliorate the negative impact of the sexual abuse and neglect they experienced. Social supports helped them manage the consequences of their abuse, and these relationships were pivotal to their success. In the difficult times during adolescence, social supports "helped them navigate the muddy terrain."[20]

When teachers work in the best interest of the child, it acts as a strong protective factor. Teachers who are supportive, caring, and have high expectations can structure a child's experience in and outside the classroom in order to buffer risks and scaffold success.

In high school, Sadie felt isolated and alone. She had few friends in school and studied enough to "just get by." However, in tenth grade, one of her teachers took an interest in her art. Sadie was very talented in drawing and painting. Her teacher would stay after school in the studio and offer her advice, direction, and helpful critiques. Without Sadie's knowledge, her teacher submitted one of Sadie's portraits to a citywide high school competition. Sadie's won third place, and her portrait was displayed at the annual exhibition. Although Sadie's parents did not come to the opening, her teacher was there and stood by her side. Sadie was too ashamed to tell her teacher about the abuse she was experiencing at home, but somehow she thought the teacher was aware. Her teacher acted as a mentor and gave her special attention that she did not get from other adults in her life. Sadie's relationship to her teacher made her feel valued and important, helped her to temporarily forget about the abuse at home, and eased her isolation in school. Sadie feels a special attachment to this teacher, and still drops by the studio to say hello and check in.

Sadie's teacher was a support person who offered warmth, encouragement, and guidance. Mark Katz confirms the importance of a teacher's role in enhancing a student's resiliency, and states that a "caring mentor is able to transfer valuable knowledge, wisdom, and lessons of life that leave a lasting imprint."[21]

Schools can function as a protective factor and foster resilience in children with multiple risk factors, including buffering the impact of poverty, and acting as a protective device against the impact of impoverished and/or violent homes and communities. Schools can have a significant role in facilitating and promoting resiliency in youth because they can offer a place to excel, gain self-esteem, meet other people, and escape the dysfunctional dynamics of their homes. Schools can offer a safe haven, consistency and structure, and promote and encourage the individual's intellectual, social, physical, and artistic capacities, which in turn increases self-esteem and a sense of belonging. Supportive school environments can ameliorate the harmful effects of sexual, physical, and emotional abuse and neglect on children.

Schools can be utilized in a variety of ways to act as a buffer or protective factor for children who have experienced multiple risk factors. Schools can "stimulate and nourish talents that might otherwise go unnoticed, remediate specific areas of vulnerability, enhance social and interpersonal abilities necessary for friendships and other relationships to develop, [and] permanently alter the trajectories of children who would otherwise develop serious emotional and behavioral problems."[22]

After-school programs are important protective factors as well, because they offer educational remediation and act as a stabilizing force in reducing the effects of distressing experiences. Neighborhood organizations can act as "urban sanctuaries," ensuring that inner-city youngsters do not have too much unstructured, idle time that can lead to involvement in high-risk activities, particularly in the poorer and more violent neighborhoods.[23]

Belonging to a religious community and having spiritual beliefs are also protective factors that can support resiliency.[24] A spiritual belief and/or a religious affiliation can help people maintain faith in something greater than themselves, and can act to mitigate the overwhelming circumstances that at-risk children are exposed to. Being part of a religious organization can offer a spiritual community where people are connected through common values and beliefs, and can act to sustain the individual by offering support. Religion also offers an approach to understanding one's world and guidelines to monitor one's behaviors.

Religion offers structure and consistency to manage the overwhelming experience of dealing with factors associated with risk. Many of my clients have asserted that their strong religious faith enabled them to positively reframe difficult personal events and enabled them to view their negative experiences as important lessons in life and opportunities for personal growth. My clients and the mothers I interviewed felt that their strong religious faith helped them provide meaning in their life and gave them strength to deal with the adversity they experienced. Fatima shared that when she was a little girl she looked forward to going to service on Sundays because the sermons provided her a sense of solace. She believed that God was always with her, loved her, and could hear her through prayer. During her most painful times, prayer offered a safe place to gain a sense of peace and detach from her worries. She said her belief in God was the light in the darkest moments of her life.

ASSESSING RESILIENCY

Oftentimes resilient capacity is assessed through evaluating an individual's adaptive behaviors and their achievement of developmental milestones, such as graduating from high school and/or college, obtaining consistent employment, having financial stability, managing personal responsibilities, and maintaining close relationships with significant others. However, caution should be used when assessing resilience based on using only overt behaviors such as these. While a child or an adult may appear high-functioning, they may still be struggling with emotional problems.

Emily's Story

When Emily entered my office for the first time she was well-groomed, she wore brand-name clothes, and her hair was cut to perfection, not a strand out of place. At five-foot-eight, she stood erect with an aura of self-confidence and intelligence. When she sat on the office couch, she crossed her legs and was poised and cautious in her movements. Her clothes were meticulous and her mannerisms and verbal interactions were careful and composed. On first appearances, Emily was a little intimidating. She appeared self-reliant and self-assured.

It was Emily's husband, Dylan, who prompted her to come to therapy. Dylan was supportive but concerned because her job responsibilities were causing her stress and were interfering with caring for their four-year-old son, Noah. Since Emily spent long hours at the office, Dylan and the nanny were the primary caretakers of Noah.

During therapy, I learned that she and her husband were lawyers and together they owned a profitable consulting firm. Emily spent ten to fifteen hours a day at the office. Her life was consumed with work; the majority of her waking hours were spent either at the office or traveling on business. Her workload had begun to interfere with her physical and emotional health. Emily went to bed worrying about work responsibilities and woke up in the middle of the night with anxiety. She revealed that she was struggling with feelings of apprehension and not being good enough; she could not sleep, and felt disconnected from her husband and child. Although on the surface she looked successful and competent, internally she said she felt "vacant and lost."

Over time, Emily realized some of the reasons for her over-involvement with work. Her initial reason was that she wanted to make sure she could provide for her son and give him more than she had growing up. The other reason, which was more difficult for Emily to share, was that her preoccupation with work was a way she could avoid mothering her son because she feared that she did not have the skills or models to be a "good mother." Emily went on to explain that her own mother was an active alcoholic, as well as physically and emotionally abusive. As a child, Emily and her mother lived with her grandmother in an apartment complex. Her grandmother's neighbor and friend, Sal, was Emily's perpetrator. Emily said she did not feel like she knew how to mother, and thus forfeited the care of Noah to her husband and the nanny. She realized that her hectic work schedule was a means of compensating and escaping from mothering, an area where she felt inadequate

Norman Garmezy coined the term *functional adequacy* to explain how, like Emily, some individuals may appear competent on the surface, but the external functioning and appearance of being resilient do not necessarily reflect emotional stability or life satisfaction.[25] Adults may superficially cope and function well with everyday tasks, but emotionally they may be experiencing feelings of sadness and despair. By understanding the external behavior in combination with internal emotional states we can gain a more holistic assessment of a person's coping abilities, degree of competence, and resilience.

CONCLUSION

Resiliency is the ability to recover from difficult life circumstances and prevail despite the adversity one encounters. Traumatic and stressful events place children at risk and make them vulnerable to short- and long-term physical and psychological problems. The more stressors there are, the greater the child's vulnerability. Poverty, family instability, physical and sexual abuse, neglect, or a primary caretaker with an untreated mental illness or active addiction are major risk factors in a child's life.

However, protective factors can aid in resiliency, and certain variables continually emerge as factors which ameliorate the long-term consequences of risk. Those factors include physical, intellectual, and psychosocial competence of the child; a secure attachment to a primary caretaker; and/or the presence of a significant person who acts as a confidant and offers support and affirming connections. Although Lia did not see her aunt frequently, they shared a caring bond that sustained Lia during the tumultuous times of her childhood; Hannah's grandmother was attentive and affirming, providing her with a reprieve from violent family dynamics; and Sadie's teacher reached out and took Sadie under her wing. Resiliency is a balancing act, and if the number of protective factors exceeds the number of risks or stressful events, the child has an increased chance of sustaining satisfactory functioning.

The stories of Claire, Fatima, and Emily reveal the overwhelming effects of childhood risk factors on early and later development. As a child, Claire struggled with poverty, a disengaged mother, and a stepfather who sexually abused her from the age of five to sixteen. Claire dropped out of high school and left home at sixteen, and at the age of eighteen became a mother. As an adult, in order to regain custody of her son, Claire was compelled to confront her addictions and get therapeutic intervention for her PTSD. Fatima is coming to terms with the discrepancies between having supportive and loving parents who did not protect her from sibling abuse and the sexual abuse by her uncle. Fatima is examining how her childhood experiences are impacting her functioning as an adult and a mother. Emily appears to be high-functioning, and on the surface seems self-assured, hardworking, and successful; however, she struggles with anxiety, fears she is incompetent, feels inadequate as a mother, and abdicates the care of her young son to her husband.

Claire, Fatima, and Emily are contending with their childhood experiences in order to disrupt negative patterns from the past that hold them back and interfere with their abilities to effectively mother their own children. Extended-family members, teachers/mentors, and deep spiritual beliefs have helped these women examine the childhood experiences that are negatively impacting their current lives and mothering experiences, and are assisting them on their path to recovery.

4

MOTHERING
Challenges and Risks

When Angela first came to see me for counseling, she was determined to "heal her past abuse" so that she could be a better mother to her daughter. When Angela's daughter turned five years old, the age Angela was when she was abused, her memories of child sexual abuse surfaced while she attended to her daughter's physical and emotional needs. When her daughter climbed onto her lap to have a story read or to be comforted, Angela's memories of her own abuse would emerge and she would become rigid and shut down, unable to express spontaneous affection. Although many years have passed, I vividly remember the session when Angela declared that she had experienced child sexual abuse and wanted to put her past behind her in order to raise her child differently than the way she was raised. Similar to other clients, Angela said that while the perpetrator never experienced any repercussions from his acts of abuse, she had to experience the abuse twice—once in childhood, and again in therapy. To ensure that her daughter's emotional needs were met, Angela was willing to revisit her abuse and reclaim her past so that she could come out "healed" on the other side.

My clients and the women I interviewed stated that they wished to be better parents to their children than their parents had been to them, and that they had made a conscious decision not to treat their children the way they had been treated.

Hannah made a commitment to mother her child differently than her mother had done when she was growing up: "My mother abused me, sexually, physically, and emotionally. I had many abusers in my life, but she was one of them. I had no models of what a mother was really supposed to be. I knew I didn't want to be the mother that I had. For me, I just kept that in my mind, all the time, even as an adult when I matured. I just didn't want to be the kind of mother I had. It took a lot of work not to be."

Mothers with child sexual abuse histories have difficulties parenting and express a number of challenges and risks in mothering their children, including holding negative views of themselves as mothers, mental health concerns, difficulty with physical and emotional caregiving, struggles with discipline, fears associated with their children being abused, lack of external supports, managing multiple responsibilities associated with mothering, and financial instability. In order to describe the challenges and risks mothers who have experienced child sexual abuse encounter, this chapter will incorporate the existing research studies, my private-practice experiences, and interviews with mothers who experienced child sexual abuse.

NEGATIVE PERCEPTION OF SELF AS MOTHER

Mothers who experienced child sexual abuse want to mother their children appropriately and desire to provide their children with better parenting than they received as children. However, they hold strong negative perceptions of themselves in their parenting roles and lack confidence in their parenting abilities.[1] Mothers feel less self-assured and are generally overwhelmed when caring for their children. Mothers feel inept and have difficulties balancing how to be emotionally available for their children without smothering them, and how to set appropriate limits and boundaries without feeling they are being oppressive and abusive. In general, mothers maintain that mothering their children does not come naturally and state the reason they lack parenting skills and knowledge is because they did not have positive parenting models growing up.

Fatima stated, "Sometimes I wonder, if I had more support, guidance, and protection as a child, I might not have had to face so many struggles, and my path would have been easier or smoother." She also stated that growing up in poverty and living in a chaotic home made her feel "less than others," and added to her negative self-appraisal. As a result of her childhood history, she makes deliberate attempts not to replicate the negative home life she experienced, and she is more protective of her daughter than her mother was of her:

> I grew up in a chaotic house with yelling and fighting and abuse, where I was not always protected. I think that is why I do not have a lot of confidence in raising my daughter. I question and doubt myself. I don't know how to be a mother, but I know not to be my mother. Today, I do things differently than my mom. I keep the house peaceful without fighting, and I am also careful about who comes into my home and who takes care of my daughter. It is not easy, but I am committed to my daughter.

MENTAL HEALTH STATUS OF MOTHERS

As examined in chapter 2, mothers who were victims of child sexual abuse are at higher risk of experiencing isolation, low self-esteem, complicated grief, self-mutilation, drug and alcohol abuse, and mental health concerns. Mental health concerns include depression, anxiety, and post-traumatic stress disorder. Mothers say their mental health symptoms interfere with their stamina and desire to be emotionally available and attentive to their children.

Celia discussed how she struggled with undiagnosed depression while she was attending Alcoholics Anonymous (AA) meetings to work on her recovery from alcohol addiction. Celia describes how her depression and addiction impacted her mothering:

> I was a recovering alcoholic, and for many years I had no idea I was depressed. My twin sons were teenagers before I was diagnosed with depression. I would question why I would have these numb periods and sometimes I would feel extremely sad. I attended AA meetings that would stress principles like, "Do not drink, keep sober, keep it green, one day at a time." That was supposed to solve everything, and I believed that. Not one doctor had told me I had depression, and I had gone to many trying to find out why I felt like I had low energy and little stamina.

I love my boys, and I loved when they were born, but there were moments and certain times when I just couldn't maintain being emotionally available to my sons. They had a lot of energy and were always on the go. It was difficult to keep up with them. I was a stay-at-home mom, and I would sit home during the day and find it very difficult to just keep the interaction with them. It wasn't always that way, but it was that way a lot. My depression made it difficult to connect with my sons. I tried to push myself out of the depression states so I could be more emotionally available to them. However, I was not always successful.

Zoë discusses the impact of her depression on her mothering:

I have dealt with depression a lot throughout my life, and it definitely affects my mothering. When I am depressed I feel like I don't want to do anything but sleep or curl up in a ball and shut out the rest of the world. The depression affects my mothering by making me more emotional at times. Sometimes I feel that I don't know if all my struggles are worth it. Sometimes it makes me somewhat withdrawn from my daughter and other people. I fight with not letting the depression take over, and try to think about positive things to help me get out of it.

Elaina shared similar feelings. She felt her present experiences with anxiety and depression mirrored her early days of recovery, when she felt emotionally fragile. As a result, Elaina went on medication so she would be able to function as a mother:

Last year, I was experiencing anxiety and depression and it was getting in the way of both work and taking care of my daughters. It was not a very good period of time for me. It reminded me of the fragility I felt in my first years of recovery from alcohol and drug addiction. I went on medication because I hated the idea that I could not be the mother I wanted to be. My mental health was deteriorating, I could not sleep at night and I was having anxiety. In the past I would have alcohol and smoke marijuana to manage my feelings. Now I have a strong recovery background and an AA support system, so I know that I will never go down the path of addiction again. However, I did need to go on prescribed medication to alleviate my anxiety and depression so I could better care for my two daughters.

Fatima discussed how she experienced feelings of guilt over how her depression and anxiety were interfering with her mothering. She talked about the actions she took to protect her daughter from being impacted by her negative emotional states:

> Sometimes I may feel depressed or anxious because I have so much to balance and I would like a little break. Sometimes I go into small depressions, but I get out of them soon enough. But the mood does get in the way of me being more alive or being more available to my daughter. I try to push past the mood, but sometimes I just need to sleep and take a break, and in a few days it subsides. When I do get in these moods I am not as emotionally available as I would like to be, or I may get easily frustrated and not be as patient. I may raise my voice; it is rare, but it happens. I always feel guilty when it does happen. I have made a commitment not to be outwardly angry or yell at my daughter. Instead, I will leave the room and not talk about the issue until I have more of a grip on what is going on with me.

PHYSICAL AND EMOTIONAL CAREGIVING

Mothers who were victims of child sexual abuse struggle with various aspects of physical and emotional caregiving. Some mothers report feeling more anxiety with the physical and intimate aspects of parenting, such as bathing, toileting, and dressing their children. Intimate aspects of physical caretaking can elicit memories related to their own abuse histories, and mothers may begin to "feel an uncomfortable identification with their own abuser."[2] As a means of managing emerging memories of abuse, mothers will "distance" from their children emotionally and mechanically respond to the needs of their children, and/or relinquish portions of their parenting responsibilities to others.

Several of my clients said that when their sons reached adolescence mothering became more difficult. They stated that their son's physical changes associated with puberty and the growth of secondary sex characteristics triggered memories of their own sexual abuse. In chapter 2, Laura shared that mothering her adolescent son was further complicated when her son's physical strength and growth made it difficult for her to set limits and maintain an authority role with him.

Mothers who experienced child sexual abuse also have difficulty with the emotional aspects of caregiving. In therapy, mothers have shared that they have trouble comforting and nurturing their children. Mothers perceived themselves as emotionally absent in their parenting roles, feeling numb, dissociated, and emotionally unavailable to their children, which interfered with their ability to function adequately as parents.[3]

Mothers have also reported difficulty with communicating, listening, and expressing feelings. Communication may be particularly difficult for survivors because dysfunctional family interactions and communication patterns are learned from one's family, and their own families had not modeled appropriate communication skills.[4]

Mothers who lack an adult confidant or are dissatisfied with their spouse or adult partner are more likely to engage in role reversal and depend on their child to meet their emotional needs.[5] Instead of the mother being emotionally attuned and available to her child, the child provides the mother with companionship and attempts to satisfy her emptiness and compensate for her lack of adult friendships. Role reversal thwarts appropriate developmental and generational lines of the mother–child dyad, and while the child listens and contains the mother's feelings and thoughts, the child abdicates their own feelings, needs, and wants.

Johanna worries that she did not adequately meet her children's emotional needs when they were young. She fears that the lack of emotional connection may have negatively impacted her children's ability to function. Johanna's two daughters are adults now, and she retrospectively describes how her inability to be emotionally available for them may have impacted her children:

> I fear that my children will be hurt by something I have done, or failed to do. I sometimes see my daughters struggling with personal issues and wonder if [I'd been] a better parent, would they not be struggling. My oldest daughter is overweight, has really low self-esteem, and is a single parent of three small children. Her boyfriend and the father of her children is emotionally abusive to her and is chronically unemployed. My daughter goes to work to financially support the family. I think she is overweight because she has self-esteem issues. I wonder if she stays with her emotionally abusive and

exploitive boyfriend because she saw me being abused by her father when she was growing up, and now she thinks it is normal.

My youngest daughter is also a single mother. She struggles financially and works all the time. I am pretty much raising her daughter, my granddaughter. My youngest is emotionally shut down and seems to be depressed. I take care of her daughter because I am worried that my daughter is not an attentive mother and is neglectful. I wonder if that is my fault, because she feels that I did not give her emotional warmth and nurturing. I was not a very warm or emotionally affectionate mother. I took care of their physical needs for food, clothing, and shelter, but I was not spontaneous and emotionally expressive. I am trying to compensate for my failures as a mother by being a more attentive and available grandmother.

DISCIPLINE

Women who experienced child sexual abuse have difficulties with discipline and often vacillate between using permissive practices and harsh punishments. Some mothers have difficulty managing their anger, act impulsively, and use harsh physical punishment to manage parent–child conflicts. Marjorie Saltzberg found that her clients had a tendency to overreact emotionally to their children's misbehaviors, and also expressed fears that they might harm their children and reenact the abuse they experienced as children.[6]

Susan Mapp explored the relationship between a woman's experience of child sexual abuse and the risk of physically abusing her own children. She suggests that the experience of sexual abuse is not directly linked to an increased risk of perpetrating physical abuse. Instead, she found that a mother's level of depression and minimal locus of control were the greatest predictors of a mother's likelihood of physically abusing her children. Mapp concludes that "the only path from experiencing child sexual abuse to the risk of committing child physical abuse is through the level of depression currently being experienced by the mother."[7] Similarly, Pamela Schuetze and Rina Das Eiden indicate that a mother's use of harsh discipline with her children is associated with maternal depression and her own current experience of partner violence.[8]

Many mothers who have experienced child sexual abuse have a tendency to be permissive. A permissive parenting style entails being inconsistent with rules, having problems with setting clear limits, following through on consequences, and difficulty holding their children accountable to external standards of behavior. Mothers have a tendency to be lenient in their discipline and have difficulty setting appropriate limits and following through on consequences. Mothers may also avoid physical punishment because it triggers memories of their own childhood experiences of abuse.

Mothers stated they were lenient in their parenting practices and had a tendency to be overprotective and excessively nurturing, and had difficulty letting their children be independent. Ayelet Meron Ruscio speculates that a lenient parenting style is utilized because "survivors may so carefully try to avoid forceful or punitive parenting that they move to the other extreme, avoiding directedness and discipline, withholding criticism, and ignoring misbehavior."[9]

Natalia struggles with being consistent, setting boundaries, and following through on consequences:

> Sometimes memories resurface when I have to set limits with my son. He is not an easy child. He always questions me and tests the limits. Sometimes he wears down my patience. I try to be kind and explain why I am asking him to do something, but I feel like I am talking to a wall. I try to explain everything to him but I have trouble following through with consequences. I feel like I do not have the strength to carry through and maintain the limits. Most of the time we end up in power struggles and he always wins. Then I get angry and yell and feel guilty afterwards. I will try to make up for our negative interaction by being kind, but eventually we end up in a battle. I do not know how to get out of the cycle. I want to be careful not to be like my parents, who were abusive to each other and to me. I just do not know how *not* to replicate what I have seen modeled all my life.
>
> I know my son needs limits and structure, but I do not have the skills, models, or support to be effective at setting consistent limits. He suffers as a consequence. He has difficulty in school, and is in a class with students who have social and emotional issues. I am in therapy and I take parenting classes. I am not giving up on him, or on myself. I want to be a good mother and give my son what he needs. I

will take all the support I can get to be a successful mother. I love my son and I want the best for him.

Wendi Cross reported that mothers who were victims of child sexual abuse experience problems dealing with the child's need for independence, confusion with boundaries, difficulty setting limits, and implementing appropriate developmental expectations, either by pushing their children toward developmentally inappropriate autonomy, or toward dependency.[10] These mothers tend to be fearful of hurting their children and reenacting the abuse they experienced. As mentioned earlier, this lenient style is a compensation for the punitive parenting the women received as children.

Fatima also has difficulties with setting clear boundaries and following through with appropriate limits:

> I feel like I do not set limits well. I get confused between setting limits and squashing my daughter as a person, so I have a tendency to be permissive and not follow through. I know that is bad and I continue to work on it. I have a fear that I have not given my daughter enough structure in her life. I find keeping to a structure very difficult. I did not have a structured life when I was growing up, so it is difficult to have one as an adult. I find that I am too relaxed and in the moment with my parenting, and my daughter can easily talk me out of the limits I have set. I know intellectually that this is not a good thing, but it is the hardest thing for me to do.

Johanna also had difficulty with discipline and following through on appropriate consequences. When asked what she found difficult in mothering her children, she answered:

> I was so overwhelmed that I did not follow through with my girls. I would verbally threaten limits but I did not carry them out. Sometimes I would verbally threaten these irrational long-term consequences that were unfair and impossible to follow through. I would get angry, and out of anger set an unrealistic limit, like grounding them for a month and not allowing them to use their cell phones. Of course, the consequence was unrealistic—unrealistic because it did not fit the behavior I was trying to correct, and unrealistic because there was no way I was going to be able to monitor their phone usage or to keep them grounded for a month.

After my divorce, I was working full-time, and sometimes I worked overtime to earn extra money. I was not always at home. My girls knew it, and they would not respect my limits, or me. What made matters worse is that when I did come home from work, they would lie to me and say that they did not go out or use the phone. I would find out later that they went out behind my back.

Zoë also finds discipline to be a challenging aspect of mothering. She attributes problems with discipline to being a single mother without a supportive partner: "I find discipline and raising my child alone to be the most difficult. Sometimes not having someone else to talk things over with stresses me out. I have to trust myself that I am making the best decision for my daughter. I have a hard time because I am tired all the time, and sometimes that makes it worse if I need to discipline."

FEARS ASSOCIATED WITH MOTHERING

Mothers express strong fears that they will not be able to protect their children from harm, and specifically from sexual abuse. The fear that their child could be sexually abused may emerge when their child reaches the age at which they themselves were abused as children. Mothers who were victims of child sexual abuse have intense worries and fears that their children will be sexually abused, are overprotective in their mothering, and have difficulty trusting others.[11]

Jessie has a "lack of trust in others," and as a result is overprotective:

I realize in my head that I might be a little overprotective, but I think you can never really be too overprotective. I'm also petrified of drop-ping her off at people's houses if there are men around. One time I dropped my daughter off at my friend's house and their closest friend, a man, was there, just to watch her two girls while my friend went to the store. She was going to be back in a few minutes. I just sat there and waited till she got back. I would not leave her alone with him. I don't know if that's being completely overprotective, but I don't really care. I just said to him that "I'll just sit here and wait." Was I late for work? Yes. Oh well, what are you going to do? So I am late for work. I trust my friend, but that doesn't mean that I trust my friend's friends.

> I vow to be overprotective of my daughter for her whole life, in order to make sure she never experiences any kind of trauma. That is better than being pissed off at myself for being under-protective and naively trusting someone. So I try to weigh the situation. I can trust the person 90 percent, but still, you just never know, so you always have to be cautious. It drives me nuts, because it could be anybody. It could be her father, it could be anybody, and it drives me insane, it really does, so I have to say to myself, "All right now, calm down."

Fatima also distrusts people and is fearful that her child will be sexually abused or abducted. When Fatima's daughter is not in her direct care, she fears for her safety, which creates an excessive amount of anxiety for her:

> I am always with her and I do not put her in the care of others. When she is away from me I get all kinds of nasty images of what might happen to her, and it is very uncomfortable and makes me very uneasy. The time off is not worth the tension I am experiencing when she is not with me. I do not think that it is normal, so I do not talk to other mothers. I worry about her safety. When she is away from me I am always scared that she is going to be hurt, or die. I know it sounds crazy, but I have fears that she is going to be raped or kidnapped. It is an over-excessive fear, but it is there. I know from my experience that you cannot trust anyone, and the surface picture is not the whole story.
>
> I also fear that she will be sexually abused. I am a bit overprotective of her. I do not let her go out alone or to sleep over people's houses. I am afraid that she will be abducted, so I am very cautious. She complains that I am overprotective but I do not care. I let her complain and then I agree with her. I am not going to change. It only takes once for her world to turn upside down. I think my abuse has made me paranoid and overprotective. I do not trust anyone, and they have to prove themselves to me over a long period of time.

Zoë expressed that she also does not trust many people. In order to protect her daughter from potential abuse, she does not let other people care for her daughter:

> Seeing how beautiful she is makes me more aware that I cannot trust anyone. I won't put her in "bad" situations where she is not protected and is open game for bad things to happen to her. I am not so

trusting and not so naive about men and women. Family or no family, I don't want to put my daughter in a bad situation. I won't let my daughter sleep over at anyone's house. I don't ever want my daughter to be in a situation where someone will harm her. I spend a lot of time with my daughter, and I think that is the reason why I don't want her away from me.

Even though Fatima trusted her boyfriend, she struggled with thoughts and fears that he might abuse their daughter:

I used to have these thoughts and fears more when my daughter was younger. I was very afraid that my boyfriend, her father, would abuse her—not because he did anything for me to be concerned about, but because I did not trust men. I did not trust that just because you are the father means that you are a safe person. I would ask him on occasion if he would ever abuse our daughter. He was very good about it. He would say that he is not an abuser, and has never had a history of abusing anyone, and he had never abused me. He also would say that he would never want his daughter to be abused, and if he had any feelings he would leave the house and go to therapy. That soothed me. It helped me to know that he never had a history and he would get help. Now, I should explain: If I really thought he was an abuser, I would not be with him. It was just a fear, and he knew it was a fear based on my background.

VIGILANT MONITORING

Mothers state that they monitor their daughters closely in and outside the home. As a consequence of their fears that their children might be abused, mothers engage in vigilant monitoring of their children.

When Magdalena's daughter returned from the babysitter, she questioned her daughter about her activities and paid close attention to her child's nonverbal communication in order to assess whether or not she had been abused in her absence. In order to ascertain if her daughter had been abused, Magdalena would question her daughter about her experiences when she was in the care of others:

I don't think I would ever give her a leading question like "Did anyone ever touch your vagina?" I would not give her any leading

questions like that. I just say "Did you have a good time? Who did
you play with?" I know it is weird. I don't ask her any leading questions and I wouldn't even insinuate anything. I would never ask her,
"Where did you sleep?" That's too far for me already. I just ask really
playful questions and I assess her answers. I don't want to start anything in her head. I just try to read her and I just ask her random
questions. I'll say, "Tonight we're going to go to Tom and Jane's
house," and I will try to read her body language to see if she really
wants to go there. It really drives me insane sometimes. Then I think
I do not care because I don't think there is such a thing as being too
overly protective.

In order to manage her fears and protect her child from potential
abuse, Magdalena states that she is vigilant about monitoring her
daughter. After her daughter is in the care of another, she questions her
and checks for physical signs of sexual abuse, carefully monitoring her
daughter's body for signs of abuse:

> When we go shower I look at her vagina. I don't sit there and say,
> "Let me see if anything happened," but I look, and it is, like, "All
> right, everything looks normal to me." I just dry her off with the
> towel and act like it is okay and there is nothing out of the ordinary. I
> am, like, "Jesus Christ, do I have to do this?" And I wonder—do I
> want to know what happened? I wonder if women who have not
> been sexually abused do that. Of course, you worry about your child,
> but do you actually go to the extreme by trying to read her body?

STRATEGIES USED TO PROTECT CHILDREN

To protect their children from potential sexual abuse, mothers teach
their children appropriate words for body parts and educate their children about "good touch and bad touch." They also encourage open
communication, so their children will not be embarrassed to talk about
abuse if it should occur. Magdalena felt that this would alleviate any
shame and embarrassment that might interfere with her child's willingness to discuss abuse with her if it were to happen:

> My sexual abuse makes me know that abuse can happen to anybody.
> So I am preparing her world and I want her to be completely com-

fortable. For instance, the whole anatomy thing is going to be correct. We are naming everything on her body because I want her to have the vocabulary, because if anything ever happened I want her to know how to express herself. I want her to know her body parts and have as many ways as possible to express herself if anything would ever happen. I want her to be as open as possible. I want her to be able to say all the body parts out loud and not be embarrassed. And it's weird, because I'm, like, preparing—but good God, I hope I'm not preparing her because something's going to happen. But I want her to be ready if anything does happen. Is that ridiculous? I don't know if people who have never had any sexual abuse, if they would stress that. I wonder if they do! That is why I make sure my partner also supports me in using the right words for body parts.

Johanna educated her children to use the appropriate names for their body parts, as well as taught them about sex. She also encouraged open communication with her children:

I also discussed sex with them in developmentally appropriate ways and times. In addition, I cautioned them about touching, good touch and bad touch, and how to be cautious of friends and strangers who really seem too nice. I told them that they could always come and talk to me and that I would protect them. I let them know that even when—or especially when—someone threatens them, that is a sign that they should really come to me.

Similarly, Zoë promotes open communication with her daughter: "I have to teach her to always speak up for herself, and if she is scared, that she can come to me and I will protect her."

LACK OF EXTERNAL SUPPORTS

Many mothers who experienced child sexual abuse lack the support of an extended family network. The mothers I interviewed and the clients in my practice were afraid to expose their children to the same family members who sexually, physically, and/or psychologically abused them as children. Mothers do not let their children have a relationship with their own perpetrator(s), and report strained relationships and limited contact with their extended families. Many of the family members are still actively using drugs or alcohol and have untreated mental illnesses. Mothers expressed regret that their children do not have the care of and contact with extended family, but the dysfunctional dynamics continue to exist in many of their families, making it difficult or impossible to spend time with or trust family members to care for their children. Therefore, they are unable to have ongoing and mutually supportive relationships.[12] [13]

Zoë and Elaina feel their mothers were not protective, were emotionally unavailable to them as children, and are still unable to offer safe and consistent support. As a result, they do not rely on them for emotional support, advice, or assistance with caring for their children. Zoë stated:

> I do not know my father because he left when I was only a child. So in terms of family, it is my mother. I would like to rely on her for help but she puts me down more than supports me. She thinks that supporting me is telling me what is wrong with me and what I need to do different with my child. I find my mother to be aggressive and a bit of a bully. She comes into my house, she is loud, and tries to take over. In her eyes, I do not seem to do anything right.

Elaina could not depend on her mother for consistent support because her mother is not mentally stable, or reliable:

> My mother suffers with bipolar disorder and she does not take her medication consistently. She is not high-functioning. Even though she says she loves my daughters, I would never leave them alone with my mother. For weeks my mother will go into deep depressive states and she will not answer the phone, eat, bathe, or get out of her T-shirt. During these times I worry that she will commit suicide. It is a huge burden for me.
>
> When I was younger my mother tried to commit suicide. I came home from school and she had overdosed on her medications and slit her wrists. I came home from second grade to see my mother on the floor with a puddle of blood surrounding her. I called 911 and they revived her and brought her to the psychiatric hospital. I temporarily went to foster care until my mother received treatment and the foster care system decided it was safe for me to return home.
>
> During her current depressive episodes, I visit her to make sure she is alive, try to convince her to take her medication and eat, and to

clean her apartment. She will be on the couch with the shades down, and from her despondent state blames me for calling 911 when I was six years old. It is exasperating to me. I am the one that should be mad! I would never leave my daughters with my mother; she is not a support to me as a mother. If anything, I take care of my mother.

Nieves and Johanna are raising their children without the involvement of their children's fathers. They stated that the lack of commitment and involvement from their children's fathers made the experience of mothering more difficult. Nieves shared that she is raising her daughter without the father because they separated when he learned she was pregnant. She expressed concerns and guilt about her daughter's lack of relationship with her father:

> When I had my daughter I naively thought she would not need a father in her life and it would not matter. I remember saying to a friend, how could my daughter miss something she never had. However, at age five, when she went to kindergarten, I realized that I was wrong and the realization caused me a lot of pain. It caused me pain because I saw the pain and confusion it caused my daughter. In school, she saw her classmate's fathers drop them off before class and pick them up after school. When she went to play dates at friends' houses, the fathers would be there. That is when my daughter started to ask me about her father.
>
> I did not know what to say and I was not prepared to handle her questions. I noticed that my daughter was becoming very needy and clingy to her friend's fathers. She would stand close to them and would want a lot of attention from them. This made me really uncomfortable. My daughter's father disappeared from our lives. When I found out I was pregnant he told me to get an abortion and left.
>
> I decided not to terminate the pregnancy and to raise the baby on my own. I had no one, and I was alone. I felt this pregnancy gave me the opportunity to start my own family. I was happy I was pregnant and I began to dream of a better life. When I was six months pregnant I met Jackie. She was caring and supportive of me during the pregnancy and in the first few months of my daughter's life. She was even there for the birth of my daughter. Eventually, we decided to live and co-mother together. I am a lesbian and I raise my daughter with Jackie, my life partner. I feel bad that I cannot answer my daughter's questions about her father, but I do not know what to tell her. I do not feel I can tell her the truth. I just keep repeating, "You

do not have a father; you have two mothers who love you." I know that it is not enough, but how do I tell my daughter that I did not know her father very long, and when he found out I was pregnant he wanted me to abort her, and then left, never to contact us again?

Johanna's two daughters have different fathers, and neither father is presently involved in their lives. Both fathers were addicted to drugs and alcohol, and both physically and emotionally abused Johanna and had affairs outside the marriage. When Johanna's daughters were young, they both witnessed physical abuse of their mother and persistent verbal fighting. Johanna realizes her abusive relationships negatively impacted the mothering of her two daughters:

Both my daughters' fathers were involved with drugs and drinking, and I experienced a lot of physical and emotional abuse from both of them. The relationship with my first husband lasted for three years. The relationship with my second husband lasted eight years. I stayed with my second husband because I was afraid to raise the girls on my own. I did not have the ability to financially support myself and my daughters. I was also afraid to be alone and without a man in my life. My second husband had a good income and provided well for us. We had a nice home in the suburbs, and food on the table; my daughters dressed well, and went to good schools. I had made a conscious decision that I was willing to get beaten three to four times a year in order to keep the current standard of living my husband provided for me and my daughters.

I kept thinking that I might be able to improve the relationship by attending to his every need. I cooked, I cleaned, I kept the girls "from disturbing him," and I gave in to his sexual advances. In order to avoid explosive episodes, I was extra attentive to him. Most of my energies went into trying to appease him, and I did not spend much time or give much attention to my children.

Finally, my husband left me for another woman. When I asked him why he left, he said, "You let me get away with so much, I lost all respect for you." When he said that to me I went speechless and numb. I stayed in that state for a long time. In retrospect, I realize there was nothing I could have done to stop him from his unpredictable rages and violence. He was an active addict and an abuser. I regret that my girls had to witness their mother being abused and to hear the constant fighting and yelling. I am very guilty and painfully sorry my daughters have never had a positive relationship with their fathers.

MULTIPLE RESPONSIBILITIES

Women who were victims of child sexual abuse report that they find the daily demands of mothering overwhelming, and that this negatively interferes with their mothering. Mothers state that they find it very stressful to balance the tasks of managing home and work schedules with parenting responsibilities. Mothers feel exhausted with the multiple tasks involved in caring for their children. They express that working full-time while managing household and mothering responsibilities leaves them feeling overextended, and limits the physical and emotional energy they want to provide to their children.

Fatima finds the daily demands of mothering to be stressful. She feels besieged and tired by the multiple responsibilities of mothering her daughter, completing household tasks, and working full-time:

> There is a lot to do when you are a mother. There is a lot to coordinate, think about, balance, and manage. Sometimes it gets overwhelming, and it is too much for me. Going to work, planning three meals a day, shopping for food and then coming home and cooking and cleaning, getting the clothes washed and dried and folded and put away. Doing homework and working out schedules like dance lessons, parties, dental and doctor appointments. It is a lot to balance, and there is no time for me.

Fatima wishes she did not have to work so she could have more time and give more attention to her daughter:

> I wish that I did not have to work and I could be supported. I would like to be a stay-at-home mom. If I could stay at home I would be able to keep the house clean, do the laundry, cook good wholesome meals, and have energy to be more attentive to my daughter. I wish that I could have more energy to spend time playing with her and doing activities with her. Being a mother is hard work, and I wish that I did not have to work an eight-hour day, because I feel it stretches me so thin that I cannot fully be the mother I want to be.

Zoë also finds being a single mother and managing the multiple tasks of household chores and mothering to be stressful:

> The most stressful part about being a mother is being a single mother. There is no one else but you to cook, clean, do grocery shopping, do laundry, or make all the money that is supposed to cover the bills. It gets very stressful and scary when you have a child dependent on you to care for and protect them.

Elaina finds the responsibilities associated with mothering and working challenging:

> Working full-time is challenging because it uses up so much of my time and energy that I would like to give to my daughters and myself. I do not get a lot of sleep. Making lunch, getting school clothes ready, cleaning, paying the bills, shopping, and being attentive to my children; it's a lot, and I do it by myself. I am not complaining, but since you asked . . .

In retrospect, Johanna spoke about feeling overwhelmed with "taking care of everything, keeping the house clean, working to pay the bills, shopping for food, cooking, cleaning, homework, laundry, fighting amongst the girls, doctor and dental appointments, and trying to take care of the girls."

FINANCIAL INSTABILITY

A primary risk factor in the United States is poverty.[14] Poverty is often synonymous with poor outcomes in health, nutrition, education, and employment. Fatima states that her limited income and financial stressors interfere with being an effective mother, and she does not always have the energy to nurture and offer quality care to her daughter:

> I always worry about money and not having enough. I pay my bills, but I live on a month-to-month basis. Sometimes I want more things, like a reliable car, a house, or new clothes. I do not want to have to worry about money, but I do. I think money issues are always in the sidelines, and create anxiety for me. I have a lot of responsibilities. I work two jobs and I am tired when I come home. I do not get to rest.

I have to make sure that my daughter gets individual attention. I want to find out what her day was like, what happened in school, what she learned. I also need to make supper, clean, make sure that her homework is done, get her to bed, and have her clothes ready for the next day. It is a lot when you consider that I work fifty hours a week.

Zoë also feels overwhelmed with balancing household responsibilities, employment, and mothering. She discussed how she makes choices regarding paying essential monthly bills, and how financial stresses negatively impact her self-esteem and sap her energy:

Sometimes I am so stretched and tired and I get cranky with my daughter. I worry a lot about bills and money and how I am going to pay for the rent, heat, gas for the car, food, and clothes. Sometimes I just want to give up, but I know that I can't. I worry about money all the time, and not having enough. So everything is on my shoulders, and there is just not enough. Last week I needed the car repaired so I did not pay my heating and electric bills.

My hope was that my daughter would not have to "feel" the struggle of being with a single mother that didn't have enough money to go around. I get extremely stressed out. It plays out all these fears, and I feel like I can't provide for my daughter and give her all she needs. I feel like a failure—like I can't keep us safe, fed, or happy. I feel bad because I want to sign her up for different activities but I can't because I do not have the extra money. I try not to let it affect me too much, because I don't want my daughter to feel bad, but it is a big problem. Sometimes, I have to be careful to not let all of my fears consume my every breath, and be thankful for what I do have, and what I am able to do for us.

Several participants feel that their employers are not supportive of them in their roles as mothers. Elaina's supervisor frowns upon her taking time off from work when her children are ill because her job duties as a teacher make it important to be available to students. "Because I am a teacher and work in education," Elaina noted, "there is a really high expectation to always be in the classroom. When I cannot because my children are sick—which, thank God, isn't often—they get upset."

Zoë does not have medical or dental insurance, and does not earn enough to pay for after-school care or babysitters when her daughter is sick. "I do not make enough money to pay for after-school care, and I do not get a lot of sick or vacation time. In fact, they talked to me about getting a babysitter when she is sick. The problem is that even babysitters do not want to take care of a sick child in fear that the other children in their care will get sick. My employer also does not offer family insurance coverage or dental, so I do not have health coverage."

After her divorce, Johanna lacked financial resources and had to leave her children with babysitters with whom she did not feel comfortable. "It was difficult to get time off when they were sick. I had to leave them with a woman who took care of a lot of kids and was a screamer, as I couldn't afford to lose any more time or money."

CONCLUSION

Mothers who have experienced child sexual abuse are challenged with a number of mothering concerns. Many hold negative views of themselves and express harsh judgments about themselves in their mothering roles. Mothers also struggle with drug and alcohol abuse and mental health issues, including depression, anxiety, and PTSD. Celia talked about how her addictions and depression interfered with being emotionally available to her two sons. Mothers also state that they have difficulties with nurturing and comforting their children, as well as difficulties expressing and communicating feelings. Johanna fears that she was not emotionally available to her daughters when they were young, and is concerned about the ways it may have negatively impacted them as adults.

Mothers who have experienced child sexual abuse have difficulties with discipline; they may use harsh physical punishment, or be permissive and struggle with setting limits and following through on consequences. Natalia avoids setting limits with her son to avoid triggering memories of her own abuse. Many of the mothers say that following through on consequences is difficult because they are already overwhelmed with the multiple tasks associated with mothering.

Mothers express fears that their children will be sexually abused, and are hypervigilant in ensuring that they protect their children from the abuse they experienced. As a result, they are overprotective in their caretaking and closely monitor their children. To compensate for their anxiety, mothers educate their children about abuse and create safety plans for their children in case they find themselves in an abusive situation. To ensure their children's safety, many mothers do not leave them in the care of others. Jessie and Fatima are overprotective, and Fatima said that when her daughter is away from her, she experiences so much anxiety about her child's safety that it outweighs the benefits of having time away from her daughter. To protect their children from potential abuse, Magdalena, Zoë, and Johanna have made sure that their children know the appropriate names for their body parts; they have discussed "good touch and bad touch" so that if they were abused, they could articulate what occurred without shame and embarrassment. They also foster open communication so their children will feel more comfortable revealing abuse if it occurs.

Many mothers who were victims of child sexual abuse lack external supports and are isolated in their mothering roles. Marginalized relationships with extended family members increase a mother's stressors associated with caregiving. Hannah, Elaina, and Zoë have frictional relationships with their own mothers and cannot rely on them for assistance or support. Absent fathers who are uninvolved in their children's lives create stress for mothers who then have to manage raising their children in isolation and without support. Nieves is co-mothering with her life partner and struggles with what to tell her daughter about her father, who abandoned her. Mothers find it very stressful to balance home responsibilities, work schedules, and caring for their children. Fatima and Zoë struggle with financial problems and trying to balance work, paying bills, and being emotionally available to their children. They find money to be a constant concern, as they work full-time to meet the basic needs of food, clothing, and shelter while simultaneously trying to provide quality care and positive attention to their children.

5

MOTHERING

Sustaining Resiliency

Despite risks associated with experiences of child sexual abuse, familial relationships can be significant protective factors that offer nurturing bonds and provide a reliable support system. Women share that supportive spouses or life partners, parents, grandparents, and/or siblings are sources of strength in their roles and responsibilities as mothers. A supportive spouse or life partner contributes in ameliorating the negative impact of child sexual abuse on mothering by diminishing stressors and increasing a mother's confidence and esteem. Spouses and life partners support mothers by acting as confidants on personal issues as well as helping in raising and caring for the children.

Parents, grandparents, and/or siblings also play significant roles in these mother's lives. Many of the women I interviewed stated that their fathers and mothers play an important and supportive role in their mothering. Olivia stated, "My mother helps with taking care of my daughter and is always willing to assist me." Mothers also said that as children, their grandparents—and in particular, grandmothers—were nurturing, and offered a respite from a dysfunctional home life, and as adults, these women continue to receive assistance from their grandparents. Grandmothers offer support by contributing finances, child care, and emotional support. For others, siblings offer valuable friendships and encouragement.

Mothers find friends to be important and a positive influence on their mothering. Girlfriends act as positive role models and increase their abilities to cope with the stressors associated with mothering. Friends offer direct support with child care and advice on child rearing, and act as confidants for personal issues not pertaining to mothering.

Mothers who lack role models for effective mothering educate themselves on parenting issues by taking college courses, reading books, and watching television. These external resources provide information on the developmental needs and stages of children and help mothers learn realistic expectations for their children. Higher education also affords mothers the credentials to obtain better-paying jobs so that they can adequately provide for their children and avoid the tension and pressures associated with poverty.

Many of the mothers I interviewed have found religion and spiritual beliefs to be important in helping them move past their abusive childhood experiences. Their faith has allowed them to reframe their negative childhood experiences and gain meaning and strength from the struggles associated with their past. Their belief in a loving and protective God or higher power helps to create a sense of calm and strength in difficult times and quell their anxiety and periods of depression. A religious community also offers long-term friendships.

FATHERS OF CHILDREN / LIFE PARTNERS

For mothers who have experienced child sexual abuse, a supportive spouse or life partner can be a strong protective factor that helps to cushion the emotional stress and burdens related to raising children. Mothers state that fathers or life partners who are actively involved in co-parenting can create an important support system that offers assistance in balancing the daily demands and burdens associated with mothering. Mothers report that a supportive partner who positively contributes to the family functioning by cooking, cleaning, and direct care of the children is essential, and eases the stressors associated with caring for the children.

When these mothers have strong family support, including actively involved fathers or life partners, they are more responsive to their children's needs and can employ positive parenting practices. Women who rely on their spouses or partners for companionship tend not to engage in patterns of role reversal with their children, and are less likely to depend on their child to fill their emptiness as a friend and/or confidant.[1]

Tasha states that her life partner is supportive and helps her co-parent their daughter. She feels that this affords her relief in the demands of mothering. Tasha shares how her life partner encourages her in her mothering role as they work cooperatively together to raise their daughter: "My partner always says good things about my mothering. As a child he was really hurt, so he leaves a lot of the parenting decisions up to me, and follows my lead. He supports me as a mother and is definitely very important. He doesn't criticize me and I don't criticize him. We talk together and discuss how to discipline and how to best raise our daughter."

Similarly, Fatima chose a "kind and gentle" man who is an involved and supportive father. She asserts that her ability to mother more effectively is associated with having a caring man in her life:

> I believe I am a successful mother and a better mother because I picked a good man to be my daughter's father. We have a home that is calm, without fighting and yelling. I picked him because he was kind and gentle and reliable. When I am overwhelmed I can ask him to take over the care of our daughter, and he does. He is always levelheaded and considerate. He is a really good listener, and he likes to do things with her. They go for nature walks and hikes with our dog; she loves that. They are very bonded and enjoy [their] time together. If it was a conflictual relationship, I would ask him to leave. Father or not, I will not live in a house with conflict. I have made a commitment that I will not let my daughter grow up in conflict like I did.

Fatima elaborated on the positive impact her relationship with her daughter's father has had on her. She says she finds her partner helpful in "healing" her past:

> My boyfriend is very helpful in raising our daughter. He really loves her, and I can take that love in vicariously. When I watch the two of them together I feel like I get healed. To watch a man be invested and devoted to his child, to have a man I can trust will not abuse his child, makes me feel so fortunate. I feel I get healed. I also get to see

another model of a man—a man who is not abusive, but kind and nurturing.

Grace is divorced from her children's father, but says she finds his involvement and consistent visitation schedule with the children to be beneficial. "I think one of the things that helped with my mothering was when the girls' dad started taking them on a regular schedule. Visitation helped me immensely, because I knew that whatever stressors I may be experiencing from all my responsibilities would be lessened on the weekend. All I needed to do was hang on until then."

PARENTS: FAMILY OF ORIGIN

Some of the mothers I interviewed had positive childhood experiences and fond memories they wanted to replicate with their children. Their own mothers and/or fathers were supportive when the women were young, and continued to play a supportive role during their adulthood, offering child care and relief from the stressors of mothering. These mothers felt that their parents had modeled a number of positive qualities that they desired to emulate in their own mothering. They said that their parents' compassion and caring was essential in overcoming the effects of their child sexual abuse.

Tasha had positive memories of her childhood and attempts to repeat those positive experiences with her daughter. When she was asked who her models were for being a good mother, she responded:

> My mom and dad were great. They spent a lot of time with me, and I think it's important to spend a lot of time with your kids. My mother was a stay-at-home mom, and my dad had a day job. However, he would take off from work and be there for school events and to watch us play sports. He was involved in our lives and his children always came first. My dad and I would go for walks to the park; I would ride my bicycle, and he would push me on the swings. Those are the moments you take with you when you get older—the time you spend together with your parents.

Many of the mothers I interviewed said that their compassion and ability to love their children was learned from their interactions with their own mothers. Olivia stated, "I got my compassion from my mother, and I have come to recognize that my mother's compassion and caring was essential in helping me manage the abuse I experienced. My mother put her children at the center of her life, and I do that for my children."

Similarly, Fatima shares the importance of her mother's love and dedication: "My mother was a good mother. We always knew that she loved us, and she was always available to us. In fact, she was able to give me some of the same things that I am able to give my daughter. That I can freely tell my daughter I love her comes from my mom, and that I can be attentive to her comes from my mom, and that I can be physically comforting comes from my mom."

Tasha's parents also provide a kind, caring, and nurturing relationship to her child: "I know that when I visit my parents things are easier for me, because the responsibility of caring for my daughter is shared, and my dad and mom take over. It is really appreciated. When my daughter visits them they give her a lot of time and attention. They cook with her, take her for walks, and play with her."

GRANDPARENTS: FAMILY OF ORIGIN

Having positive relationships with grandparents can be a critical component in resiliency. In both childhood and as adults, grandparents play a critical role for survivors of child sexual abuse. A connection to a grandparent is an important element in promoting resiliency, and can help to compensate for abusive and/or neglectful parents.[2] The mothers I interviewed said that their grandmothers were positive influences and were kind and gentle, which cushioned the difficult times in childhood. They also stated that it was their grandmothers who acted as models of how to be good mothers. Thoughtful, tender, and sympathetic grandmothers offered respite from the abuse that was occurring at home. Nurturing grandparents continue to be supportive by offering these women financial resources and emotional encouragement during their adulthood.

Zoë stated that her grandmother was an important and influential person in her life. Her grandmother was involved with raising her and provided affection and caring. Zoë's grandmother still plays an important role in her life. Her grandmother supports her in mothering her daughter by providing child care, as well as financial and emotional support.

> My grandmother helped raise me, and the love and nurturing that she gave me saved me from the loneliness and sexual abuse I experienced as a child. Today, I am a single mother, and I feel I have so many fears and burdens. Sometimes I feel so alone and that I am not going to make it. I get so depressed and I have suicidal thoughts. However, my grandmother still supports me emotionally and financially, whether it be a hug, a kind word, or some money to get groceries or pay bills. Her generosity is so needed in this period of my life. I am very thankful.

Fatima's extended family helps her in her mothering, and offers her a break from the responsibilities of parenting.

> My grandparents are very helpful to me as a mother, and I appreciate when I can get a break and know that my daughter is with safe and loving caretakers. I welcome their support and am so very grateful. When I visit my grandparents with my child I always get a warm welcome. My grandmother feeds me and my daughter, and my grandfather will take her to the backyard to play and feed the birds. So for a few hours I get to be the child again and I get to sit on the couch, be nurtured and fed, and I do not have to worry. While visiting my grandparents I get a short reprieve from the responsibilities of being an adult and a mother.

SIBLINGS: FAMILY OF ORIGIN

A caring and close sibling relationship can be a critical component in resiliency. Having a significant caring person such as a sibling in one's life can help to modify the negative impact of child sexual abuse (CSA) experiences.[3] Hannah stated that she was close to her brother throughout her childhood and into adulthood. Her brother acted as her protector in childhood and would defend her from their abusive father and mother. As an adult, Hannah continues to rely on her brother as an ally and confidant who offers emotional support.

Similarly, Eva has a strong emotional connection to her sister, Brianna. Eva shares the qualities in their relationship that bond them:

> Brianna and I have always been close. Even as children we were best friends and played together. We shared the same bedroom growing up, until I moved out of the house when I was seventeen. Since we are only ten months apart, our family refers to us as the Irish twins. As close as we were, as children we never talked about the sexual abuse by our uncle. We never said a word. Now that we are adults, we have discussed it and have both been to therapy, together and on our own. We have a pretty clear understanding of our family dynamics and how it impacts us and our choices in life.
>
> Brianna struggles with depression and anxiety, and we both have difficulty setting limits with others, and being assertive. I am not married and have a life partner. Brianna is divorced after ten years of staying in a violent marriage with an addict who was emotionally and physically abusive. Today, we are each other's sounding boards. If I ever have a problem I can go to Brianna. She is always there for me and I am always there for her. If either of us needs money, advice, or comforting, we are there for each other. We have raised our children together, and they are close. We plan family holidays and vacations together. My sister Brianna is my best friend, and I feel really comfortable with her. If I did not have her in my life, I do not think I would have come out of my family as undamaged as I did.

FRIENDS

Mothers report that positive relationships with friends and other non-family members offer guidance and emotional support, as well as substitute for the lack of caring and reliable connections within the family.[4] The mothers I interviewed feel that their friendships with other women are important in their roles as mothers, and have helped to build their self-esteem and self-confidence. Positive friendships help mothers to manage difficult life experiences and to ameliorate the negative impacts of child sexual abuse.

Girlfriends are a reliable and consistent support network. Mothers have said that their girlfriends help them to cope with the general stressors in life and in parenting, both sharing discipline strategies and offering concrete services like babysitting. Girlfriends also act as confidantes for difficulties not related to child rearing. Girlfriends listen and give feedback on problems with significant relationships and other life issues.

Fatima's friends act as role models for mothering. She pays close attention to how her friends behave with their children, and uses that as a standard of how to treat her own child.

> I have friends who show me how to set limits without being abusive, and how to be patient with my child. I have a memory of watching my friend relate to her daughter. She asked her daughter what she wanted for a snack. Her daughter did not know, so they opened the refrigerator and together discussed what the options were for lunch. The interaction went on for about five minutes. I was impressed, because it showed me that her child was first, even when there is a guest in the house, and that you can be patient with a child as they think through what they want.
>
> I do that with my child now. I am patient while she makes decisions. I do not try to rush or push her, and I appreciate working with her as she thinks things through. If my daughter needs me and wants to talk to me, I make sure that I turn off the television or turn down the radio to let her know that I am attentive, and what she has to say is important. I want to give her the message that she is significant. I want her to have the self-esteem that I lack.

Grace's friends act as positive role models and offer concrete help in the form of child care. She says that her friends are consistently loyal to her, and stand by her during difficult times in her life:

> I didn't have any role models to be a good mother. As I got older and my children got older, friends were influential if I thought them good mothers. I would ask advice and try to emulate things they had done. I would have friends that I would watch and see how they handled their kids and how they managed their homes. I had some friends that I trusted that would provide child care for my children when I needed a break. I was able to confide in my friends about my struggles with my husband. They stayed loyal to me and did not judge me. They would fill in for me and take care of my children when I was at my breaking point.

Girlfriends also act as confidantes with whom participants can discuss mothering and share strategies to improve their mothering abilities.

One mother shared her thoughts on the importance of the committed long-term friendships that have been available to her during her most difficult life experiences:

> I have friends that I can rely on. If I ever need anything, they are there for me. If I need advice or babysitting, they are there. They are also mothers and are very good role models. I am a recovering addict, and they knew me when I was active and when I became free of drugs. So they have seen me hit bottom and have stood by me and have been supportive of me during my recovery. When I need babysitters they are there for me, and I can trust that they will give my daughter everything she needs, and more, when I am not there. My friends listen to me and are present for me when I need to discuss things with them. They also share their experiences with me and use my advice, direction, and support.

EDUCATION: BOOKS, COLLEGE COURSES, AND TELEVISION

Women that lack appropriate models for mothering may augment their parenting abilities by exploring other models for mothering, utilizing books, college courses, and television to increase their parenting knowledge and skills.[5] Books, college courses, and television are resources that enhance their knowledge on child development and parenting techniques, and offer mothers guidance on how to provide structure, set limits, and manage difficult child behaviors.

Mothers with a college education said it was important and helpful to them in their mothering roles. Their education increased their understanding of the developmental milestones of children and helped them gain a sense of developmentally appropriate norms and expectations. Tasha stated, "Taking psychology and child psychology courses made it a little bit easier to understand the stages my daughter was going through. I would go to the textbook and it would show me exactly where my daughter was developmentally. It has helped me to know what is normal for her age, and not to treat her or have expectations of her beyond what she was capable of."

Fatima actively sought information about child development, and her college education was important because it taught her about parenting skills, the physical and emotional needs of children, and the meaning of "patience."

> I have learned a lot about parenting and child development from the classes I have taken in college, and I try to apply the information to my parenting. For example, knowing that you should be patient with kids because each child will learn at their own pace, and you shouldn't push a child if they are not ready. I learned the importance of being an authoritative parent that provides a structure to a child's life so they have a sense of predictability and safety, but simultaneously letting your child have freedom within the structure to make their own decisions. I learned how to manage sleep problems and temper tantrums from the psychology classes I took and the books I read.
>
> Having the knowledge and the skills to deal with children is really important. I have found that love is essential, but not enough. I learned that you use the love you have for your children to propel you to create a home life that allows a child to feel secure and safe enough to explore their world. As a mother it is my job to structure her life so she can have what she needs in the world to be successful. I have read a lot of parenting books, taken college classes, and watched friends and television so I can put together a model of how to mother my daughter and give her what I did not have.

Courses, television, and books on parenting can help by offering tips on providing structure and consistent limits for children. Olivia stated: "I read a lot of books on parenting and self-help. I feel that parenting books are helpful and give me guidance. I like the practical skills that I have gotten from reading. You get a lot of good information about the importance of setting limits and sticking to them. You see what happens to children and families if you don't."

Obtaining higher education indirectly impacts mothering because it affords mothers the opportunity to seek higher-paying jobs that enable them to provide for their children's basic needs. Success in school also helps to increase self-confidence and self-esteem. Tatianna said, "My education gave me a good profession to financially support myself and my daughter, but it also gave me a lot of self-confidence."

SPIRITUALITY AND RELIGION

Spirituality, religion, and/or a belief in God or a higher power benefits most of the women I interviewed. Belonging to a religious group and having a strong spiritual belief is a protective factor that supports resiliency.[6] A spiritual community offers its members a commonality where people are connected through collective values and shared beliefs. Being involved in a religious community connects mothers to a support system which can compensate for the lack of a supportive family network.

Many mothers feel that a spiritual and/or religious belief is beneficial, both personally and in their role as mothers. A belief in a higher power offers comfort and helps to manage times of stress and periods of depression and anxiety. Through prayer mothers find solace and the strength to deal with life's challenges. Spiritual beliefs provide guidance in how to structure their lives, and also help mothers to create meaning and gain courage and insight from their abuse experiences. Mothers find support and refuge in their spiritual beliefs and practices. Having a spiritual faith helps survivors of trauma to positively reframe their negative life experiences into valuable learning opportunities.[7]

Olivia's strong spiritual beliefs were learned during her recovery in Alcoholics Anonymous (AA), and through participating in the twelve-step process. It was in the "rooms" where she learned most of the important lessons in her life:

> There is a wealth of knowledge in the rooms. To this day the most important things I learned in life I learned in AA. There is nothing today that I know that beats the life lessons you can learn in the rooms. I learned to turn problems over to God, which is a valuable tool and lesson—a very valuable lesson. I was able to make safe connections with people, I was able to go make amends with my past, and learn how to treat people.
>
> I remember in my early sobriety and working through the twelve steps and the spirituality of AA. I grew up Protestant, but through AA I learned about real spirituality, and I learned about my own spirituality, on my own terms. It's allowed me to know what spirituality is, and I grew tremendously in terms of who I am. During one of the most painful times in my life, I was despairing and unhappy, but

I remember going to a meeting and I was heard and accepted. AA taught me how to deal with negative emotions and thoughts.

I don't know if God was looking after me, and that brought me to AA; I just know it is powerful stuff, and there is no question it works. I gained more meaning and insight by attending meetings than in any other aspect of my life. There's dysfunction in AA, but there is also spirituality—there really is. You can walk into a meeting at any hour. There's a cross section of humanity, and every kind of person in the world is there. AA offers safety and spirituality, and in these meetings, people are healed.

Celia found her recovery from alcoholism was beneficial to her mothering. She learned from the twelve-step programs how negative childhood experiences can impact adult alcoholism. She also learned the importance of expressing feelings, and that receiving emotional support from others is essential to recovery:

The healing process has given me so much that has positively affected my mothering. The twelve-step rooms helped me learn a lot. I learned the importance of having a sponsor to talk to, the importance of acceptance, understanding, and compassion. I learned that sharing your experiences and feelings with others is healing. The rooms are very powerful. You hear the stories of others, and you get to hear how people become addicts. It is usually because of a history of child abuse and neglect.

Fatima discussed how her spiritual beliefs help her in her mothering, and says that prayer offers her a time to slow down and a way to let go of the emotional burdens of her everyday responsibilities. She stated how prayer and the belief that you can give your problems to God provide emotional comfort:

I am just beginning to develop spiritual beliefs. I find it helpful and comforting to have a spiritual faith. I have a sense that I can go to a higher power and ask for help or divine intervention through prayer. I find prayer in some ways similar to therapy. A time to take a break from life and life's worries, and to go inside to take a few minutes to pray or meditate. It is helpful to me when I am struggling with a problem to put it into God's hands and to get rid of the burden. It helps me to relieve my anxieties and worries.

Fatima's religious practice offers her a community of like-minded people, and her priest offers her insight and valuable life lessons:

> I like having a community of people at church and I like going to church on Sundays. We have a good priest who talks about how to manage life from a spiritual view. He speaks about nonjudgment and how we are all God's children, and he reminds us of our blessings. Many times I think I forget how much I really have and how blessed I am. Going to church helps to remind me. A spiritual belief helps me to see how far I have come from my childhood experiences. I realize that today I am safe and I have made a very different life for me and my daughter. I am very grateful to God for allowing me the ability to break from my past and to have my own family. I have learned how to express love and caring in appropriate ways. As an adult I have learned to appreciate and achieve joy from the simple moments in life, like spending time with my daughter or watching my daughter and her father cook breakfast together. I cherish those moments, and believe that my history of chaos and abuse has allowed me to know what is really important in the short time we get to live.

Zoë feels that her spiritual and religious beliefs are important, and said she makes sure she shares these beliefs with her young daughter:

> I do have both a spiritual and religious faith that has had a major influence in my life and my role as a mother. I believe that Jesus is walking with me, showing me my path and the way I must go. My daughter and I are blessed with guardian angels in our lives and they are watching over us. I read the Bible to my daughter and talk about God because I want her to know that there is a greater power that is watching out for us, and we need to have faith and believe that we can get through our hard times, and that our struggles will only make us stronger.

Grace also finds prayer to be calming, and through her spirituality she has come to believe that life experiences can teach valuable lessons. Through her faith, Grace is able to see how her traumatic life experiences have helped her to learn about the importance of loving relationships. Through her spiritual growth she has learned self-forgiveness and compassion:

I am a very spiritual person. I believe that there is a universal power that is watching over you and that meditation and prayer can be a calming influence. I also believe that things happen for a reason, and that your experiences are about learning lessons that are important. For me, I learned the importance of forgiveness, not only for my abuser, but for myself—forgiving myself for not making the best choices in my life. I have learned a lot from my experiences. Just kicking my drug habit, I had to learn that I really wanted to live, and I wanted to live a life that was full of what really matters, like family, and loving your kids, and enjoying life. I enjoy my garden, I enjoy reading, I enjoy cooking, I have a good man in my life now, and I have loving children.

Hannah's spiritual and religious faith is an integral part of her and her son's daily life. She also feels a sense of comfort from prayer, and gives her worries to God. Her faith teaches her that God is taking care of and watching over her. She believes that God unconditionally loves her and is always there for her, even when friends cannot be. Hannah applies God's unconditional love as a model of how to mother her own child:

I try to make sure that my son has God in his life. He is respectful of people, and I believe it is because I model that for him. I have God in my life. When my friends are not available, I always have God. When I pray I feel a sense of peace. I have a strong faith that God is taking care of me and that I do not have to worry. I put my worries into his hands. I try to remember his unconditional love that he showed others. I use God's acceptance and love as a model for mothering. God is always there, even when others cannot be there when I need them. I pray every day and it gives me a sense of peace.

Hannah, a young single mother, made sure that her son was involved in the local church. She felt that the church community offered a social network that would counterbalance the lack of a supportive family network: "I believe in God very much. You don't have to go to church for that. When my son was younger I just strove for him to have as much normalcy and socialization as I could. By going to church I thought he could be around other families and around other children and participate in programs in the church. I was trying to keep him on the right track and give him a sense of community."

MOTHERING PERCEPTIONS AND RESILIENCY

Despite their difficult childhood experiences and challenges, the women I interviewed felt that they were resilient and enjoyed mothering. They consider themselves to be good mothers and make conscious efforts to not replicate the mistakes their parents made. At the end of the interviews I asked the mothers five questions:

1. How do you define good mothering?
2. Do you feel you have done well despite your childhood experiences?
3. Do you consider yourself a good mother?
4. What do you enjoy most about your mothering?
5. What aspects of your mothering would you like to increase?

The women I interviewed defined good mothering as being able to provide for their children's basic needs of food, clothing, and shelter while also being emotionally attentive and spending quality time with their children. When asked, "Do you feel you have done well despite your childhood experiences?," all the mothers I interviewed said they felt that they were stronger because of their childhood experiences, and that they had been able to turn their lives around. Whether they were recovering from alcohol or drug abuse, or dealing with the impact of depression and anxiety, low self-esteem, aloneness, or domestic violence, the women I interviewed felt they had survived and were resilient.

Fatima stated, "Yes, I think I have done well. I have gone to college and I have a full-time job and I am happy with my life that I have created." When asked the same question, Madison laughed and said, "Yes, I feel fortunate that I am alive." Claudia stated that she also felt that she was successful despite the difficulties that she had coped with in her life:

> I think I did well in spite of my childhood experiences. I have had to struggle with childhood abuse, poverty, and racism. I am Puerto Rican and feel that my children and I have experienced racism. Sometimes I have felt that I do not have a place in the world because of my abuse, and the color of my skin. I have been treated differently, and have had to work harder to prove myself. I have worked hard

to finish college, and I am the first one in my family to complete my college degree. The college degree has given me self-worth, a well-paying job, and respect from colleagues. I have come a long way!

Johanna feels that she has done well, and although she and her children struggled with adversity in the past, they have been able to move forward in their lives: "We are overall doing well. Although I exposed my children to an adverse environment, I eventually extricated myself, and them, from that environment. In addition, I have always been very open with my children about my life choices and how it affected me, and ultimately them. I think I did pretty well, and I know they are doing the best they can. That is all I can ask for."

Mothers were asked the question: "Do you consider yourself a good mother?" All the mothers interviewed stated they felt they were good mothers, and elaborated on the positive qualities they associated with their mothering. Mothers felt that they had done well despite the negative childhood experiences, and felt that they had persevered. All of the women declared that they loved their children and put their children's needs first, and that they wanted to give their children the mothering they themselves did not have as children.

Tasha's child is the center of her world, and she enjoys spending time with her: "I do consider myself a good mother. I try to live day to day, keeping in mind what is the best for her. I want her to reach her potentials and I want her to develop as well as she can. I also think I am a good mother because I have a lot of patience with her. She likes spending time with me and I do take time for her. I put her as the center of my world. Hopefully this will have a positive effect on her."

Celia's children are also the center of her life, and she views her children as gifts: "I think that I'm a good mother. When the boys were born they were just amazing gifts, and I treated them as gifts. I had such joy having my children and everything revolved around them. My whole role has been about taking care of them. I think I've been a good mother because I've been able to teach them about things in life, and I've been able to model for them, to impress upon them about making a difference in other people's lives."

Hannah feels that she was a good mother because she provided for her son's basic needs of food, clothing, and shelter, and she was emotionally available to him: "I am a good mother because I was there for my son. I made sure he had shelter, he had clothing, food, and a home. I was there for him to help him with his homework and I played with him. I provided things for him that I never had. And it's not just about the material things. I've always been there and loved him."

Zoë believes she was a good mother because she loves and supports her daughter and exposes her to new situations: "Yes, I do consider myself a good mother. First of all, I truly love my daughter and I do everything I can to show her that I love and care for her. I take my daughter and introduce her to new experiences. I talk to her and listen so that she knows that I love her. I love her unconditionally, no matter what she does."

Tatianna states that her child's positive personality is confirmation of her good mothering: "Yes, I do believe I am a good mother. Not perfect, but definitely good. Her spirit is partly a reflection of the way I have mothered her. She is very bright, she is kind to other kids, and to animals. She is respectful of people, and I believe it is because I model that for her."

Mothers were asked the question: "What do you enjoy most about being a mother?"

Hannah said she is proud of her son's accomplishments and enjoys being in a family: "I take pride in my son when he accomplishes things. I love him, and to me it is like having a family I never had. I have someone to share things with and we do things together. I can let my [inner] kid out with him. I could never do that when I was a child."

Fatima stated: "I enjoy everything about mothering. I enjoy looking at her. I look at her and I am enthralled that I have made such a smart, kind, funny, and pretty creature. I like watching her grow up, and I enjoy when she learns new things. I enjoy being with her and talking to her. I enjoy learning about who she is."

Similarly, Zoë enjoys interacting with her daughter and engaging her in a variety of activities: "I enjoy the time I get to spend with my daughter. I enjoy snuggling with her, watching a movie, cooking, and dancing. The list goes on. She is so much fun, and I feel so blessed to have her to do things with. You just cannot replace any of the time that you have with your children—it is so precious. I truly am lucky to have such a lively, vivacious child in my life."

When mothers were asked what aspects of their mothering they would like to increase, all of them said they wish they could spend more quality time with their children. Hannah stated, "If I could increase anything, it would have been the time we got to spend together." Similarly, Fatima said, "I would like to be more attentive and to give more time to my daughter." Zoë wanted "to be able to find more of a balance and make sure I get some quality time in every day. I want my daughter to look back and remember the times that she spent with her mom." Lastly, Tatianna wants to be "doing less of the managerial caretaking and household responsibilities and spending more quality time with my child."

CONCLUSION

Supportive relationships with significant people—including father of the child, life partner, parents, grandparents, siblings, and friends— help to alleviate the many demands of mothering. Involved and active fathers help by sharing child care and participating in disciplinary decisions; their helpful presence improves the overall functioning of the family. Fatima found that co-parenting with a nurturing partner was helpful in healing her early abuse because she was able to witness a nurturing, positive father–daughter relationship, and this vicarious relationship assisted in her healing. Olivia, Tasha, Fatima, and Zoë found that their parents and/or grandparents were invaluable supports that offered comfort, advice, and direct care of their children. Hannah's brother protected her as a child from her parents' abuse, and still remains her friend as an adult.

Positive and reliable friendships are essential supports for mothers. Friends are confidants and offer guidance and emotional support on both mothering and personal concerns. These outside relationships compensate for the lack of caring and supportive connections within the family, and serve as protective factors to buttress the negative impacts of child sexual abuse on later mothering.

Spiritual beliefs and religious practices also help mothers manage the daily demands of mothering and feelings of anxiety and depression. Some of the mothers find solace in a spiritual belief and/or a caring God who watches over them. Olivia and Celia expressed the importance of their involvement in twelve-step programs that offer concrete guidance and a spiritual conviction that they use to guide them in their life. A spiritual community also offers a support system that reinforces spiritual principles and provides friendships and community to compensate for the lack of a partner and/or extended family. Zoë, Grace, Fatima, and Hannah find that their spiritual beliefs and church offer solace and comfort, spiritual understanding to manage difficult times, and a social network which compensates for the lack of a supportive family.

Many of the mothers said that although they lacked positive parenting models, they have found alternative supportive models for mothering. Women who do not have good support systems scaffold their parenting practices by using courses, television, and books for appropriate parenting models. Mothers looked at television and observed friends, attended parenting classes, and read books on parenting in order to develop models of positive parenting behavior.

Mothers stated that even though they are tired, overworked, and balance a multitude of responsibilities, they enjoy many aspects of mothering experiences, including spending time with their children and watching them develop. Johanna, Celia, and Claudia have endured much adversity, but despite their challenges they feel successful in life and in their mothering roles. When mothers were asked if they could increase one thing in their mothering, they all wanted to change their lives so that they could spend more time with their children. Due to the responsibilities associated with employment and the daily demands of raising children, mothers feel that quality time with their children is often sacrificed.

6

THE THERAPEUTIC RELATIONSHIP
AND ITS IMPORTANCE TO
RESILIENCY AND HEALING

Twenty-five years ago, I was asked to speak on a panel with five other therapists. The topic for the panel discussion was "What do I bring to my practice working with women survivors of sexual abuse?" After accepting the offer to speak, I went to the library to research what other professionals in the field had written on the topic. I wanted to get a framework to help prepare my presentation. To my dismay, I could not find any relevant information. Although it seemed simple on the surface, it would have been easier to discuss the *clinical issues* and *strategies* related to working with survivors of child sexual abuse (CSA). I realized that the answer to the question "What do I bring to my practice?" had to come from within, and from the heart. I have to admit that the thought of speaking from my heart to colleagues at a professional conference left me feeling vulnerable. Still, this revelation shifted my approach on how to prepare for the panel discussion: I needed to get out of my head and into my heart; I needed to breathe and be silent, and to allow the answer to surface.

The answer that emerged was that to effectively work with women survivors of child sexual abuse, it is not only necessary to have the clinical skills and knowledge, but also the personal qualities that enable one to build a therapeutic relationship with women who are seeking guidance and relief from enduring pain. For a survivor of CSA, it is their perpetrator's betrayal of the relationship that caused them hurt and confusion, and therefore, the therapeutic relationship becomes an important path toward beginning to heal the hurts of betrayal that occurred with the abuse.

The therapeutic relationship necessitates certain qualities in order to be effective, and include kindness, acceptance, warmth, nonjudgment, and empathy. With these qualities, the relationship with the therapist becomes a corrective experience for the client, and in time, trust replaces fear, gentleness replaces anger, clarity replaces bewilderment, connection replaces aloneness, and caring replaces feelings of vulnerability.

I am glad that I was offered the opportunity to speak on the topic. As a helping professional it gave me the opportunity to reflect on and gain insight into the "use of self" in creating and sustaining authentic relationships, which is an integral part of the therapeutic process. A therapist must have the intellectual capacity to earn a degree and gain credentials to work in the helping professions; however, a competent therapist also needs to possess self-awareness and the ability to create meaningful relationships. The relationship between the client and therapist is significant to therapeutic outcomes.[1] Gentleness, kindness, understanding, and the willingness to join the path and journey of another are key to a therapist's ability to create the dynamics that will lead to healing. This can be particularly challenging when the path the therapist is about to join is tumultuous and comes with stories that are filled with sadness, hurt, torture, and pain. The mothers I interviewed agreed that in adulthood, an attentive and caring relationship with their therapist was critical in their healing and recovery process, which simultaneously improved their capacities to mother their children in more appropriate and loving ways.

Essential to resiliency of CSA survivors is having a person in their life who is thoughtful, caring, and attuned to them. For adult survivors, a positive relationship with a therapist offers the conditions necessary to establish and support resiliency. Carl Rogers summarizes the importance of the therapeutic relationship: "When the other person is hurting, confused, troubled, anxious, alienated, and terrified; or when he or she is doubtful of self-worth, uncertain as to identity, then understanding is called for. The gentle and sensitive companionship of an empathic stance . . . provides illumination and healing. In such situations deep

understanding is, I believe, the most precious gift one can give to another."[2]

The therapeutic alliance helps women who were victims of child
sexual abuse rebuild the trust that was broken by the abuse. The client
can tell her story and be heard without being censored, corrected, or
judged. The therapeutic alliance is the contradiction of the experience
of growing up in a family fraught with dysfunction. By treating the
client differently than she was treated as a child, the therapist assists in
re-creating trust and showing the client that she is valued and has significance.

One of the most important qualities of a therapist is the ability to
demonstrate empathy. Empathy is the ability to step into the life of
another person and experience what it is like to be them, to live in their
world, and, for a moment, view life from their perspective. The ability
to empathize is not a passive skill but an active process that takes energy
and sustained focus. Empathy demands attention and commitment on
the part of the therapist. It takes energy to be fully present and attuned
to another person, and it requires a commitment to momentarily sus-
pend your own thoughts, judgments, and evaluations in order to be
open to another person's lived experience. It is in these moments between therapist and client where connections and corrective experiences occur.

Achieving real empathy is important because most clients can discern whether or not the therapist understands them, or, as one of my
clients says, "gets it." When a client senses that the therapist understands her perspective, it works to support the therapeutic alliance and
increases the client's willingness to reveal more personal information
and to share feelings on a deeper level. An empathetic therapist vali-
dates the client's internal experiences and facilitates the client's development of a stronger and more flexible sense of self.

Chloe's Story

Chloe was referred to me after spending six weeks in an intensive day
treatment program. Chloe was diagnosed with post-traumatic stress disorder (PTSD), which had severely limited her ability to accomplish
basic daily living tasks. She was unable to function at work or at home,
and was unable to care for her ten-year-old daughter. She presently

lives with her life partner, Marilyn, who helps co-mother their daughter. Chloe experiences flashbacks, panic attacks, and exaggerated startle responses that are triggered by environmental stimuli. At the completion of the six-week day treatment program, it was recommended that Chloe continue therapy in order to maintain the gains she had made in the program.

Chloe is petite at five-foot-five, and weighs 118 pounds. Her blonde hair is cut very short and she typically wears a black leather jacket, a T-shirt, and jeans. She appears androgynous except for the row of three small diamond earrings in her right ear. When therapy started, Chloe appeared emotionally quite fragile, and only talked when she was spoken to. Her answers were brief and barely audible.

In therapy, Chloe revealed that when she was a child she was physically and sexually abused by her stepfather, whom her mother had married when Chloe was five years old. Chloe's new stepfather, Sam, was an active alcoholic, and Chloe was the target of his rage. Shortly after Sam moved in, Chloe began to experience constipation and severe stomach cramps. She would frequently cry in pain. When her crying disturbed her stepfather, he would beat her. However, as a precursor to Chloe's physical abuse, she would hear fighting between her mother and stepfather as her mother attempted to prevent the impending violence. Her mother's screams warned little Chloe that she would be next. To avoid the fury of her stepfather and with the hope of becoming invisible, Chloe would hide under the blankets and push herself tightly into the corner of the bed. Chloe said, "I remember trying to stop Sam from hurting me by softening my cries to a whimper so I would not be heard and disturb him." Chloe's mother's attempts to control her husband's drunken rages and to protect her daughter were futile, and Chloe was frequently beaten. With the ultimate goal of shielding Chloe from future beatings, Chloe's mother started giving her sleeping pills so she would sleep through the night and not anger her stepfather.

When Chloe reached the age of eleven, Sam began sexually abusing her. She disclosed to me that her stepfather's demeanor changed during the sexual abuse encounters, and he became gentle with her. Chloe said, "I realized the sexual encounters were inappropriate, but I secretly preferred the sexual abuse and kindness than my stepfather's wrath." The dilemma of Chloe preferring the sexual encounters over the physical abuse and violence added an extra layer of confusion and shame for Chloe.

In my office, Chloe initially presented as fragile, scared, and restrained. In our therapeutic sessions, there were often long silences; and when Chloe did speak, she was barely audible. During sessions, Chloe sat at the farthest end of the room, maintaining the physical distance between us. As therapy progressed, we slowly revisited her childhood. Chloe discovered that the message she received as a child was, "If I am visible or heard, I will be killed." As a child, in relation to her stepfather, the message was accurate. However, as an adult, this message was severely interfering in Chloe's overall functioning and her effectiveness as a mother. Chloe came into therapy because she yearned to "get better" so she could reengage in mothering and caring for her daughter. Chloe's goal in therapy for herself was "to find my voice and to be visible without fear."

When Chloe would share her past and talk about the abuse she experienced, her body language revealed elements of the effects of the abuse, and she presented as a frightened, forlorn, and vulnerable five-year-old child. Whenever she recounted her abuse, her head was down, she did not make eye contact, her voice was faint and at times would fade away into silence, her shoulders were slouched, and she held her arms across her stomach. While describing the events of her childhood, she would reexperience aches and cramping in her stomach, as she had when she was younger.

When Chloe arrived at my office for her first visit she appeared wounded and frail. For her, letting someone get physically and emotionally close to her was frightening and caused extreme discomfort. In order not to overwhelm Chloe and to earn her trust so she could feel safer and more secure in our relationship, I mirrored her verbal and nonverbal behaviors; her soft speech, slow movements, and long silences. I imitated her pace and slowed down, and I was soft-spoken and patient.

In order for Chloe to feel protected and allow her to let down her guard and defenses, the conditions of safety needed to exist. She was listened to, cared for, understood, and validated. She needed permission to express the sadness, rage, fear, and her sense of the betrayal and deep shame. Therapy gave Chloe the opportunity to tell her story without fear of blame or condemnation. By sharing her story with me, several effects were occurring simultaneously: a) Chloe was contradicting her lived experience and beliefs that "if I am visible and heard I will be killed"; b) she was having faith in the theory that revisiting the past and becoming vulnerable would bring healing; and c) she was trusting that she would be safe and I would be able to care for her while she was at her most exposed and helpless. As much as Chloe was suffering, she maintained a glimmer of hope that her life could be different from the nightmarish experiences of her childhood.

In the process of revealing early abuse experiences, clients are sharing the most vulnerable part of themselves and allowing the therapist to be a witness as they delve into their darkest and most unprotected inner spaces. During this process of sharing there is a union between the therapist and client; time stops, the therapist is silent, there are no words, no fixing or saving, just being present. To join another individual in this way is a privilege, and these moments are sacrosanct. It is in these moments where the therapist and client are attuned to one another and healing occurs. To this day, I remain impressed with Chloe's incredible strength and courage to enter my office to seek support and treatment.

THE THERAPEUTIC RELATIONSHIP AND MOTHERS WHO HAVE EXPERIENCED CHILD SEXUAL ABUSE

The therapeutic relationship is critical to resiliency and is a driving force in supporting mothers who were sexually abused as children. When I interviewed mothers and asked what helped or currently helps them to persevere, all of them stated that in adulthood, their therapist is a critical support in their life. Many said that their therapist is the mother they did not have and an exemplar of how to be kind and caring. Their therapist models how to be a good friend to others, which helps them to create long-lasting and supportive friendships. The therapeutic relationship shows them how to communicate effectively, and how to manage conflict and deal with feelings appropriately.

The mothers I interviewed stated that their therapists have been important and influential figures in their lives, and in many ways compensate for a lack of positive mothering models. They stated that their therapists are sympathetic and nonjudgmental, and show them how to appropriately mother their children.

Zoë shared how her therapist supports her in her role as a mother:

> The way my therapist treats me is a model for how I treat my daughter, particularly since I did not have a very good mother. My therapist listens to me and doesn't judge me; she supports and encourages me. I try to do the same for my daughter. When I had my daughter I had many ideas about being a good mother and what I wanted to do as a mother. However, working with my therapist has opened me up to more of the interpersonal relationship that I want to have with my daughter—sitting with her, taking time to talk and ask about her day, spending time with her even though I may have cleaning or cooking to do. What I have learned from my therapist has helped me in child rearing.

Sadie's therapist acted as a model for positive mothering and helped her to manage personal issues unrelated to mothering. Her relationship with her therapist enabled her to "heal," which in turn enabled her to be a more effective mother: "Therapy was really to heal me so I can be a real mother to my daughters. She mothers me and I can mother my children. I did not have a good model with my mother, but my therapist is everything a mother should be. She is there for me, she understands me, and she gives me good advice."

The therapeutic alliance helps to counter the negative family dynamics experienced by clients. Fatima stated that her therapist acts as a confidante and mentor, which helps her to increase her self-esteem: "My therapist has been caring and supportive. My therapist offers me direction in life and has helped me work on my self-esteem. My therapist has re-parented me and taught me the life skills that I needed for survival that I did not get from my family. I feel that I am able to transfer those life skills in parenting my daughter. My therapist is helping me move toward [becoming] the woman and mother I dream of [being]."

Grace discussed how the therapeutic relationship is important in modeling a caring relationship. She has been able to transfer the positive qualities intrinsic in the therapeutic relationship to her children. "With my counselor, I feel like I have someone who is interested in me and cares about me. I have a place to talk about my struggles and get listened to. He gives me advice and models how to be attentive and how to manage feelings. I am able then to give that to my children. I never had it in my family, so I did not know what it was like. When I did know, I was able to give it to my girls."

The therapeutic relationship is important for modeling healthy and affirming relationships. Therapists help the mothers I interviewed to manage interpersonal problems with significant others, and teach them the skills needed to create healthy relationship with others. The women have been able to transfer these skills to their mothering practices. Magdalena stated, "I was taught during therapy to express my feelings and to put labels to certain feelings, like sad and happy, so I try to do that with my daughter too. I try to teach her to use words to label feelings, like, 'Are you mad, sad, or scared?' I try to give her tools to express herself. I was never really taught how to do that until I went to therapy. Therapy lets you know what is normal and appropriate."

Grace stated that her therapist was important in treating her for her drug addiction, which ultimately led her to mother her children more effectively: "I got into therapy and stopped doing drugs. That turned me around. I was able to think more clearly and parent better. I was able to get down to a child's level and understand my daughters better. Now, I appreciate and value them more."

Grace said that her therapist not only offered a positive and affirming relationship, but also offered specific strategies to apply to difficult interactions with her children. "My counselor, when I finally went to counseling, was also there for me and did not judge me. He was kind and supportive, but he also gave me concrete advice on how to handle situations. Concrete steps were really important—do this and say that. I appreciated it. Insight was not enough; I also needed the skills and tools in order to manage situations that came up that were overwhelming."

An affirming and trusting therapeutic relationship can enhance and support the social/emotional development of the client. A relationship that is warm and accepting and where the therapist displays genuineness helps to facilitate healthy client development and supports success in meeting therapeutic outcomes. The mothers I interviewed stated that the therapeutic alliance serves to buffer the effects of childhood trauma and poor role models, and helps to interrupt the intergenerational cycle of abuse.

The therapeutic alliance goes beyond the traditional role of the therapist as expert and advice giver and offers a more comprehensive alliance. My interviews with mothers who were victims of child sexual abuse indicate that the therapeutic relationship is fundamental to the success of mothers as they manage the developmental needs of their children and the complexity of tasks associated with parenting. The therapeutic alliance helps to remediate their vulnerabilities and work through their issues of low self-esteem, depression and anxiety, drug and alcohol addiction, isolation, and lack of support systems. Therapists who offer guidance, warmth, support, and encouragement, as well as concrete advice and guidance, support women as they work to become more effective in their relationships and in their mothering. A positive and affirming therapeutic alliance is significant in mitigating the long-term effects of multiple adversities faced by mothers who have experienced child sexual abuse. It is through the therapeutic relationship that the therapist can utilize "self" to share information, expertise, and practice wisdom, and teach relationship skills by modeling effective listening and communication.

GROUP THERAPY

Resiliency is associated with strong social support systems, and group therapy is a modality that can be used to promote social supports and sustain resiliency. Group therapy is a major treatment modality for trauma survivors and is important in helping survivors deal with the effects of sexual abuse. In order to develop safety and trust, successful groups employ rules about confidentiality and protocols to guide interactions between members. When safety is created, group members have the opportunity to share their stories and break the secrecy and seclusion that surrounds the sexual abuse. Through dialogue women can recognize commonalities and offer the encouragement and acceptance needed as part of the healing process. Support groups are helpful for building relationships with other survivors, learning to tolerate the feelings associated with the abuse, exploring the skills necessary to maintain relationships, and providing an environment to engage in reflection, insight, and understanding.

Resiliency is fostered in reciprocal relationships where one can accept support and advice from others but also have the opportunity to give back. Group offers the arena for members to both provide and receive support. Paula Poorman found that "Thriving was not just viewed as an autonomous activity, but rather an interdependent one in which [participants] not only drew support from, but returned it to others."[3] Her study found that women gained personal power not in terms of accomplishments or successes that could be measured directly, but rather from the relational process where one was able to accept the support of others and also have the opportunity to give back to others. Reciprocity allows for a mutual exchange that enhances a sense of trust in others and a trust in oneself. The ability to give helps to build self-confidence, and helps survivors realize that due to the adversity they have faced, they have the capacity to offer support, advice, and compassion to others. Reciprocal interchange is empowering for survivors; it is a model for mutually fulfilling and respectful relationships; and it promotes healthy ways of relating.

In group, Chloe heard stories from other survivors that were similar to hers. As members gave voice to their experiences, Chloe was able to find the words to describe and express her own story. In the safety of the group, and for the first time, Chloe was able to formulate her traumatic past into words and create a meaningful personal narrative that afforded her the opportunity to express her grief and past abuse to others. With the support of the therapist and group members, Chloe had the opportunity to change her belief that "it was dangerous to be seen and heard." She began to speak about her feelings, ask for her needs to be met, set appropriate boundaries, and use her power effectively. In turn, she offered encouragement, support, compassion, and valuable insight to group members.

By bearing witness to others' stories and offering comfort and understanding, Chloe was able to externalize her own pain in a healthy way, and reduce the shame associated with her abuse. She also grew in her understanding of the dynamics of the abusive relationship with her stepfather, and over time was able to be forgiving and show compassion toward herself. The cohesion and caring of the women in group helped to build Chloe's resiliency and supported the conditions necessary for her to become "visible" and "heard."

STRENGTHENING THE THERAPEUTIC RELATIONSHIP: IMPORTANT CONSIDERATIONS

A number of qualities and skills assist a therapist in creating a strong client–therapist connection, which is critical to successful outcomes in therapy. Steven Ackerman and Mark Hilsenroth found that "personal attributes such as being flexible, honest, respectful, trustworthy, confident, warm, interested, and open were found to contribute positively to the alliance. Therapist techniques such as exploration, reflection, noting past therapy success, accurate interpretation, facilitating the expression of affect, and attending to the patient's experience were also found to contribute positively to the alliance."[4]

In addition to possessing the appropriate personal attributes, the therapist can make a conscious effort toward establishing and maintaining a positive therapeutic alliance. The therapist can develop and enhance the therapeutic relationship by actively creating rapport, working collaboratively with the client, utilizing self-disclosure, having congruency between verbal and nonverbal communication, and treating the client with respect, as well as obtaining further training and engaging in supervision.

The remainder of this chapter will explore the skills that enhance the therapeutic relationship, which in turn supports safety and trust, the two main conditions for an atmosphere in which survivors can explore and share their inner experiences.

Creating Rapport and the Therapeutic Alliance

One of the primary roles of a therapist is to engage the client in a relationship built on safety and trust. When a client feels safe and trusts the therapist, she will be more comfortable discussing difficult and sensitive issues.

The initial session is where engagement and treatment begins and first impressions are formulated. This initial session is the beginning of the client–therapist alliance, and it is important that the therapist exhibit feelings of empathy, warmth, and genuine concern and respect; as well, the therapist must convey that they have the knowledge and skills necessary to assist the client with their concerns. Creating a rapport with the client is critical because the relationship between the client and therapist is the thread that weaves through and impacts the entire therapeutic process.

A therapist can also support the development of trust and a sense of safety by creating a structure with protocols regarding confidentiality, the treatment process, and appointment times. The structure provides a level of safety so the therapeutic work can begin.[5] Predictability, consistency, and rules help to support a sense of security and safety, which is significant for survivors who have frequently experienced chaotic lives and unpredictable relationships with adults and authority figures. Maintaining consistency and predictability teaches the client that she can have confidence that the therapist is dependable and reliable. For some clients, therapy sessions are a refuge and the only secure place they have to express their thoughts and feelings, explore issues in their lives, and be heard and supported. In therapeutic relationships there will inevitably be times when failures in communication and misunderstandings occur, and having a strong rapport and sense of trust strengthens the potential to mend and reestablish ruptured relationships.

A Collaborative Therapeutic Relationship

Collaboration occurs when the therapist and the client work together to identify problems, set goals, and resolve issues. Ackerman and Hilsenroth affirm that "If a patient believes the treatment relationship is a collaborative effort between her/himself and the therapist, s/he may be more likely to invest more in the treatment process and in turn experience greater therapeutic gains."[6]

In order to help the client gain autonomy and personal power, it is important to minimize power differentials inherent in the therapist role. In a joint collaborative effort, the relationship between the client and the therapist is egalitarian, and the client is seen as the expert of her own experience. The assumption is that the client is the authority and essentially knows what she needs. The therapist offers a general structure to guide the clinical process, but therapy sessions are open and mutually shaped as an outgrowth of the client's stated goals and needs. In the beginning phase of therapy, the therapist may guide the sessions, particularly with trauma survivors who are new to therapy, who are cut off from their feelings, and/or who dissociate during sessions. However, the basic assumption is that the client knows the direction she needs to take and the therapist supports the client until she is comfortable and more skilled at influencing the content discussed in sessions.

To equalize the power dynamics, the therapist needs to capitulate the role as expert. Even the best therapists do not have the capacity to fix someone; there are no instant cures, and healing takes time. However, while the therapeutic relationship is a partnership, the therapist does not relinquish their knowledge and skills, and is still influential in moving therapy in the direction of therapeutic goals. The therapist's expertise is evidenced by the tools and skills the therapist brings to the session, as well as the questions the therapist asks, and the new meanings and understanding that are co-created through dialogue.

Working in collaboration helps to minimize the power imbalance inherent in the therapist–client relationship and ultimately empowers the client to perceive herself as an active agent, both in therapy and in her life. In this way, therapy provides a corrective experience and gives the client an opportunity to tell her story and to be the subject of her life. This is particularly important for women who were sexually abused as children and whose power and autonomy were usurped in the exploitative relationship with the perpetrator.

I have learned that the biggest gift I can offer both to myself as a therapist and to my client is to set aside my ego and, knowing that healing from trauma unfolds over time, to let go of the desire to fix the client's problem, or to always say just the right words. When I am "trying" to be a proficient therapist, I am rendered less effective. The best sessions have occurred when I stayed connected to the client, kept it simple, listened, allowed silences, and took the client's lead. As a therapist, one of my main goals when I meet a client is to secure a safe and trusting environment and to bear witness to my client's unfolding story.

Therapeutic Use of Self-Disclosure

Self-disclosure occurs when the therapist shares personal information with a client, going beyond the roles of listening and offering insight, support, and/or advice. Disclosure on the part of the therapist needs to be done with care and must be purposeful. Self-disclosure is an important component of a strong therapeutic alliance that is empowering to the client. However, discerning the degree and the amount of disclosure needs to be done thoughtfully.

Nancy Bridges advises on the parameters a therapist should use when revealing personal aspects of self, and states that the therapist needs to "guard against excessive disclosures, and disclosures that shift the focus away from the patient."[7] Many clients appreciate their therapist's self-disclosure because it helps to normalize the dilemma they are struggling with, eases their sense of aloneness, increases awareness, and/or supports the client in making a positive shift in their perspective on the problem. Therapist self-disclosure improves the client's ability to feel connected to their therapist and strengthens the overall therapeutic relationship. When the therapist reveals aspects of their personal life, it assists in equalizing the relationship between client and therapist. Clients see their therapists as "more real," and feel that their self-disclosures "humanize" them without diminishing their role as a helper.[8] However, some clients do not want the therapist to be revealing, and feel that therapist self-disclosure takes the focus and attention away from them. In these instances, the therapist should be respectful of a client's desire to maintain firm boundaries.

While most clients appreciate a therapist's self-disclosure, only under certain conditions are disclosures helpful. Clients feel that the potency of therapist disclosure is enhanced by its *infrequent* occurrence.[9] Clients can become confused by a therapist's self-disclosure, and the therapist should wait until later in the therapeutic relationship, when a level of trust and safety has been established in the therapeutic alliance. Clients find therapist self-disclosures helpful when the self-disclosure is relevant to and reflective of the client's current concern. Clients also report feeling uncomfortable when the therapist exposes private aspects of their life they are currently struggling with, but find it helpful when the therapist discloses past issues that have already been resolved, and they are able to share the skills, lessons, and insights learned from the resolution of the experience.

Awareness and Congruency in Communication

The majority of mothers I have worked with who experienced child sexual abuse are very sensitive, aware, and intuitive when it comes to reading the emotions of others. They are astutely aware of spoken words as well as unspoken ones, interpreting the meanings embedded in silence, and are attentive to the moods of others. For many of my clients, words are not as important as the nuances of communication, and they are very skilled at observing body language, facial expressions, and tone of voice. Some of my clients have the uncanny capacity to recognize incongruences in verbal and nonverbal behaviors and cues. In homes where abuse occurs, children receive double messages, and as an adaptive skill for survival and self-protection, CSA survivors become adept at perceiving emotions and being attentive to incongruences between verbal and nonverbal communication. As a result, many clients are aware if the therapist is only physically and/or intellectually present but not emotionally attuned to them. During sessions, it is important for the therapist to be fully attentive and present and to ensure that their internal and external states are congruent.

Congruency in communication occurs when our words, tone of voice, and body language are all in alignment. Congruency is an active process whereby the therapist is aware of their own thoughts and feelings and at the same time is attuned to the client's process. Leslie Greenberg and Shari Geller have written extensively on the importance of congruency and effective therapeutic presence, and state that "the therapist needs to be fully present in the therapeutic encounter in order for congruence to be therapeutic. Therapists cannot bring extraneous personal baggage, needs, or even agendas for therapy into the encounter. Being able to be fully present to the other is a highly developed skill that requires a letting go of preconceptions and full attention in the moment."[10]

The sexual abuse experience is damaging because the perpetrator treats the victim as an object for their own personal gain. When working with sexual abuse survivors, therapists need to be sensitive to the impact their behavior and inquiry may have on their clients. Carl Rogers believes that it is important to maintain a genuine and authentic relationship with a client, and warns of making the client into an oddity or an object. He wrote: "I enter the relationship not as a scientist, not as a physician, who can accurately diagnose and cure, but as a person, entering into a personal relationship. Insofar as I see him only as an object, the client will tend to only become an object."[11]

Congruency in communication is also associated with the questions that we ask our clients. Questions can help to increase the therapeutic alliance and to show the client that the therapist is involved, interested, and cares; however, questions that are devoid of empathy and caring only act to objectify the client and, to some degree, reenact the exploitative relationship and the client's original core hurt.

In the first agency where I worked, in order to gain access to counseling services, clients went through a formal intake interview which lasted an hour. The client was told that the questions and their responses would aid in assessment, formulating a diagnosis, and creating the initial treatment plan. I sat at the desk with the intake form and pen in my hand so I could write the clients' responses to the questions. The intake interview ascertained basic identifying questions like the client's name, age, and marital status, the number of children, where they worked and lived, and income level. After obtaining the basic information, the next step was to address the client's presenting problem, needs, and services they would require. I noticed that when I asked a series of questions to delve into the client's concerns, I was directly contributing to the client's feelings of discomfort and objectification.

When a client is dealing with domestic violence, rape, divorce, depression, and/or anxiety, it is essential to avoid bombarding the client with a series of questions that are emotionally loaded. The therapeutic process is a balance between understanding the presenting issues and joining the client in a relationship. It is important to carefully gather information without overwhelming the client and heightening her distress and discomfort from the interchange. Asking a barrage of questions can result in a client feeling like an object and exacerbate her emotional state, especially if attention is not given to the feelings that arise when the client attempts to answer. When a therapist meets with a client, it is important that the therapist does not re-create conditions that would make the client feel objectified, and to explore the client's inner life and experiences with sensitivity and awareness.

Heal Thyself: Supervision and Training

No one goes through life unscathed, and everyone has a story related to childhood and/or adult experiences that have been hurtful and have left an enduring impact on their worldview and possibly the degree and quality of their functioning. When therapists have the opportunity to examine and work through their own personal issues, they invariably become more effective therapists. Many treatment strategies are taught experientially so the therapist has the opportunity to simultaneously work on their own healing while learning therapeutic theory and skills. A clinician is more effective in intervening with clients when they have worked on their own emotional blocks and/or dysfunctional individual or family patterns. How can you take a client where you dare not go yourself? Within training groups, therapists practice with one another the skills and techniques they are learning, based on the belief that clinicians need to heal their own wounds so they can be more effective with their clients.

A therapist who has made a commitment to examine "self" in a therapy milieu will concurrently learn important therapeutic skills and improve their competency as a therapist. Personal work helps the therapist to understand the vulnerability of being a client and the impact one feels when revisiting the past and examining the places they have been hurt. When a therapist works on their own issues, their experiences can make them both more sensitive and better able to ascertain when to push past their client's fears, and when to be respectful of defenses; the importance of listening; and the necessity of a strong therapeutic alliance. Therapy and/or experiential training helps a therapist learn to be more comfortable with expressing their own feelings and accepting the feelings of others. It also increases the therapist's ability to tolerate strong feelings, and, therefore, enhances their ability to create a safe space for their clients to express a range of emotions, including pain, anger, and sadness.

It is extremely important that therapists who work with survivors of complex trauma do not practice in isolation. Supervision can support the therapist in their capacity to manage and contain the stories of clients, which include horrific, distressing, and many times explicit details of abuse and neglect. Invariably, there will be moments when the therapist is rendered incapable of moving forward in the session with a client and will not know the best therapeutic direction to take. There will be times when a therapist is challenged by a client, but the key is to know when one is "stuck" and to reach out for supervision in order to regain clarity and focus. When a clinician has utilized all their skills and tools but remains at an impasse with a client, it is crucial to use supervision for guidance. It is important for a therapist to have a good rapport with a supervisor and colleagues with whom they can safely share personal issues that may be triggered by clients. Supervision, whether formal with a designated supervisor or informal with colleagues, can both help illuminate issues that might interfere with the ability to be objective with a client and help a therapist clarify the appropriate therapeutic direction.[12]

CONCLUSION

Mothers who have experienced child sexual abuse confirm that their therapist has a positive influence on their mothering. Their therapists offer support, compassion, and understanding, which help them to foster resiliency and emotional endurance. The therapeutic relationship offers a "corrective" experience where mothers receive the nurturing and attention they did not get as children, and act as a positive role model for mothering. These women state that their therapist helps them work through issues related to past abuse which in turn enables them to be more effective mothers. Zoë, Sadie, Fatima, Grace, and Magdalena share that their therapists play a critical role in their mothering by offering concrete advice on how to manage parent–child conflicts and acting as models for positive mothering.

The therapeutic relationship offers an opportunity for clients to learn how their past abuse experiences have interfered with their current adult functioning. A trusting therapeutic relationship affords the mothers I interviewed the opportunity to engage in introspection and learn skills necessary to maintain supportive relationships. Therapists assist mothers in managing the long-term impact of CSA, mental health concerns, alcohol and drug addictions, and current problems with significant adult relationships.

Building a trusting and safe therapeutic alliance is important and helps to support the therapist and client in exploring sensitive and personal issues. The therapeutic relationship is enhanced when the therapist collaborates with the client, effectively uses self-disclosure, and acquires training and supervision.

Sexual abuse survivor groups are important because women are able to share commonalities with other women who face similar challenges. There is a strength in knowing one is not alone in experiences and feelings. Group therapy allows members to look at the abuse and the adversity that they have endured with others who have similar stories. Receiving support is significant in one's growth; it is also empowering and healing to have the capacity and the desire to give back to others. It is in giving to others that members can see themselves as capable, and it helps to assist them in their social and emotional growth. Supportive bonds that are fostered among group members helps to break the isolation and shame related to the abuse.

Chloe was able to build her self-confidence and strengthen her communication skills in the protection and safe boundaries of individual and group therapy. In an environment of acceptance and support, Chloe was able to explore new ways of thinking, feeling, and behaving. Utilizing the relational skills modeled in individual and group therapy, Chloe was able to use her new skills outside the therapeutic milieu. With encouragement and practice, she used these skills outside the therapy office in her everyday life with family, friends, and colleagues at work. With the combination of individual and group therapy, Chloe was able to build strong relationships and transform herself into a creative and resourceful woman; as a result, she felt empowered to make personal change, and to continue an active role in co-parenting her daughter.

7

A LEGACY OF TRAUMA

Mechanisms for Intergenerational Abuse

My experience working with mothers who were survivors of sexual abuse began when I worked in a home-based family therapy prevention program. The program was designed to prevent the placement of children into foster care, or to facilitate the return of children already placed in foster care to their families by improving and stabilizing family functioning. I worked closely with a team of service providers that included a supervisor and caseworker from Child Protective Services (CPS), a family court judge, a law guardian, a consulting psychologist, and foster parent/s. I counseled clients with a range of concerns, including domestic violence, child abuse and neglect, parent-child conflict, and marital problems. All of the families I worked with were court-mandated to participate in counseling and were working-class/poor and marginalized members of the community. The families struggled with the chronic traumas of abuse, neglect, and poverty across several generations. The clients referred to our agency were predominantly the poorest of the poor, and came from economically depressed inner-city neighborhoods with inadequate housing, high levels of crime and violence, and academically low-performing schools. The physical poverty that my clients contended with reflected a poverty of spirit that resulted from cumulative traumas and generations of familial abuse and neglect, along with social poverty, racism, classism, and sexism.

This was my first experience in my new role as a social worker, after graduating with a master's degree in social work. This population of clients is considered difficult to work with because counseling services are court-mandated rather than voluntary, and clients are usually angry that the consequence of not abiding by the court order is the loss of custody of their children. Since family treatment is mandated by family court, most clients perceive the team of service providers as threatening and intrusive, and service providers are often faced with clients' hostility and resistance.

For the professionals who work with this population, the hours are long and the pay is low. Family sessions occur in the client's home and usually in the evenings, when all family members can be present. Workers frequently encounter dangerous situations with threats of violence from families who feel powerless, angry, and violated by court systems and social service agencies that they perceive as impinging on their family and threatening to take their children.

On my first day of work my supervisor welcomed me to the agency and informed me with a smile and a forewarning that the job was the "trench work of social work, but you have to start somewhere." Regardless, I was committed to working with mothers and their children, underserved populations, and at-risk families.

My first client was a nineteen-year-old mother named Clara, whose ten-month-old daughter Lily had been placed in foster care. In order to regain custody of her daughter, Clara had to successfully fulfill the reunification requirements outlined in the court order, with the following conditions:

- Maintain weekly supervised visits with her daughter;
- Maintain weekly appointments with the CPS worker;
- Maintain weekly appointments with the family therapist;
- Attend weekly parent support classes;
- Maintain a stable residence for at least six months; and
- Maintain a steady income from employment or public assistance.

Clara's Story

Clara's mother left Clara when she was three years old with her father and two older brothers. When Clara was twelve, her father died of lung cancer, her fourteen-year-old brother went into residential treatment, and her eighteen-year-old brother moved out to live on his own. Clara went to live with her paternal aunt and her husband.

When Clara was a child, she and her family were considered the outcasts of their community—"trailer trash," as she described herself. Clara and her family grew up in a rural area isolated from friends and neighbors. They rented a two-bedroom trailer in which her brothers shared one bedroom, she had the second bedroom, and her father, who was diagnosed with emphysema and relied on an oxygen tank, slept in the living room on a reclining chair. Her older brothers got into trouble with the police for vandalism and petty theft. As the female of the house, and the parentified child, Clara was responsible for housework and caring for her ailing father, particularly toward the end of his life, when he was unable to walk by himself and needed help with dressing, eating, going to the bathroom, and taking his medications.

Clara's older brother Liam sexually abused Clara from the ages of nine to twelve:

> I was never really mad at Liam for molesting me because I knew that he was struggling, and was just as lost and scrambling as the rest of the family. Even though I knew what he did to me was wrong, I also recognized that he tried to take care of my brother and me. Liam protected me at school when I was teased by other kids. He also had a part-time job working at the neighbor's farm, and took his earnings and bought me clothes for school and presents for my birthday. Liam would save food from his school lunch and give it to me and my brother when he got home.
>
> Liam seemed to be the most impacted out of all of us, and started smoking pot when he was in middle school. After Dad died and the family split up, Liam told me he was sorry. Till this day I am not sure what he was sorry for. I do not know if he was sorry for molesting me, or for not being able to keep the family together, or for our entire life and what we had been through.

When I asked Clara how she had survived, she could have chosen a number of ways to answer this question, but she replied:

> When my brother was molesting me, I was thinking that he was testing me to see if I was a "real princess," and I imagined that if I was a real princess, that everything in the house would change and

everything at home would be better. I imagined that if I was a real princess, the family would have money and we would be rich and live in a big house, and Mommy would be happy and come back, and Daddy would get better from the emphysema.

However, when I woke up and walked into the living room, I saw Dad smoking a cigarette, the house was a mess, and my mother had not returned. At that moment I realized that I was not a princess, and I was not going to be able to save my family. My body became heavy and I felt despair as I realized I was totally alone. I had no one to go to, not my father who was dying, or my mother who had left years before.

As a child Clara was ostracized and did not have friends. Her father lacked the funds to pay for school field trips, purchase school pictures, or buy snacks for recess. Clara recounted how she felt "like disappearing into the floor" as she watched her classmates get on the bus to go on a field trip while she sat in the principal's office for the day. Isolation, fending for herself, and the shame associated with growing up poor and as an outcast in her community was very familiar to Clara, but the feelings of not being accepted and the social rejection always remained painful, and never got easier for her to manage.

Clara's paternal aunt Helen and her husband Al took custody of Clara. They did not have children of their own and Clara felt welcomed and grateful to them. Clara left the community that scorned her and her family, and had a new beginning. Unlike living with her brothers and father, Clara's burdens and responsibilities were minimized and she was no longer expected to clean and cook. Even though Clara missed her family, she was also relieved that she was no longer responsible for caring for her ailing and dying father. Clara settled into her new school and was able to devote her time to her studies. She received high marks in school and made new friends. Her aunt and uncle gave her everything she needed and were generous and caring. Clara was relatively happy except that she worried about the circumstances of her two brothers, with whom she had lost communication.

After a few years of living with her aunt and uncle, her uncle started taking Clara fishing on his boat, a hobby Al was passionate about, but which did not interest Aunt Helen. At sixteen, Al took Clara for driving lessons. It was during these boat and car outings, when Clara and Al were alone, that he sexually abused her.

At the age of sixteen, Clara decided to quit school and ran away from her aunt and uncle's home. Clara shared,

> I instinctively knew that if I revealed to Aunt Helen that her husband was molesting me, I would be blamed. I knew that Aunt Helen's allegiance was to Al, and I would be held responsible. I could not spend another Christmas in that house, pretending to be part of a happy family and grateful for everything I was given. I hated Al, and I started hating my aunt for being so stupid. I started to wonder how she could not know what Al was doing to me. He took me away every weekend on fishing trips and several times a week for driving lessons. On numerous occasions I resisted going with Al and used the excuse that I had a test to study for, or that I was not feeling well. It did not matter, and most times I ended up going. I even tried to find a weekend job at the mall so I would have a legitimate excuse to stay home. I could no longer live a double life pretending to be indebted to both of them and pretending everything was fine.
>
> Aunt Helen would constantly tell me and the neighbors what a good uncle Al was, how he helped me get my boating license, took me on fishing trips, and was teaching me to drive. If I had to listen to her high-pitched, hysterical voice describing our idyllic relationship, to me or to someone else, I was going erupt. So I made the decision to leave. It was finals week at school and I did not have it in me to study. I felt worn out and did not have much energy for anything, especially the stamina to keep up the charade of my happy life with my aunt and uncle. So I decided to leave. I did not write a note and I did not tell any of my friends. I just wanted to quietly disappear with no drama.
>
> I had just turned sixteen; it was December, two weeks before Christmas. I left school at lunchtime. I dumped my schoolbooks in the trash, walked to the highway, and put my thumb out. I knew of the potential dangers of hitchhiking but I didn't care. I didn't care if I died. Dying felt a lot easier than living. I guess I was not brave enough to kill myself, but I was not going to stop it from happening. Death would have been a welcome relief from my life.
>
> The first person who picked me up was an older man. He asked me where I was going and I said to him, "I am going to wherever you stop driving." I said the same thing to each person that gave me a ride. In one week I went through three states. Sometimes the people that picked me up gave me money or went through McDonald's and

bought me something to eat. I slept in bus and train stations and I panhandled for money.

I met Dante at the train station while I was panhandling. He gave me money to pay for a motel room for a few days and told me to get some rest and a shower. That next morning, he came to the motel and took me out for breakfast. After a few days Dante said it was getting too expensive for him to continue paying for a motel, and he invited me to stay at his apartment. He promised I would be safe and he did not want anything from me. He said I could leave anytime I wanted. I went with him to his apartment and as promised, he never asked anything from me. I cleaned the apartment and made him coffee and breakfast before he went to work. I had to do something in exchange for living at his place for free. After a month we started to live together as boyfriend and girlfriend.

Dante worked in an auto shop and sold drugs to supplement his income. One day Dante asked me to deliver a package to a friend on the other side of town. When I arrived at the apartment the police were inside and everyone, including myself, was arrested for sale and possession of a controlled substance. I was sure Dante would come bail me out and get me a lawyer, but I never heard from him again. I was told by Dante's friend that he set me and his friends up in order to get a plea deal for himself. I don't know what to believe, but I know that Dante was there for me when I was at the bottom.

I was sentenced to a year in jail. At the time I was sentenced I found out that I was pregnant, and had my baby in jail. I named her Lily. Lily was taken from me at birth and put into foster care. Now I am trying to get my daughter back. It has been eighteen months since she has been in foster care, and fourteen months since I have been working with Social Services to get her returned to me.

I had been meeting with Clara for over a year. She was conscientious about keeping her appointments with me and her visits with her daughter. Clara was bright and I enjoyed working with her. Although she had a somber demeanor, she was intelligent and articulate. She was insightful and motivated to make changes in her life and meet the requirements in the court order so she could get custody of Lily.

One day I went to Clara's house for our scheduled weekly home visit and she did not answer the door. I tried calling her on the phone and left a message that I was at the house for our appointment, and that I would wait on the porch until she returned. It took five minutes for

Clara to answer the door, and she immediately said that she did not want to see anyone, and the only reason she had come to the door was because she was "court-ordered, and she did not have a choice."

It was 10:30 a.m. and Clara was still in her pajamas; clearly, she had just gotten out of bed. We sat for a while in her living room and I mentioned that her mood had changed since I had last seen her in the parenting group. During the last group session, Clara had energy, her mood was uplifted, and she had seemed hopeful because her CPS worker had informed her that she was going to have her first weekend overnight visit with Lily.

During group, Clara shared how she had decorated her daughter's bedroom, bought food, and was going to bake cookies with Lily and bring her to the park. I asked her what had happened in the past two days to change her mood. She did not reply; her breathing became shallow, and she postured as if she was angry. The silence filled the room and the energy was intense. I did not know if she wanted to cry in pain or scream in anger. I asked Clara again what she thought might have changed her mood. She acknowledged the change in mood but could not discuss the reason for the significant shift in her demeanor.

I remembered that her CPS worker had told me that Clara had an appointment to recertify for public assistance and food stamps. I asked Clara if she had gone to that appointment, and she started to cry. There were no words, just sobs and tears. I sat with her as she cried. At some point, I gently asked her to make eye contact with me. I told her that it was good to cry, but not to get lost in the pain. With encouragement she was able to make eye contact and share what had transpired at the appointment with Social Services:

> When I arrived at the public assistance office I was instructed to update my identification card. The woman taking the picture asked me to stand in front of the camera and, while laughing, requested that I look into the camera and "smile, and say 'sex.'" I looked in the camera but I did not smile and I was silent. The woman was stronger with me and said, "Smile and say 'sex,' or I will not take your picture, and you will not get your identification card or food stamps."
>
> On the surface, the woman appeared playful and was laughing. I reluctantly smiled and said "sex," but I was devastated and felt humiliated. I crumbled inside and felt like worthless trash.

After the picture was taken, I was directed to the fifth floor Paternity Unit. I sat with five other women in the waiting room. After an hour a large man in a suit and tie called me into his office and closed the door. He informed me that he was going to ask a series of questions that would help to locate the father of my daughter, in order to establish paternity and attain child support. He asked Lily's age and name; whether I was married, single, or divorced; who the father of my daughter was; when did I have sex with the father; was I having sex with any other men during that time frame; has the father of my daughter claimed legal paternity; did I know where he was living and where he worked; and did he have contact with me or my daughter.

There was a long silence. Clara's breathing was superficial, and her eyes were vacant and expressionless. I asked Clara if she was willing to go inside and discover what was going on. It was an exercise we had done in the past, and she was familiar with it. (Note: "T" stands for Teresa, and "C," for Clara.)

T: Take a few moments and breathe into your body. What part of your body wants to talk now?
C: My chest.
T: How do you know your chest wants to talk?
C: It feels tight.
T: Anything else?
C: It feels tight, like it is in a vise.
T: Your chest feels tight, like it is in a vise. Anything else?
C: No.
T: If you could give the tight feeling in your chest a feeling, what would the feeling be?
C: I don't know.
T: Breathe. Would tight like in a vise be mad, sad, glad, or scared?
C: I don't know.
T: Breathe into the tightness in your chest and give it permission to relax. Relax the tightness only for a moment, and then you can tighten up again. Breathe, and from the tightness in your chest, answer this question: Do I feel sad, scared, mad, or glad?
C: I don't know.
T: Breathe into your chest and take a guess.
C: It feels sad.
T: Anything else?
C: Mad.

T: Anything else?

C: No.

T: Breathe into the tightness in your chest and give it permission to relax. You only have to relax for a moment, and I will ask another question, and then you can tighten your chest again. What would happen if you let yourself feel sad and mad? Breathe.

C: I feel like I would go crazy and split into a thousand little pieces.

T: What would happen if you split into a thousand little pieces?

C: I would disappear.

T: What would happen if you disappeared? Breathe. Let the answer come from the tightness in your chest and not your head.

C: I would not exist anymore.

T: So the tightness in your chest protects you from going crazy and splitting into a thousand little pieces and disappearing?

C: Yes. I can shut down, and I do not have to feel.

T: Is it okay if we explore a little deeper and ask the tightness in your chest some more questions? We can just take a peek, and we can go together.

C: [Nods her head yes.]

T: From the tightness in your chest and not from your head, have the tightness in your chest finish this sentence: I feel sad because . . . ?

C: I feel sad because I hate my life, I feel so alone, and I do not have much hope.

T: Breathe and have the tightness in your chest finish this sentence: I feel mad because . . . ?

C: [Starts to cry.] I have no more fight left in me. I feel like giving up. [While sobbing, Clara put words to her internal experience that until this moment had been outside of her awareness.] It is unfair that Lily was taken from me. I understand why they took her from me when I was in jail, but it has been a year and I still do not have her. I never once hurt Lily; I do not raise my voice when I speak to her, I do not hit her, and I have never denied her food or attention. In the past year I have given her more than I ever received as a child. How come I am considered a bad mother?

[Angry and still sobbing, she continues.] No one was there for me: My mother left me, my brother molested me, and my father continued to smoke until he died of lung cancer. Then Social Services left me in the custody of my aunt and uncle, where I got raped for years, and now they have the audacity to tell me I am a bad mother and I have to prove myself to get Lily back. Where was Child Protective Services when I needed them? I have never treated my daughter the way I was treated. I love Lily with all my heart, and if I lose her, I will have nothing. For over a year I have done everything the judge has asked me to do, and it's still not good enough. It's so unfair. No one was there for me. I suffered abuse and neglect. How can they say that I am like my parents—like my aunt and uncle?

There was silence. In front of me I saw a slim, overwhelmed, and burdened little girl. Her torso and shoulders were rounded as if she was carrying the world on her back; her mousy brown hair was thinning around her hairline, and tears were rolling down her face. I sat in the silence as she cried. I told her that I was sorry, and that in the past year I had observed how much she loved her daughter, and was impressed with how determined and focused she was in getting her home.

After Clara's recertification, she decided to get off public assistance and find a job. She found the interactions with the workers at public assistance to be belittling and shameful. For several months, Clara looked for employment, but she did not have a high school diploma, job skills, or an employment history. She was tenacious, however, and after three months Clara found employment as an aide in a nursing home. Even though the work was hard, Clara was surprised how much she enjoyed working with the elderly. She was paid $10.50 an hour and had the 4:00 p.m. to 10:00 p.m. shift, a total of thirty hours a week. Clara would have preferred full-time employment, because as a part-time employee she was not eligible for overtime pay, health benefits, or vacation time.

Clara did not own a car and used the bus to get to and from work. On the days when her supervisor asked her to stay late to help with patients, she was fearful that she would miss the last bus that left at 10:15 p.m. If she missed that bus, she would have to walk the two and a half miles home on a major road that did not have consistent sidewalk access. Clara told me that several times she ran to catch the bus only to watch it drive away. There were times she had to walk home in the dark, in rain or snow.

Clara was granted overnight weekend visits with Lily, and after a few months was going to be awarded full custody. Lily would attend day care from 8:30 a.m. to 2:00 p.m., and Clara needed to be home in the mornings and from 2:00 p.m. onward to care for her daughter. Clara asked her supervisor at the nursing home if she could switch to a day schedule, but there were no day shifts available. Clara was conflicted because she liked her job and did not want to resign from her current position, and she was committed to staying off of public assistance. However, the court order mandated that Clara be available to her daughter before and after day care and that she have a steady income that afforded her the basic staples of food, clothing, and shelter. Clara decided that her primary goal was to get custody of Lily, so she resigned from her position and reapplied for public assistance.

One morning, I was walking down the street toward Clara's apartment for our weekly appointment. The houses were close together and the porches were slanted from settlement. They were two- and three-family homes; single-owner-occupied homes had long since disappeared.

On this spring morning the sun was shining, the grass was green, and the trees had new buds. I arrived at Clara's house and knocked on the door for our home visit. Clara opened the door and was very excited; she wanted me to see this really "hot guy." She took me by my hand and pulled me across the living room floor and opened the curtain a few inches so I could look out of the window. Across the street was a man I frequently passed on the way to her house. He was short in stature and thin, his chest was bare and sunken, he had a cigarette hanging out of his mouth and a tattoo on his arm—a green snake with a long, thin, red tongue that forked. The snake wrapped around the word "Mother." He was working on a car that did not have tires and was positioned on four concrete blocks. He was under the open hood, and I noticed a six-pack of beer on the ground and an open can of beer on top of the car. His jeans were held up by an extra-long belt, his pants hung below his buttocks, and his boxers were showing.

As we both looked out the window, Clara blurted, "I wouldn't mind having his sneakers under my bed."

I could not believe this was the man Clara thought was "hot" and wanted to have an intimate relationship with. We had spent many sessions talking about Clara's dreams and discussing how she wanted her daughter out of foster care and living with her. We had discussed how she hoped for a house, a yard, and a fence so Lily could play safely in the yard, protected from the older neighborhood children who appeared to enjoy bullying the younger ones, and safe from the pit bull who frequently freed himself from his leash and terrorized the residents. Clara wanted to be married and have a family, and to have more children.

I was startled when Clara showed me the man she thought would save her and offer her the life she dreamed of for herself and her daughter. Why did she think the man across the street would be willing or able to save her? Why did she not see the potential red flags and signs that this man was not going to help her change her desperate circumstances, particularly since it was apparent he was struggling with his own difficult situation?

I used this moment to review her dreams of a husband, and giving her daughter what she herself had not had growing up, and always longed for: a family, a home, and safety. After reviewing her dreams we discussed her attraction to the man across the street. Clara shared that she felt alone and was scared about getting her daughter back, and caring for her without the support of family or friends. She said she did not feel that she had many choices in life, and since he also appeared to be alone, perhaps the two of them could offer each other friendship and family.

I pointed out the potential warning signs and suggested that this man may have a problem with alcohol, because I had often noticed that he drank beer early in the mornings, and often had a six-pack not far from him. I mentioned he may not have a job because he was outside working on his car during the day when most people are working. Clara defended him and said he may have a night job. Out of my own anxiety I pushed the issue and mentioned that for the past several weeks I had been watching him work on the car with no tires, sitting on cinder blocks, and thought it reflected his situation of being "stuck and not going anywhere."

In a short period of time it was clear that Clara was angered by our conversation and was incensed that I was discrediting the man as a potential partner and someone who would support her in raising her daughter. She was angry because questioning the potential relationship was dimming her hope of having a family, because she did not believe she could manage raising her daughter on her own, without support.

I quickly realized that dismissing this man may have reminded her of the treatment she and her family received from the community where she grew up. As a result, she grew more fervent and protective of the stranger across the street. All of a sudden I became aware that I was the enemy, and I embodied the families, teachers, and police that had criticized, judged, and treated her family as if they were "worthless trash." While I understood, I felt that I could not leave our conversation there. I was hooked into my fear that pursuing this man would complicate her life and undermine her goals. I felt it was important to use the moment to help Clara understand the potential consequences of her decision to pursue this relationship.

Clara had the ability to be insightful and make connections from her past to her present. I was hopeful for her future, but I had a strong feeling that a connection with this man would not offer the safe and nurturing connection she wanted for herself, and that instead it would severely interfere in her efforts to meet her goals of creating a stable and safe home for herself and Lily. In fact, I was feeling more fear for Clara than Clara was feeling for herself. This was my warning sign: I was emotionally hooked, and needed to take a few steps back.

Clara did have an intimate relationship with the man across the street, and in four months her home pregnancy test was positive. Before he left the area he gave Clara half the money needed to pay for an abortion. He reasoned that "he only had to come up with half the money for the abortion because she was responsible for half the pregnancy." During our next session together, Clara was confronted with three choices: to terminate the pregnancy, surrender the child for adoption, or have and raise the child on her own. Clara chose to keep the child because she felt that this pregnancy would give her a second chance at being a mother, and this time she would care for her child from birth. Clara said she wanted a chance of having her own family and to make up for the family she never had.

Clara gained legal custody of Lily, and soon after gave birth to a baby boy named Billy, in memory of her father. Six months later, Clara's case was dismissed and her counseling services were discontinued.

A few years later I met up with Clara's caseworker from CPS and asked her if she knew what had become of Clara and her two children. She said that right before Christmas, Clara had left her two children at day care and never returned to pick them up. After many attempts to reach Clara, the day-care teacher called the police and her children were taken into state custody and placed in foster care. Clara's parental rights were eventually terminated and her children were adopted.

INTERGENERATIONAL TRANSMISSION PROCESS

Family patterns are passed down through the generations without conscious awareness, and the dysfunctional dynamics that occur in one generation contain symptoms that reverberate horizontally across generations and vertically from one generation to the next.[1] The mothers in my practice and the women I interviewed recognized that their history of child sexual abuse was severely compromising their capacity to mother, and they made a conscious and deliberate decision to put an end to the dysfunctional family dynamics and stop the intergenerational patterns of dysfunction.

To understand the intergenerational transmission process, I will reference Clara's story, because it reflects the lives of many young single mothers with histories of child physical and sexual abuse, neglect, abandonment, and violence. These mothers may also endure the insidious effects associated with poverty, classism, sexism, and/or racism.

The remainder of the chapter will examine several mechanisms that contribute to the intergenerational transmission of abuse, including exploring intrapsychic dynamics, poverty, and risk and protective factors.

Intrapsychic Dynamics

As mentioned in earlier chapters, child sexual abuse has both short- and long-term consequences. These effects last long after the victim leaves home, as she carries the symptoms into her relationships with her intimate partner, friends, colleagues, and with her children. Selma Fraiberg and colleagues, in their paper "Ghosts in the Nursery," examined the intergenerational transmission of trauma and the mechanisms for the passing down of a mother's traumatic wounds to her children. They questioned why some mothers with histories of abuse repeat and reenact the patterns of abuse with their own children, while other mothers are able to shield their children from abuse and offer emotional and physical protection and comfort. Fraiberg and her colleagues contend that a mother's inability to meet and respond to her child's needs is a "mother whose own cries have not been heard."[2] A mother's unresolved childhood trauma can prevent her from feeling the pain, sadness, anger, and/or deep distrust connected to her own child abuse. When these feelings are repressed, it creates a barrier between her and her child which interferes with the mother's ability to express compassion, be responsive, and show empathy.

During the abuse phase, defense mechanisms are used to protect against overwhelming and threatening feelings. However, the defenses a mother employs as a child to ward off the feelings of powerlessness, despair, fear, and/or anger during and after the abuse are the same defenses that later render her incapable of responding to her children. The degree to which a mother reenacts her abusive past with her child is related to her ability or inability to access both the memory and the feelings associated with the abuse. A mother who is numbed and disconnected from the feelings related to her abusive past may have difficulty displaying warmth, exhibiting empathy, and responding to her children's physical and social/emotional needs. A mother may also become immobile and unable to respond to her child's distress because it triggers her own unresolved childhood feelings of discomfort and pain. Thus, to avoid and protect herself from emergent feelings, she ignores her child's call for help and comfort.[3] Unwittingly, a mother's use of defenses interferes with her capacity to form a secure attachment and to offer physical safety and emotional comfort to her child.

Children perceive threats from a variety of cues in the environment, including "loud noises, strange people and objects, large or unfamiliar animals, rapid approach, darkness, being alone, and other stimuli associated with the increased probability of danger."[4] It is the caregiver's task to regulate a child's physiological arousal, and to protect and soothe the child from these perceived and/or real threats of danger. If not, chronic physiological stress on the body can change a child's biochemistry and the functioning of the brain, leading to both short- and long-term problems with adaptation. A child who is deprived of the safety that occurs with a secure attachment to their caregiver may exhibit symptoms of depression, anxiety, aggression, and learning problems. These children may also somaticize their distress with upset stomachs, headaches, nail-biting, sleep disturbances, and other physical symptoms with no organic causes. Additionally, they may display acting-out behaviors such as truancy, drug and alcohol abuse, violence, rebellion against authority, and school failure. Hence, the child becomes the newest symptom-bearer of the mother's pain, and the repetition of trauma is carried into the next generation.

Conversely, a mother who is able to resolve and heal from her abuse and has a strong support system is more capable of being attuned and responsive to her children, and better able to develop a secure mother–child attachment.[5] The women I interviewed and counseled sought therapy because they were aware that their history of child sexual abuse was interfering with their mothering, and they had made a conscious decision to heal their past in order to ensure that their pain would not be reenacted with their children. These mothers recognized that their unresolved pain and grief placed them at greater risk for passing their emotional injuries and inner conflicts on to their own children, and they were committed to removing the barriers that had interfered with their abilities to be more loving, attentive, and responsive to meeting their children's needs.

Poverty-Related Trauma

Research has examined the long-term negative consequences of child sexual abuse, but the discourse on the psychological and physical wounds of poverty is not as prevalent in the dialogue as the more overt types of abuse. It is part of the human condition to be challenged and experience pain, but those who live in impoverished economic conditions encounter and bear a larger biological, psychological, and social burden than their counterparts with economic privilege. According to Paul Farmer, "the poor are not only more likely to suffer, they are more likely to suffer in silence."[6] Chronic poverty impacts every aspect of a person's life and is a risk factor for unsatisfactory outcomes, as it disposes individuals to multiple stressors, including food insecurities, poor housing, violence, and increased vulnerability to physical and mental health problems.[7] Poverty negatively impacts self-esteem, disempowers people by limiting their choices, has detrimental effects on mother–child relationships, and increases one's susceptibility to victimization. The harmful impact of poverty is further exacerbated when it merges with the damaging consequences of child sexual abuse.

In the United States, single motherhood is often synonymous with poverty, and severely restricts and interferes with the mother's ability to meet the most basic physiological needs of food, clothing, and shelter. The federal poverty level for a family of three, one adult and two children under the age of eighteen, is an annual cash income of $19,337.

Currently, there are 43.1 million Americans living in poverty, and approximately one in three female-headed households, and one in five children, live in poverty.[8]

Like Clara, women with a history of child sexual abuse are at a higher risk of not completing their education, teenage pregnancy, single parenting, and living in poverty. In fact, women with a history of child sexual abuse are 80 percent more likely to live in poverty than women who have no such history.[9]

To assist Clara with her finances, her caseworker helped her to construct a monthly budget. Clara was employed as an aide in a nursing home, worked thirty hours a week, and earned $10.50 an hour. Although Clara wanted full-time work, the agency only offered part-time positions for entry-level aides. As a part-time employee, Clara did not receive health insurance, sick and vacation time, or overtime pay when she worked extra hours. Her monthly budget included rent, heat and utilities, travel expenses to and from work, food, telephone, and household supplies. Money for clothes, cable television, and miscellaneous expenses was omitted from the budget. Once completed, the budget revealed the fragility of Clara's financial situation: Clara did not earn enough money to cover her basic monthly expenses, and there was no money available for emergencies. Clara was advised to apply for public assistance to obtain food stamps, health insurance, and Section Eight housing subsidies.

For mothers with a history of sexual abuse, economic stressors related to material deprivation are compounded by living in unsafe neighborhoods. Extremely impoverished neighborhoods are frequented with problems associated with crime, gang violence, drug use, vacant housing, vandalism, inadequate public transportation, and underperforming schools. These neighborhoods leave the most vulnerable, such as the elderly, disabled, women, and children, at risk for harassment and violence. Often, impoverished neighborhoods lack access to supportive services to offset the cumulative risks, including adequate police protection, mental health services, after-school activities for children, and neighborhood associations.

Economically disadvantaged neighborhoods can eventually affect the physical and mental health of their residents.[10] Violent, chaotic, and disordered neighborhoods expose residents to danger and victimization, as well as heightening states of fear, fragility, insecurity, and a diminished sense of well-being. High-risk neighborhoods erode the capacity of residents to form reliable connections, making it more difficult to develop a support system, and thereby decreasing the protective impacts that a social support network can provide mothers and children. Poverty has been associated with increased depression, anxiety, and post-traumatic stress disorder, as well as physical illness such as diabetes, respiratory disorders, cardiovascular disease, and cancers.[11]

Social supports and friendships can decrease the negative impact of troubled neighborhoods and poverty on a mother and her children. A supportive social network can act as a protective factor that scaffolds individual and family functioning by reducing a mother's isolation, alleviating stress, increasing coping mechanisms, and enhancing potential sources of help in times of need. A social support network, whether it be friends, members of a church, or neighborhood organizations, can act to increase a mother's overall physical and psychological well-being and her ability to care for her children in developmentally appropriate ways.

Conversely, poverty, cumulative stressors, and complex trauma can result in the experience of learned helplessness. When repeated attempts to positively change one's life circumstances are thwarted by interpersonal violence, economic poverty, inadequate social supports, and/or limited opportunities, it can lead to defeat and immobilization. When one's efforts continually do not yield favorable outcomes, it generates the belief that "No matter what I do or how hard I try, it does not make a difference." Clara did not have the resources or skills to overcome the insurmountable challenges she confronted, which eventually led to her capitulating and giving up her efforts to create a home for herself and her children.

Women with a history of child sexual abuse are at greater risk for revictimization as adults. According to Bridget Klest, "traumatized individuals living in the context of poverty may be particularly vulnerable to revictimization."[12] Survivors of child sexual abuse are twice as likely to experience revictimization as an adult and at four times greater risk of experiencing adult sexual assault.[13] Survivors of child sexual abuse are also at higher risk of experiencing domestic violence and for becoming homeless.

Revictimization has been attributed to symptoms of emotional dissociation and/or hyperarousal diagnosed with post-traumatic stress syndrome. The latter two responses of emotional numbing/dissociation and hyperarousal are also the mechanisms associated with a woman's vulnerability to revictimization. The defense mechanism of dissociation, used to protect oneself against the overwhelming physical and emotional effects of child sexual abuse, is the same mechanism that allows for continued revictimization. As an adult, when faced with cues in the environment and/or in interpersonal interactions that resemble the past traumatic event, the survivor may again elicit the defense of dissociation. This dissociative state that protected the defenseless little girl does not serve the same protective function as an adult. Instead, it leaves a woman unable to identify potential danger in the environment and prevents her from taking appropriate precautionary action, making her and her children more vulnerable to danger.[14]

Similarly, a woman who was sexually abused as a child often takes a subordinate and compliant position in her relationships. Compliancy and passive behaviors may have been used to protect herself as a child by not escalating the abuse by the perpetrator. As an adult, this pattern of relating to people can thwart her abilities to act assertively, leaving her powerless to employ protective actions. In addition, appeasing others to avoid conflicts leaves her at risk of denying and silencing her own feelings and needs. Often, perpetrators seek out mothers who are submissive because they can easily be taken advantage of and exploited. Low self-esteem, faulty judgments, and unhealthy boundaries make these mothers and their children susceptible to further victimization.[15]

On the other end of the continuum, mothers diagnosed with PTSD may have hyper-aroused physiological states, causing them to be vigilant, easily provoked, and inept at maintaining a sense of calm under stress. Their bodies are primed to respond to potential threats and they may overreact to benign encounters and situations that remind them of the trauma. From a hyper-aroused position these individuals misinterpret and respond to environmental and interpersonal cues with a high degree of emotional intensity. Their interactions with others are governed by strong feelings and misperceived threats rather than intellect and logic. Highly charged reactive behaviors can antagonize others and result in occurrences of verbal and/or physical aggression, thus reinforcing their position of victim and their need to maintain a defended stance toward others.

Chronic hyper-aroused states are physically and emotionally draining, and over time can diminish one's ability to sustain attention and
focus, make rational and effective decisions, and discern between real
and imagined threats. This reduces the individual's ability to respond
effectively to real threats, leaving them vulnerable to revictimization.[16,17]

Women with a history of child sexual abuse may misuse alcohol and
drugs to numb feelings and alleviate emerging memories linked to their
past abuse.[18] However, substance use also interferes with a woman's
ability to discern risk and dangerous situations, thereby diminishing her
ability to protect herself against potential perpetrators. Substance use
increases a woman's risks of revictimization, and is connected to higher
rates of physical and sexual assault.

Revictimization in adulthood predisposes and/or exacerbates mental
health concerns, including symptoms of post-traumatic stress disorder,
depression, anxiety, substance use, and suicidal ideation.[19] Increased
symptomatology resulting from revictimization further compromises
and impedes a woman's mothering capacity to care for her children.

Poverty combined with a history of child sexual abuse increases the
stress of parenting. This is particularly true for mothers, like Clara, who
are isolated and bear the economic burdens and the responsibilities of
child rearing on their own. Stressors associated with poverty can have a
negative influence on mothering behaviors, and have been linked to
child maltreatment and neglect. The connection between poverty, maternal stress, and increase in the use of negative parenting practices
makes poverty another path for intergenerational abuse.

A mother's distress restricts her emotional and physical availability
to her children and interferes with her ability to function effectively in
her role as a caregiver.[20] A mother who is overworked, stressed, and/or
struggles with mental health concerns will have difficulties being attentive and responsive to her children, thereby greatly diminishing the
quality of her interactions. When a mother's physical energies are
drained with the daily demands of work and caring for her children, it
interferes and limits her ability to engage in conversation, be attentive,
and create a stimulating home environment that fosters learning and
sustains healthy child development. Poverty, a history of child sexual
abuse, and a mother's isolation from support systems undermines her

coping mechanisms, and are the elements that increase the potential risks of child neglect and abuse.

Although poverty and/or a history of child sexual abuse are not always connected with abusive parenting, they do increase the risks of reactive and neglectful parenting.[21] Like Clara, other mothers I counseled and interviewed with a history of child sexual abuse expressed feeling stressed and overwhelmed with the lack of economic resources and the daily demands of working full-time and caring for their children. They felt that poverty inhibited their ability to provide for their children's basic needs of food, clothing, and shelter, and interfered with caring for their children by restricting the amount of time and the quality of care they could offer. They felt anxious when they were unable to cover the monthly expenses, and were often left with deciding between paying utility bills or paying the rent. If there was an emergency or extra expense, it would create further hardship.

Mothers expressed feeling inadequate, and had profound regrets that their economic situation made it difficult to provide a better life for their children. My clients who were single mothers with insufficient incomes would borrow money from family and/or friends to tide them over to the next paycheck. However, their low incomes were severely inadequate to meet their basic needs, and they were continually confronted with the pressures that accompany living with chronic poverty. Many of the single mothers I counseled and interviewed worked overtime in the evenings or on weekends to supplement their incomes. The responsibilities of a second job were an added encumbrance for an already-burdened mother.

Risk Factors and Protective Factors

Clara did not have the protective factors in her life to help her overcome the numerous risk factors that she was confronted with, both as a child and as a young adult. Increased risk factors in a child's life greatly diminish the potential for resilient outcomes, and heighten the risk of transmitting dysfunctional family patterns to the next generation. As a child, Clara experienced multiple risk factors, including poverty, abandonment by her mother, physical and emotional neglect, parental divorce, death of a parent, and sexual abuse by her brother and uncle. As a young adult she experienced homelessness, school failure, teenage pregnancy, and incarceration. When I was working with Clara, she was twenty years old, a single parent of two young children under the age of three, and involved with Child Protective Services.

Many of the professionals working with Clara were committed to serving at-risk populations and families in crisis, and were caring and respectful. However, inherent in our roles is a contradiction and power imbalance that Clara was keenly aware of, and she addressed her concerns related to this in our sessions. From Clara's perspective, the professionals in her life who acted as supports were simultaneously threatening and intimidating because they were affiliated and aligned with the agency that had custody of her daughter, and would ultimately decide whether or not her child would be returned to her. Clara also expressed feeling angry and confused because the system that left her in the care of her aunt and the uncle who sexually abused her was the same system that had placed her daughter in foster care. Clara felt she was being treated unjustly, and could not understand how she could be compared to her aunt and uncle when she had never abused or neglected her daughter.

Although Clara was compliant and fulfilled the expectations outlined in the court order, the inherent duality in our professional roles made it difficult, if not impossible, for her to feel safe and to fully trust the workers in her life. Paradoxically, the only supportive and consistent adults in Clara's life *were* the professionals overseeing her "case." However, once the treatment goals were met and the family was stable enough so Clara could be reunited with her daughter, services were discontinued and Clara and her children were left without a support system. Limited funding and large caseloads did not allow for the deeper and ongoing therapeutic work and supports Clara and her children would have benefited from.

A mission of the Department of Social Services (DSS) is to provide services and assist the most disadvantaged members of our communities. The two workers employed by Social Services who were supposed to support Clara also caused her harm. The worker who insisted Clara "smile and say 'sex' " in order to get her food stamps was harmful in her interactions with Clara, and, I am assuming, a host of other women with histories of trauma who had come in for services. This inappropriate interaction, which seemed to be amusing to the worker, was demeaning and instilled a deep sense of humiliation in a young woman who was already unprotected and vulnerable. In a similar manner, being interviewed by the male worker from the Paternity Unit was a demeaning experience. He requested that she enter a small office, and, behind closed doors, he questioned her on the identities of the sexual partners near the time she had conceived her daughter. Clara felt shamed by these interactions, which shared characteristics with the sexual abuse and denigration she had suffered as a little girl.

During times of significant stress, our internal resources become challenged and place one at risk of reverting back to past events that were experienced as overwhelming and defeating. Clara had many vulnerable experiences, but when her former caseworker told me that two weeks before Christmas, Clara had left her children at day care and never returned to pick them up, the image that surfaced was of the sixteen-year-old who ran away from her aunt and uncle's home to escape sexual abuse. I recalled the moment she shared with me that even though she was aware of the dangers of running away, she felt "death would have been a welcome relief." I can only speculate on her emotional state and sense of defeat at the moment she made the decision not to pick up her two children from day care.

Early termination of services and the lack of natural support systems left Clara and her two children vulnerable. Clara lacked the protective factors of an understanding and committed partner who could act as a confidant and ally in raising her children, and the guidance and protection of family members and/or friends who could support and buttress her through the hardships and daily challenges of poverty and mothering two young children. Clara did not have the internal resources or external supports to reinforce her desire to provide her children with a better life than what she had experienced as a child. The overwhelming risk factors and adversity Clara encountered contributed to the repetition and reenactment of her past with her children.

Clara left her children when her daughter was about the same age Clara had been when her mother left her, and at the same time of year when she ran away from her aunt and uncle's house. The nodal event that surrounds Christmas is unknown, but conceivably it was the same time of year her mother had left her, her brothers, and her father. I can only speculate as to why Clara never returned to pick up her two children at day care. Perhaps the responsibilities of mothering had become too difficult and overwhelming, or possibly leaving her children was her attempt to give them more than she had had as a child, and more than she felt she could provide for them. I may never know, but it rekindled a deep sadness within me as I brought Clara back to life by retelling her story.

It became clear to me that whatever part of Clara's spirit had not been broken by her childhood sexual abuse and neglect had finally been shattered as a young adult by systems that attempted—but failed—to provide the safety and ongoing economic and emotional support necessary to address the underlying causes of her vulnerabilities. Clara had an intense desire to love and care for her children. Although her intentions were strong, they were thwarted by multiple risk factors and minimal protective factors, a Social Services system that terminated services early, and in some instances contributed to her pain, and a political structure that endorses public policies that create economic and social inequities and sustain marginalization for women and children.

I can remember as a little girl sitting on my mother's lap and attentively listening to her and Mother Teresa, my namesake, converse about her work with "the poorest of the poor." Mother Teresa recognized the suffering caused by material poverty, but she expressed that the worst poverty and suffering comes from being alone, and the feeling of being unloved.

CONCLUSION

In order to understand the intergenerational transmission process and how a mother's childhood trauma is passed down to her children, this chapter examines the relationships between intrapsychic dynamics, poverty, and the hardships associated with multiple risk factors. Child sexual abuse experiences "are generally unrecognized and become lost in time, where they are protected by shame, by secrecy, and by social taboos against exploring certain areas of human experience."[22] When a child experiences sexual abuse and does not receive the protection and support of a caring adult, they are at high risk for immediate and continuing problems with mental and physical health. The lasting effects of a mother's adverse childhood experiences places her own children at risk for neglect and abuse.

The term *feminization of poverty* refers to the concentration of poverty among women, particularly women who are female heads of households. Poverty is one of the highest risk factors because it impacts so many aspects of mothers' and children's lives. Poverty interferes with a mother's ability to provide for basic needs. Poverty limits the choices of neighborhoods where her family can live, the schools her children can attend, and the quality and quantity of food she and her children have access to. Poverty results in numerous stressors that impinge on a mother's quality of life, and her history of child sexual abuse compounds and exacerbates the ramifications of poverty. Poverty and a history of child sexual abuse are both linked to a mother's increased symptoms of depression and anxiety, potential for revictimization, and neglectful and punitive parenting.

Living in impoverished neighborhoods is another chronic stressor that impacts mothers and their children, with the associated crime, gang violence, inadequate housing, diminished supports among residents, and lack of police protection. Neighborhood chaos increases the feelings of vulnerability and stress, and is linked to mental and physical health concerns, further eroding a woman's stamina and mothering capacities, while placing her and her children at risk. A mother who is struggling with symptoms of depression, PTSD, anxiety, adult victimization, and/or poverty is less capable of forming a secure attachment with her children. When a mother's physical and mental energies are confronted by chronic stressors, she will have difficulty responding to the emotional and physical needs of her children, which in turn compromises her ability to adjust and function. Poverty and child sexual abuse contribute to the repetition of trauma and enables the abuse to continue through the next generation.

A common thread I observed in the mothers I interviewed and saw in my practice was the multitude of traumas they had experienced as children and adults. Yet, all of them had a desire to mother and engage in warm and loving relationships with their children. This desire should be utilized to assist and support mothers in strengthening and fostering healthy families. Intervention efforts should focus on increasing protective factors for mothers and their children while simultaneously working to influence the political and economic structures and policies that deny and restrict opportunities and keep mothers marginalized and disadvantaged.

8

IMPLICATIONS FOR TREATMENT AND POLICY

Strengthening Resiliency

To effectively intervene and treat adult survivors of child sexual abuse (CSA), helping professionals must be aware of the long-term symptoms in child sexual abuse survivors that may affect their mothering abilities. To ensure that treatment interventions are successful and to alleviate the long-term consequences for this vulnerable group, it is critical to understand the continued effects of childhood trauma on the next generation, and to promote resilient capacities among mothers sexually abused as children.

Interventions designed to accommodate the psychological, emotional, social, and spiritual development of this group of mothers can decrease the risks associated with intergenerational abuse. Integrative and comprehensive services can seek to ameliorate the effects of abuse that interfere with mothering capabilities. Professionals can promote protective factors and increase resiliency by enhancing the supports they offer mothers, including enhancing the therapeutic alliance, treating mental health and/or substance abuse concerns, teaching mothers how to manage and regulate the consequences related to their traumatic life events, helping mothers build their natural support systems by creating positive and affirming connections with family members, friends, and community resources, and teaching relationship and communication skills. When it is deemed necessary, mothers may participate in parenting classes where they can receive guidance to enhance their mothering skills.

The first half of this chapter will review and summarize the ways helping professionals can support at-risk mothers and their children, as well as offer mothers approaches to increase their resilient capacities. The remainder of the chapter will examine policy implications and changes that need to occur on a political and social level in order to support mothers and future generations.

PROMOTING PROTECTIVE FACTORS AND INCREASING RESILIENCY

Therapy and the Therapeutic Alliance

Practitioners can increase the effectiveness of therapy and facilitate positive outcomes by enhancing the therapeutic alliance.[1] A therapeutic alliance can serve to buffer the effects of child abuse and the consequences for the next generation. A relationship that is warm and accepting, and where the therapist displays genuineness, assists in facilitating healthy client development, supports success in meeting therapeutic goals, and supports women in their mothering roles.

Participating in an encouraging and supportive therapeutic alliance is significant in alleviating the long-term effects of the multiple difficulties women encounter in their life and in their mothering. Therapy can help mothers to move past limitations in their mothering capacity by focusing on issues of low self-esteem, depression and anxiety, substance abuse, and lack of support systems. The mothers I interviewed and saw in my practice struggled with child rearing, mental health concerns, domestic violence, isolation, and/or poverty, and they said they found therapy to be beneficial. They reported that their therapists offered direction, warmth, and caring. Mothers also found it beneficial when their therapists offered concrete advice and skills for navigating difficult parent–child dynamics.

Therapeutic Groups

Therapeutic groups serve a multitude of purposes. Groups can be a place where survivors share their common experiences, validate their difficulties, and support one another. Positive group experiences can act to amplify client strengths and improve resiliency. Joining with others with similar concerns, interests, and experiences can aid participants in propelling and sustaining their commitment toward change. Group therapy can be a critical component in moving past the negative outcomes of child sexual abuse, breaking the silence and shame, and creating connections forged around common concerns.

Groups offer opportunities for mothers to develop and practice communication and problem-solving skills in a supervised and safe setting. For some clients, these skills may be new and different. Group members can be coached on how to enhance effective and affirming relationships, and then apply these skills outside the group milieu. Groups can increase mothering expertise among participants through an added educational component. Clients can modify their expectations of their children by learning about developmentally appropriate milestones. Group leaders can teach child-rearing skills and help mothers to create a predictable home structure, set limits, and manage their children's challenging behaviors. Members can increase their parenting abilities by sharing common experiences and strategizing solutions to problems related to mothering.

Parenting Education and Early Intervention

Mothers who have experienced child sexual abuse find that mothering is the most demanding and challenging during the first five years of their child's life. Therapists can employ carefully developed and thoughtfully planned interventions that include working in collaboration with educators and health-care providers to ensure that comprehensive services would begin in these most difficult, early stages of mothering. During these early years, professionals in the field of infant/ child mental health can be instrumental in supporting mothers in all areas of child development, and facilitating techniques and skills to promote attachment and bonding. Early interventions can encourage positive mother–child interactions which are critical to long-term biological, psychological, and social growth. Professionals can support mothers in meeting their children's basic physical needs of food, clothing, and shelter, while enhancing their abilities to meet the emotional needs of their children. Treatment strategies can act to promote and encourage the creation of secure and connected relationships.

The quality of mother–child attachment is critical to development and is established when a mother is attuned to her child's emotional and physical needs and is competent in her caregiving. Secure attachment is a critical element in fostering healthy psychosocial development and resiliency in children. It is important to teach mothers the skills needed to care for the overall well-being of their child, including how to create warm and enduring bonds. Mothers can promote resiliency in their child by offering warmth and comfort, responding appropriately to the child's needs, and engaging in developmentally appropriate interactions.[2]

To stop the cycle of abuse, specialists can assist parents in attachment and bonding by encouraging appropriate interactions and teaching mothers how to utilize facial expression, eye contact, and vocalization to soothe and comfort their children.[3] A strong and secure mother–child relationship is an important protective factor, and has been shown to scaffold intellectual functioning, social/emotional growth, and resilient capacities in children. It has been found that "sensitive and responsive caregiving moderates the effects of high-risk environments and promotes resilience and positive change for children who have experienced poverty, family stress, and maltreatment."[4] A mother who is attuned and attached to her child is more apt to protect the child from danger and potentially traumatic experiences. If the child should suffer a traumatic event, a caring and supportive mother or caregiver is a critical influence in diminishing the negative impact.

Infant–Parent Psychotherapy is a relationship-based intervention utilized to promote positive parent–child interactions and to form safe and secure attachments for children in the first five years of life. In this approach, the therapeutic relationship is the "secure base" and a critical component in supporting positive mothering. From this "secure base," the therapist models attentive and empathic connections, assists the mother by making links between her own childhood experiences and how they shape her current interactions with her child, and offers insight and feedback while teaching the mother to be sensitive and responsive to her child's developmental needs.[5] Infant mental health providers and other professionals can decrease the risk factors linked to mothers who are isolated by involving significant and caring others in the therapy process, including parents, stepparents, siblings, and grandparents.[6]

A number of mothers talked about the important role education and books played in helping them to recognize the developmental stages and needs of their children. Education afforded them the knowledge to attend to the physical, cognitive, and psychosocial development of their children. In each stage of childhood, a child must master particular developmental tasks. The psychosocial task of toddlerhood is "autonomy vs. shame and doubt." This stage is marked by a toddler's desire to pursue independence and autonomy from caregivers. This psychosocial milestone simultaneously occurs alongside the physical milestones of mastering walking and toilet training and the cognitive milestone of talking. During this time, the child moves away from being totally dependent on caregivers to asserting their own preferences and decisions.[7]

When I worked with young single mothers in a family outreach prevention program, I saw that toddlers in this stage of development were at risk of physical abuse by inexperienced and uninformed mothers who interpreted the child's desire for independence as defiance. As mentioned in chapter 7, one reason Clara wanted to mother was to help her cope with her deep feelings of loneliness and emptiness. She wanted a family to make up for the one she did not have. Clara shared with me that she liked infants because "they can shape to my body, and they are warm and cuddly. I do not like children as much when they get older and can talk."

Parenting a toddler can be challenging because, unlike infants, toddlers have the capacity to both verbally and physically resist as they try to assert their independence, as when they insist on dressing and feeding themselves. For a young, single mother who is isolated, without supports, and in particular feels her child is there to meet her needs, the behaviors in this stage of development are seen as an affront to the relationship, and as rebelliousness. The favorite word for toddlers is "no," which can be misinterpreted as disobedience by the immature mother who expects her child to comfort her and meet her needs. These mothers can be taught that a child who says "no" is not being defiant but is setting a boundary with their caregiver in order to assert their independence and acquire self-sufficiency. The word "no" is the child's verbal attempt to gain autonomy from the caregiver, rather than the child being "bad" or deliberately misbehaving.

The psychosocial stage of adolescent development is "identity vs. role confusion," and is marked by a second surge of independence as the adolescent attempts to develop an identity separate from their parents'.[8] The physical milestone of adolescence is the growth of secondary sex characteristics related to sexual maturation. In chapter 2, Laura struggled with mothering her son when he reached adolescence; her son's physical changes associated with puberty triggered memories of her sexual abuse. Mothering an adolescent boy was further complicated because her son's physical strength and growth intimidated her and made it difficult for her to set limits and maintain a role of authority.

Mothers sexually abused as children find that learning about developmental stages and having realistic expectations of the abilities and behaviors of their children is helpful in understanding and tending to their children. It is useful for mothers to have the knowledge of how each developmental stage might challenge or hinder their abilities to parent.

Significant Relationships

Supportive and affirming relationships are powerful protective factors that help to ameliorate the risk factors that confront mothers with histories of child sexual abuse and their children. Mothers who have experienced child sexual abuse are more resilient and are better able to maintain psychosocial competence if they have stable and secure attachments with other adults. Significant social supports are critical resources and serve a protective function, and they help to ameliorate the adversity and struggles faced by mothers and their children. The women I interviewed stated that their relationships with a caring mother, father, grandmother, husband or life partner, and/or friends were essential in overcoming the effects of the sexual abuse and alleviating the stressors associated with mothering.

Caring and attentive people who are accessible act as strong protective factors that decrease the adverse long-term effects linked with CSA. Supportive spouses and life partners, extended family members, and friends who are loving, kind, and competent can be critical influences and valuable resources for successful mothering. Integrating natural support systems into their lives helps mothers build resiliency. Learning to create natural support systems and sustain healthy relationships can also enable mothers to wean themselves from reliance on the therapeutic relationship.

Specifically, mothers state that their husbands or life partners offer them relief from the demands of mothering and provide emotional support and a sense of security. They act as confidants, share in the stressors associated with raising children, help with household chores, are caring and reliable, and share in the essential daily responsibilities of parenting.

For many mothers with histories of child sexual abuse, building connections and developing close relationships does not conjure up experiences of safety and comfort. Instead, close relationships are associated with apprehension, fear, terror, and mistrust. When a child experiences interpersonal violence, "there is a profound disconnection, a violation of human relatedness and meaningfulness in relationships that cuts deep. Finding ways to reestablish the caring connection or the belief in the possibility of love as a response to vulnerability is essential."[9] A necessary aspect of creating and sustaining warm and positive connections is allowing oneself to be vulnerable and open, and to engage in reciprocal relationships. Many of the mothers I saw in my practice equated vulnerability with being unprotected and exploited. In the safety of therapy, mothers learn to feel comfortable sharing difficult feelings and experiences, which makes it possible to reexamine and reframe what it means to be vulnerable and have close and caring connections.

Individual and group therapy can help mothers develop the skills to be competent and successful in relationship building. However, many mothers, because of the violations they experienced as children, do not always have the skills to discern who they should allow or not allow into their lives and the lives of their children. Mothers may need support and guidance in creating and sustaining meaningful and affirming connections with others. Effective communication skills, managing stress, deescalating conflict, problem solving, and regulating emotions are essential competencies that can be modeled and taught in the therapeutic milieu.

Religion and Spiritual Supports

Mothers who were sexually abused as children find that their spiritual and/or religious beliefs are beneficial to them both as individuals and in their roles as mothers. Their spiritual beliefs provide relief and solace in times of stress and when feeling overwhelmed. Mothers gain comfort through prayer, along with the strength to deal with the challenges they experience both in their lives and in mothering their children. Spiritual beliefs can also offer individuals guidance about how to structure their lives. Some of the mothers I interviewed said that their religious beliefs have helped them to gain valuable life lessons from their struggles and to positively reframe the adversity they have faced. CSA survivors who are able to create meaning and gain strength from their abuse experiences show more resilience and overall competence in adulthood.[10]

Additionally, belonging to a religious group offers a caring social network. Mothers find that a religious community provides supportive people with shared values.[11] Being involved in a religious community fosters faith and connects mothers to a support system that can compensate for a lack of strong supportive relationships in their nuclear or extended families.

TRAUMA AND THE HUMAN NERVOUS SYSTEM

Alice Miller, psychoanalyst and authority in the area of child abuse, wrote, "If we do not work on three levels—body, feeling, mind—the symptoms of our distress will keep returning, as the body goes on repeating the story stored in its cells until it is finally understood."[12]

Body

When working with CSA survivors, it is imperative that the physical body is included as an integral part of the treatment intervention. For many survivors of child sexual abuse, talk and insight therapies are insufficient modes of treatment because they fail to recognize the impact of trauma and the concurrent neurophysiological changes that occur in the body.

In our first session, Fatima exclaimed, "I have read all the books, I understand all the theories, I know it is not my fault, I realize that I was just a little girl, but I still feel tortured." Fatima was bright, understood the long-term consequences of child sexual abuse, and was involved in counseling for a number of years. However, her symptoms persisted because the feelings and physiological responses associated with the trauma were still held tight and bound in her body. In order to alleviate Fatima's symptoms of depression and anxiety, her body needed to be incorporated into the therapy process.

Understanding the ancient brain's threat-protection-stress system that provides for the defense strategies of social engagement, fight/flight, and freeze gives insight into how the nervous system is impacted by child sexual abuse. Structurally and functionally these strategies involve the autonomic nervous system (ANS), which includes both the sympathetic nervous system (SNS) and the parasympathetic nervous system (PNS), and the protection systems of the PNS vagal nerve ganglia, the very ancient dorsal vagal complex (DVC), and the more recently evolved ventral vagal complex (VVC), as described by Stephen Porges in his polyvagal theory. Simply put, there are three neural circuits in the autonomic nervous system that have evolved over millions of years, and each neural circuit is responsible for different physiological, behavioral, and emotional reactions in the individual. Each neural circuit is activated in sequential and hierarchical order, in which the most recent neural circuit in the evolutionary stage of development is activated before the next neural circuit in the evolutionary stage of development is engaged. All three neural circuits provide "adaptive responses to safe, dangerous, or life-threatening events or contexts."[13]

The most recently developed circuit or autonomic subsystem is the social engagement system (SES), and it is found only in mammals. As Porges describes, this system is linked to the myelinated ventral vagal complex (VVC), and affects parts of the body that are critical in creating safe relationships essential for survival. This system encompasses facial expressions, head movements, listening, and the human voice. These elements function together to express caring, empathy, and attunement to others, which are necessary in securing supportive relationships and sustaining physical and mental health.[14]

Without one's conscious awareness, the nervous system engages in a process that Porges calls *neuroception*, which operates to continuously assess and evaluate the environment for potential risks. In the regulated state, when there are no apparent or real threats of danger, and the person is experiencing a sense of safety, one feels calm and relaxed, spontaneous and flexible, and is able to engage in mutually fulfilling interactions with others. While experiencing safety, the ventral vagal pathways function to downregulate defensive actions and to dampen the activation of the sympathetic and parasympathetic nervous system defenses of fight/flight/freeze responses.[15] However, if the nervous system senses threat to psychological and/or physical safety and integrity, the social engagement system is initially involved to elicit the protection of a supportive person. If the danger prevails and no one is available to offer assistance, or if the person that is supposed to protect you is the perpetrator, the body quickly reverts to utilizing the next recently evolved neural circuit, the fight/flight actions of the SNS. The sympathetic nervous system is engaged without conscious awareness, stimulating the body for mobilization and defensive fight/flight actions, resulting in an increase in heart rate and breathing, pupils dilating, muscles tightening, and the digestive system and metabolism slowing down so that the body's energy can be engaged in the necessary behaviors for survival—that is, to react by fighting back, or by fleeing and running from the threatening person or situation.

However, for children who are sexually abused, attempts to escape or fight back are usually futile. Fearing annihilation, the most primitive and ancient survival strategy, the unmyelinated dorsal vagal complex of the parasympathetic nervous system, is activated. When this neural circuit is activated, the body shuts down and feigns death; breathing, heart rate, and metabolism decline, oxygen to the muscles and tissues decreases, the body collapses and becomes immobilized, and the person goes into a dissociative state. The freeze-immobile-dissociative responses serve to defend and protect the victim by potentially decreasing the perpetrator's pursuit and/or reducing the victim's fear and pain associated with the assault or impending death. In the same way, Sophia became immobile and limp as she pretended to sleep while her grandfather sexually abused her.

In times of danger, the myelinated ventral vagal complex (VVC) releases the "vagal brake" on the sympathetic nervous system (SNS), and the rapid-acting sympatho-adrenomedullary (SAM) and slower but longer-acting hypothalamus-pituitary-adrenal cortex (HPA) axes are activated. Both systems prepare and prime the individual to take action in the face of threat. In threatening circumstances, the hypothalamus, located in the limbic system in the brain, engages the SAM, the sympathetic nervous system's neural pathways to the adrenal medulla (the inner portion of the adrenal gland), preparing the body for fight or flight by the release of both epinephrine (adrenaline) and norepinephrine (noradrenaline). Epinephrine increases blood pressure, heart rate, and lung capacity; norepinephrine, through peripheral vasoconstriction, preferentially sends blood to the muscles of the arms and legs to promote the capacity and strength for fighting or fleeing. Also, norepinephrine released in the brain as a neurotransmitter increases one's alertness and focus, resulting in hypervigilance.

Within a short period of time of activating the sympathetic nervous system, the hypothalamus engages the endocrine system to release powerful hormones into the bloodstream. The hypothalamus produces the hormone corticotrophin, which signals the pituitary gland—the master gland in the endocrine system—to send the hormone adrenocorticotropic (ACTH) to the adrenal cortex, the outer portion of the adrenal gland, which stimulates the release of the stress hormone, cortisol. Cortisol is secreted into the bloodstream and prepares the body to respond to threats in the environment by altering physiological responses that may impede mobilization. Cortisol will shut down metabolism and digestion so that the body's energy can be used for fight/flight behaviors. However, cortisol also releases glucose in the body to improve alertness and increase the stamina necessary to defend oneself against the impending threat.[16]

Prolonged and chronic physiological stress states—resulting from situations such as ongoing and cumulative abuse and maltreatment, poverty, and chaotic and unpredictable homes and/or neighborhoods—have both short-and long-term detrimental consequences on the body. Both chronic hyper-aroused and hypo-aroused physiological states compromise the functioning of the immune system, which increases the body's susceptibility to disease, and places the brain at risk for both structural and functional impairments, impacting mental health.

Mind–Body Therapies

After the trauma, if there is no one available to help the child to calm and regulate their physiological stress state and make sense of the abuse experience, the child's body will remain in a physical state that sustains and perpetuates the traumatic experience. Instead of moving forward, the child becomes frozen, and is at risk of perceiving and responding to current experiences from a body that is wired for fight/flight/freeze. Clients who have experienced long-term child maltreatment have physiological systems that are "dominated by the immobilization/shutdown system"; and clients who have experienced an acute, single trauma are "dominated by the sympathetic fight/flight system."[17] When a person is in a hyper-aroused or hypo-aroused state, their behaviors, feelings, and internal experiences are subjugated to a physiological system braced for defense. A person cannot learn or integrate new information and experiences in a hyper-aroused state wired for attack or flight, or in a hypo-aroused state of collapse. Rational ways of thinking, behaving, and feeling are the privileges of a non-traumatized body—a body that is out of real or perceived danger.

Therapists are trained on the importance of creating a therapeutic alliance with their clients by developing a relationship of trust so that clients feel comfortable in allowing themselves to be vulnerable, and safe enough to engage in the therapeutic process. However, if a client has no memory of a secure or safe attachment to a caregiver, a therapist's attempts to create an alliance can elicit fear and suspicion. Children who are abused may conclude that the world is not a safe place and develop a deep mistrust of people. Based on their experiences of abuse, they associate closeness with being violated and hurt. In these clients, instead of fostering a therapeutic alliance, the therapist's attempts at connection may elicit fight/flight/freeze responses.[18] The therapist needs to utilize treatment interventions that promote safety in the therapeutic sessions; otherwise, the client is at risk of becoming triggered and overwhelmed. The client, frightened by the therapist's attempts to develop a therapeutic alliance, may *fight* back by displaying defensive and "resistant" responses; take *flight* by canceling appointments or terminating therapy; or, in a state of *freeze*, may show outward compliance but internally be shut down and dissociated.

Fight/flight/freeze responses have physical indicators that are revealed in one's posture, breathing patterns, amount of muscle contraction, degree of eye contact, skin pallor, and facial expressions. The therapist can utilize these physical indicators to determine which domain of the stress response system the client is currently experiencing (social engagement, fight/flight, freeze) and support the client in becoming aware of and skilled at managing the associated feelings and sensations.[19] One of the goals of therapy is to help clients feel safe while they learn to connect to their bodies and manage the physiological sensations linked to the stress states of hyper-arousal and immobilization, without re-traumatizing the client. While working to shift a client from an immobilized and a collapsed physiological state, she may experience sensations similar to what was experienced during the abuse. Tightening muscles, increased heartbeat, and sweating can trigger visual memories, feelings, and/or bodily sensations of her past abuse. In other words, the client's own physiological experiences and body can overpower and re-traumatize her.

In order to promote physical and mental health in clients with a history of child sexual abuse, the nervous system needs to be addressed in therapy, and the defense systems of hyper-arousal or hypo-arousal need to be regulated. Mind–body therapies have demonstrated a consistent picture of efficacy in working with traumatized clients by alleviating symptoms in conditions like depression, anxiety, and post-traumatic stress disorder. Mind–body therapies can restore and repair the damage caused by the chronic engagement of defensive physiological states, and show significant results in symptom reduction and improvements in mood and behavioral functioning. Once the nervous system is regulated and the social engagement system is activated, the client can experience psychological and physical safety, and emerge into the awareness that she is no longer in danger—that the threat has passed, and she has survived.

Therapists should move from working with a purely traditional model of "talk therapy" and/or medication as the primary interventions toward incorporating therapeutic methods that use integrated mind–body approaches. Trauma can influence changes in both the brain and the body, and in order to alleviate the negative symptomatology seen in survivors, treatment needs to incorporate methods that aid in physiological and affective regulation. A number of therapies utilize mind–body techniques to regulate neurophysiological states: eye movement desensitization and reprocessing therapy (EMDR), emotional freedom techniques (EFT), somatic experiencing, neurofeedback, and trauma-sensitive yoga are therapeutic interventions that recognize the impact of child sexual abuse and trauma on the brain and nervous system.[20] These interventions improve physiological regulation by activating neural circuits in the social engagement system and increasing states of calm and safety, which are both necessary conditions required to facilitate positive changes in the lives of CSA survivors.

Feelings

The expression of feelings is a critical component in the healing process. In fact, repression of feelings can cause disturbances in biopsychosocial functioning. Survivors of child sexual abuse need a therapeutic channel to express strong feelings and have them acknowledged, understood, and respected. The mothers I see in my practice fear disastrous outcomes for expressing themselves, and when they attempt to assert their needs, feelings, or wishes, they are confronted with the original traumatic experience in which their efforts at self-assertion were unsafe and/or futile.

In order to facilitate a client's ability to express herself, it is important to examine the ways in which the child was coerced into silence. To silence a child and to keep her from revealing the abuse, a common threat used by perpetrators is that the family will break up, or the child will be blamed and ousted from the family. The perpetrator may have threatened to hurt or kill the child, another member of the family, or the family pet. When the client is faced with reversing her silent and submissive behaviors, what surfaces is the original terror that created and sustained those behaviors in the first place. Therefore, the therapist needs to be sensitive and supportive in acknowledging the fears that surface when a client attempts to express and assert herself. It is helpful to remind the client that her childhood beliefs, feelings, and behaviors were a means of coping in a dysfunctional family, and that now, as an adult, the strategies that once helped are no longer adaptive. Traumatic childhood experiences that remain hidden and unexpressed continue to fester in the present. The old ways of thinking and behaving re-create childhood dynamics of powerlessness in which the child was unheard, negated, unacknowledged, and unprotected,

Clinicians need to create a safe holding environment where exploring strong feelings and the erroneous beliefs that the client has internalized about herself and her world can be recognized and addressed. Several erroneous beliefs that keep adult survivors from expressing themselves are:

If I am visible, I will be a target for other people's rage.
If I assert myself, I will be harmed.
If I express myself, I will not be liked.
If I am compliant, I will be safe.

To effectively work with mothers who were sexually abused as children, it is important to teach them how to identify their feelings. Clients may have survived by repressing their feelings—or, at least, the most uncomfortable ones—and may not have learned how to identify or differentiate among the various emotions. Sadness, fear, shame, rage, pain, or some combination of these was experienced during the abuse phase. The strength and range of feelings experienced by little girls who are sexually abused are too intense for them to process, and their bodies react by shutting down, collapsing, and/or dissociating.

One of the consequences of shutting down and dissociating is that the person becomes disconnected from a wide range of experiences and feelings. As time passes and feelings begin to reemerge, clients may experience these emotions as intrusive and overwhelming, and become frightened, fearing that they may be consumed by such intense sensations. At times, the client may experience multiple and seemingly disparate feelings simultaneously, and as a result, feel overpowered by their intensity and complexity, making it difficult to articulate and work through the experience.

Therapists can assist clients to manage the emerging feelings and the memories that often accompany them. The paradigm of "mad, sad, glad, or scared" helps clients to identify basic feelings. There are hundreds of "feeling" words to capture an experience; however, to keep it simple, in the voice of the little girl who was hurt, this paradigm is effective, safe, and a good starting place. Similar to the session with Clara, described in chapter 7, exploring where feelings are experienced in the body and conversing with that part of the body, supports reconnection and teaches the client that her body is not the enemy, and can be a powerful resource in her healing.

Donnel Stern writes that "the dissociated experience is unformulated and cannot be thought out or articulated; it can only be enacted."[21] Individual and group therapy are important modalities to support women in connecting with their traumatic and dissociated experiences.

While discussing the details of her abuse, Jen's affect was flat, her eyes appeared vacant, and she was disconnected from her feelings. However, her unexpressed feelings filled the room, and group members absorbed the pain, sadness, and anger associated with her story. When Jen had finished sharing, the other women in the group responded and expressed their reactions. In doing so, group members were able to give voice to and articulate the feelings that Jen did not have access to and was detached from. This offered Jen and the other group members an opportunity to share and articulate feelings related to their child sexual abuse experiences. Group therapy offers mothers the opportunity to formulate and express their own feelings, while simultaneously teaching them to create a holding environment and bear witness to the expression of others' feelings. This is an essential skill in creating and sustaining healthy relationships, and is beneficial in improving a mother's abilities to assist her children in understanding and regulating their own feelings.

In dysfunctional families, inappropriate use of power and violence are modeled. As a result, trauma survivors often do not have appropriate role models or learned skills to cope with their feelings, or the words to describe their internal experiences. Learning how to identify, acknowledge, and express feelings in appropriate ways is vital in fostering a mother's capacity to create meaningful relationships with her children and to live a full life.

Mind

Many of my clients experience an enormous amount of emotional upheaval in their lives through cumulative traumas of abuse, neglect, violence, and losses. Acting out in the present and creating and/or being involved in continual crises helps to manage and ward off the pain of the past. To interrupt the cycle of childhood reenactments, the past must be explored, articulated, and regulated. When the client feels safe enough in the therapeutic process, the therapist and client can explore how the trauma has impacted her life, her self-perceptions, and her behaviors and choices, as well as explore the dysfunctional family dynamics that keep the client hostage to her past. These sessions may elicit thoughts, feelings, experiences, and/or memories that surround the abuse. The therapeutic milieu is a safe place to work on the abuse because clients are protected by the boundaries of a healthy therapist–client relationship. In this context, the client can be encouraged to try new ways of thinking, feeling, and behaving.

IMPLICATIONS FOR POLICY

The mothers I interviewed and counseled identified that financial instability, lack of child care, lack of education and training, and mental health concerns were major obstacles that interfered with their effectiveness as mothers. The remainder of this chapter will focus on the policy implications of these four areas, including current policies that act to impede and undermine women's effectiveness in mothering their children—the next generation.

Financial Instability

For the women I interviewed and counseled, having a limited income and experiencing financial stressors interfered and negatively impacted all aspects of effective mothering. Working full-time and feeling overextended and overwhelmed with household responsibilities and mothering tasks interfered with providing quality care and being emotionally available to their children. Some of the mothers shared that they constantly worried about not having enough money because, even though they worked full-time, they did not have the resources to pay monthly bills, and struggled with meeting their own and their children's basic needs of food, clothing, and shelter.

The financial plight of many single women who are heads of households is well documented and mirrors the financial difficulties experienced by the mothers I interviewed and saw in my practice. The employment opportunities available to women without a postsecondary education are concentrated in low-wage clerical, retail sales, factory, and service-sector jobs, referred to as "pink-collar jobs." Single women who are heads of households who work in pink-collar jobs struggle to survive on their inadequate income, and working does not afford them an income that will lead them out of poverty and toward self-sufficiency. Working mothers employed in low-paying jobs are likely to be trapped in the cycle of poverty. Furthermore, entry-level and part-time positions usually do not offer health insurance coverage to employees, making a lack of medical benefits a major concern faced by mothers in the workforce.[22]

Public policies must address the obstacles that impede women's ability to financially support their families and meet the psychosocial needs of their children. This would require a social commitment to end poverty, by providing a strong economy, a livable wage, and full employment for citizens.

Child Care

A major concern for working mothers is having access to quality and affordable child-care programs. This is affirmed by the reports of the women I interviewed and counseled. Many mothers have difficulty finding available, convenient, affordable, and quality child care and/or after-school care for their children while they are at work, and, as a result, are forced to leave their children in the care of those deemed inadequate, inconsistent, or unreliable. Child care for young children and after-school care for children over six is limited, and the need heavily exceeds the available supply. Consequently, obtaining child care poses a serious problem for mothers. Available child care is costly, and dips heavily into a single mother's paycheck. After paying this bill, women may frequently lack enough money to cover the costs of basics such as food, clothing, and shelter.[23]

Another major concern for mothers is whether the child care they are able to obtain is meeting the developmental needs of their children. When a mother is working full-time, a large portion of a child's waking hours will be spent with another caretaker, so it is important to assess the quality of care children are receiving. Bruce Fuller and his associates state that "total hours of care, stability of care, and the type of care all can have effects on children's development, but the quality of care has by far the greatest influence."[24] Professionals in the field of child development place emphasis on the importance of a nurturing and supportive relationship between the child and caregiver, as well as a child having a stimulating environment to enhance their cognitive, emotional, and social development.[25] Children can benefit from enriched environments that meet their developmental needs. Ensuring quality day care and after-school programs "not only ensures a brighter future for the children themselves, but for all of society, since we will pay the costs of educational failure, increased crime and violence, and reduced worker productivity when children fail to receive the nurturing and supports they need to achieve their potential."[26]

Quality preschool and after-school programs can act as a protective factor and counter the risks faced by children who live in poverty and/or are from single-parent homes. Barbara Blum confirms that "high-quality, stable child care can be a powerful intervention for young children and their parents."[27] Attending a quality day-care facility that offers an enriched program can improve children's social, cognitive, and language skills, even when accounting for variables related to family background and low income.[28]

Employment and Training

Mothers with a college education usually have jobs that afford them financial stability. Like Clara, mothers without an education or training are at risk of finding only low-wage jobs that do not offer health insurance. Single mothers who are heads of households working at minimum or low wages are at risk of remaining in poverty unless they are offered opportunities and access to education and training.[29] Public policy makers should support mothers in obtaining an education or receiving training in a recognized field that will offer employment security. Investing money for training and education can break the cycle of poverty and abuse, neglect, and high stress associated with poverty. Education and training promote long-term economic self-sufficiency, which is critical for labor market success, and an essential ingredient in long-term stable employment that affords a livable wage.

Mental Health Concerns

In the United States, managed care organizations oversee the majority of substance abuse and mental health services "in which central authorities use rules, standards, and procedures to regulate the nature and length of all treatment episodes."[30] The original intent for the creation of a managed care system was to control and supervise the financial costs associated with the provision of health-care service delivery. In order to rein in costs, clinical treatment plans are monitored and evaluated by managed care staff, who follow a set of regulations and rules to manage mental health and addiction treatment. These stringent regulations and rules dictate the treatment modality to be used, the treatment setting, and the treatment duration.

Opponents of managed care assert that the constraints placed on mental health and addiction intervention options are harming patients, and, to the point, quality services to this vulnerable group of mothers are compromised. In order to save costs, long-term therapy is being replaced with short-term models of treatment. Short-term therapy curbs costs by reducing the number of individual sessions offered, instead supplementing individual treatment with self-help groups. Proponents of long-term psychotherapy assert "that to abandon this modality is to compromise care."[31] The therapeutic relationship cannot be constrained, or time spent with the therapist replaced by self-help or other adjuncts, without a negative impact on treatment outcomes.

Proponents of long-term therapy emphasize that the healing of emotional wounds takes place in the context of an ongoing relationship between client and skilled therapist. They deem that short-term therapy sacrifices the qualities inherent in the therapeutic relationship, which is a key element in positive treatment outcomes. Short-term therapy focuses on treatment strategies that address the "presenting problem" rather than the underlying causes. For these reasons, short-term treatment approaches may not be beneficial to clients with childhood histories of sexual abuse. All the mothers I interviewed expounded on the importance of their relationship to their therapists. They stated that their therapists played a multitude of roles, including that of mentor, advice giver, substitute mother, confidant, and role model. Mothers strongly agreed that their therapists helped them to overcome the pain of the past and aided them in managing the challenges of mothering, depression, anxiety, addictions, and interpersonal problems with current adult relationships.

Managed care requirements that focus on treatment of the "presenting problem" runs contrary to CSA research that strongly suggests that depression, anxiety, and addictions to alcohol and drugs seen in adults are frequently the long-term outcomes of CSA experiences. By working on the symptoms and ignoring the real underlying causes, such as early sexual abuse experiences, the presenting symptoms are treated only superficially. Managed care regulations that impose time limitations and dictate treatment strategies present a threat to quality care and limit the effectiveness in making long-term and sustained behavioral changes in clients.

Lastly, managed care's set protocol used to guide treatment options and set time limits is a rigid, "one size fits all" strategy that does not take into consideration individual needs and circumstances. Although the managed care protocol may save costs, it is simultaneously prohibiting clients from receiving appropriate treatment and care. In turn, this may cause mothers to experience prolonged psychological pain and undue harm.

Although mental health service providers can negotiate with a managed care case manager to modify the regulations based on a client's individual circumstances, doing so is time-consuming, and does not always yield the desired outcome of extended treatment. In his study, Michael Sosin found that therapists manipulated their diagnoses and exaggerated clients' symptoms in order to ensure that their clients could continue treatment. Public policy makers could expand insurance coverage to include longer inpatient and outpatient treatment services. This would then put policy in line with the current research, which indicates that a longer duration of treatment prevents relapses and sustains treatment efforts for clients who are addicted to drugs and/or alcohol, and have mental health concerns that seriously interfere with their functioning.[32]

CONCLUSION

There is a great need to rethink and reevaluate how mental health providers will meet the challenges that face women with CSA histories in order to eliminate the barriers that impede their mothering abilities. Full, integrative mental health services show great promise in providing for the needs of this population and promoting the necessary supports. By identifying the aspects related to risk factors and protective factors, practitioners and service providers can plan and target interventions that are geared toward strengthening women in their roles as mothers, and assist in preventing trauma and its consequences for the next generation. Individual competence can be improved by building relationships between family, friends, and community resources. To increase resiliency, mothers can learn skills to handle the emotional consequences related to traumatic life events, learn strategies for managing stress and interpersonal conflict, and build natural support systems by creating connections to extended family, friends, and community and spiritual resources to help support them in their mothering roles.

According to Bessel van der Kolk, "Traumatized human beings recover in the context of relationships: with families, loved ones, AA meetings, veterans' organizations, religious communities, or professional therapists. The role of those relationships is to provide physical and emotional safety, including safety from feeling shamed, admonished, or judged, and to bolster the courage to tolerate, face, and process the reality of what happened."[33] A mother's functioning can be strengthened by building connections and enhancing social support systems. It is important to focus on the difficulties confronted by this vulnerable population, but it is just as critical to develop and foster their strengths and resilient capacities by strengthening the interactions between mothers, their families, and the community resources that can assist them in their mothering.

John Bowlby, famous for his research on mother–child attachment, wrote: "If a community values its children, it must cherish their parents."[34] In following his wisdom and knowledge, public policies need to address the obstacles that impede mothers' abilities to support their families, and break the cycle of neglect, abuse, and poverty by offering financial appropriations and government supports. Mental health and substance abuse services, education and training, publicly funded health insurance, and child-care assistance are necessary resources. For mothers who are part of the working-class poor and marginalized, policy makers must ensure that these women have the supports they need to maintain employment while earning a wage that will bring them and their children out of poverty.

The economic costs of child maltreatment in the United States are estimated at $124 billion a year.[35] These costs are predicted to grow as child maltreatment continues to increase and pose a major public health concern. A number of therapeutic practices have been shown to be effective in decreasing the impact of toxic stress and trauma on families. Providing monies toward preventive services targeting at-risk families would reduce the economic costs while also reducing human suffering. A comprehensive support system can address the mental health and parenting concerns of these mothers, as well as the work-related needs of mothers who are economically disadvantaged.

It will take a concerted effort on the micro and macro levels to address the real and potential problems presented by mothers who were sexually abused as children. It will take a comprehensive and combined effort to address the difficulties of this population. As stated earlier, integrative and holistic therapeutic methods are needed to accompany policy commitments that will provide the supportive services and resources needed to enhance the mothering capacities of women with CSA histories. A solid undergirding of research theory and funding must be in place in order to implement programs that will yield positive results. The information from this book can be used to inform and guide helping professionals and policy makers in ensuring that comprehensive services are available to assist in preventing the consequences of trauma from being visited on the next generation.

NOTES

I. DEFINING CHILD SEXUAL ABUSE AND THE FACTORS THAT IMPACT RESILIENCY AND RECOVERY

1. Paris Goodyear-Brown, Abbe Fath, and Lori Myers, *Handbook of Child Sexual Abuse: Identification, Assessment, and Treatment*, ed. Paris Goodyear-Brown (Hoboken, NJ: John Wiley & Sons, 2012), 4.

2. Goodyear-Brown et al., *Handbook of Child Sexual Abuse*, 4–12.

3. Robert F. Anda, Maxia Dong, David W. Brown, Vincent J. Felitti, Wayne H. Giles, Geraldine S. Perry, Edwards J. Valerie, and Shanta R. Dube, "The Relationship of Adverse Childhood Experiences to a History of Premature Death of Family Members," *BMC Public Health* 9, no. 106 (2009), 7.

4. US Census Bureau News, *Profile America Facts for Features* (Washington, DC: US Department of Commerce, 2012).

5. Joseph H. Beitchman, Kenneth J. Zucker, Jane E. Hood, Granville A. Da Costa, Donna Akman, and Erika Cassavia, "A Review of the Long-Term Effects of Child Sexual Abuse," *Child Abuse & Neglect* 16 (1992), 101–18.

6. Leslie L. Feinauer and Daniel A. Stuart, "Blame and Resilience in Women Sexually Abused as Children," *American Journal of Family Therapy* 24, no. 1 (1996), 37–38.

7. Feinauer and Stuart, "Blame and Resilience in Women Sexually Abused as Children," 39.

8. Christine A. Courtois and Julian D. Ford, *Treatment of Complex Trauma: A Sequenced, Relationship-Based Approach* (New York: Guilford Press, 2013), 56.

9. Ronald C. Summit, "The Child Abuse Accommodation Syndrome," *Child Abuse & Neglect* 7 (1983), 183.

10. van der Kolk, Bessel A. *The Body Keeps the Score* (New York: Penguin Group, 2014), 163.

11. Victoria L. Banyard, Linda M. Williams, Jane A. Siegel, and Carolyn M. West, "Childhood Sexual Abuse in the Lives of Black Women: Risk and Resilience in a Longitudinal Study," *Women and Therapy* 25, no. 3–4 (2002), 45–58.

12. Robin Karr-Morse and Meredith S. Wiley, *Scared Sick: The Role of Childhood Trauma in Adult Disease* (New York: Basic Books, 2012), 189.

2. THE LONG-TERM IMPACT OF CHILD SEXUAL ABUSE

1. David Finkelhor, *A Sourcebook on Child Sexual Abuse* (Beverly Hills, CA: Sage Publications, 1986), 183.

2. Sarah Hartley, Carly Johnco, Marthinus Hofmeyr, and Alexis Berry, "The Nature of Posttraumatic Growth in Adult Survivors of Child Sexual Abuse," *Journal of Child Sexual Abuse* 25, no. 2 (2015), 201–03.

3. Christine A. Courtois, *It's Not You, It's What Happened to You: Complex Trauma and Treatment* (Longboat Key, FL: Telemachus Press, 2014), 38–40.

4. American Psychiatric Association (APA), *Diagnostic and Statistical Manual of Mental Disorders: DSM-5* (Washington, DC: American Psychiatric Publishing, 2013), 160–67.

5. APA, *DSM-5*, 168–70.

6. APA, *DSM-5*, 271–77.

7. APA, *DSM-5*, 271–77.

8. David DiLillo, "Interpersonal Functioning among Women Reporting a History of Childhood Sexual Abuse: Empirical Findings and Methodological Issues," *Clinical Psychology Review* 21 (2001), 64–65.

9. APA, *DSM-5*, 189.

10. Suzanne Abraham, *Eating Disorders: The Facts* (New York: Oxford University Press, 2008), 19–29.

11. Abraham, *Eating Disorders*, 26–27.

12. Abraham, *Eating Disorders*, 31–33.

13. Susan M. Hannan, Holly K. Orcutt, Lynsey R. Miron, and Kristen L. Thompson, "Childhood Sexual Abuse and Later Alcohol-Related Problems: Investigating the Roles of Re-Victimization, and Drinking Motivations among College Women," *Journal of Interpersonal Violence* 32, no. 14 (2015), 2131–32.

14. Vincent J. Felitti, "The Origins of Addiction: Evidence from the Childhood Experiences Study," Department of Preventive Medicine, Kaiser Perma-

nente Medical Care Program (San Diego, CA: 2003), 1–8. Published in German as: Felitti VJ. Ursprünge des Suchtverhaltens—Evidenzen aus einer Studie zu belastenden Kindheitserfahrungen. Praxis der Kinderpsychologie und Kinderpsychiatrie, 2003; 52: 547–59.

15. APA, *DSM-5*, 483–90.

16. APA, *DSM-5*, 663.

17. APA, *DSM-5*, 664.

18. Christine A. Courtois and Julian D. Ford, *Treatment of Complex Trauma: A Sequenced, Relationship-Based Approach* (New York: Guilford Press, 2013), 32–33.

19. Robin Karr-Morse and Meredith S. Wiley, *Scared Sick: The Role of Childhood Trauma in Adult Disease* (New York: Basic Books, 2012), 260.

20. Vincent J. Felitti, "The Lifelong Effects of Adverse Childhood Experiences," in *Chadwick's Child Maltreatment: Sexual Abuse and Psychological Maltreatment*, ed. David Chadwick (St. Louis, MO: STM Learning, 2014), 203.

21. Felitti, "The Lifelong Effects of Adverse Childhood Experiences," 206.

22. Vincent J. Felitti, Robert F. Anda, Dale Nordenberg, David F. Williamson, Alison M. Spitz, Valerie Edwards, Mary P. Koss, and James S. Marks, "Relationship of Child Abuse and Household Dysfunction to Many of the Leading Causes of Death in Adults," *American Journal of Preventive Medicine* 14, no. 4 (1998), 254.

23. Karr-Morse and Wiley, *Scared Sick*, 14.

24. Therese A. Rando, *Treatment of Complicated Mourning* (Champaign, IL: Research Press, 1993), 3–29.

25. Courtois, *It's Not You*, 71–72.

3. TRANSCENDING ADVERSITY AND OVERCOMING ABUSE

1. Kim M. Anderson, *Enhancing Resilience in Survivors of Family Violence* (New York: Spring Publishing, 2010), 18–19.

2. Norman Garmezy, "Resiliency and Vulnerability to Adverse Developmental Outcomes Associated with Poverty," *American Behavioral Scientist* 34, no. 4 (1991), 416–30.

3. Susan B. Fine, "Resilience and Adaptability: Who Rises Above Adversity?" *Journal of Occupational Therapy* 45, no. 6 (1991), 499.

4. Donna Greco and Sarah Dawgert, "Poverty and Sexual Violence: Building Prevention and Intervention Responses," *Prevention Coalition Against Rape* (2007), 7–23.

5. Gabriela Martorell, Diane E. Papalia, and Ruth Duskin Feldman, *A Child's World: Infancy through Adolescence* (New York: McGraw-Hill, 2014), 418–20.

6. Martorell et al., *A Child's World*, 224–27.

7. Martorell et al., *A Child's World*, 171–73.

8. Katherine Covell and R. Brian Howe, *Children, Families and Violence: Challenges for Children's Rights* (London, England: Jessica Kingsley Publishers, 2008), 63–95.

9. Thema Bryant-Davis, Sarah E. Ullman, Yuying Tsong, Shaquita Tillman, and Kimberly Smith, "Struggling to Survive: Sexual Assault, Poverty, and Mental Health Outcomes of African American Women," *American Journal of Orthopsychiatry* 80, no. 1 (2010), 66–67.

10. Alison Clarke-Stewart and Cornelia Brentano, *Divorce: Causes and Consequences* (New Haven: Yale University Press, 2006), 106–30.

11. Marion S. Forgatch and David S. DeGarmo, "Accelerating Recovery from Poverty: Prevention Effects for Recently Separated Mothers," *Journal of Early & Intensive Behavior Interventions* 4, no. 4 (2007), 681–702.

12. Paul Bywaters, Lisa Bunting, Gavin Davison, Jennifer Hanratty, Will Mason, Claire McCartan, and Nicole Stelis, "The Relationship between Poverty, Child Abuse, and Neglect: An Evidence Overview," *Joseph Rowntree Foundation* (2016), 21–31.

13. David S. Zielinski, "Child Maltreatment and Adult Socioeconomic Well-Being," *Child Abuse & Neglect* 33, no. 10 (2009), 666–78.

14. Anderson, *Enhancing Resilience*, 19–23.

15. Martorell et al., *A Child's World*, 225.

16. Melissa J. Himelein and Jo Ann V. McElrath, "Resilient Child Sexual Abuse Survivors: Cognitive Coping and Illusion," *Child Abuse & Neglect* 20, no. 8 (1996), 753–58.

17. Mark Katz, "Overcoming Childhood Adversities: Lessons Learned from Those Who Have Beat the Odds," *Intervention in School and Clinic* 32, no. 4 (1997), 209; quoting Bessel A. van der Kolk, *Trauma and Development in Children* (Video), Albany: Statewide Grand Rounds, sponsored by the Bureau of Psychiatric Services, New York State Department of Mental Health (1994).

18. Anderson, *Enhancing Resilience*, 25.

19. Lanae Valentine and Leslie L. Feinauer, "Resilience Factors Associated with Female Survivors of Childhood Sexual Abuse," *American Journal of Family Therapy* 21, no. 3 (1993), 220–23.

20. Judith B. Bachay and Pamela A. Cingel, "Restructuring Resilience: Emerging Voices," *Affilia* 14, no. 2 (1999), 169.

21. Katz, "Overcoming Childhood Adversities," 209.

22. Katz, "Overcoming Childhood Adversities," 205.

23. Katz, "Overcoming Childhood Adversities," 207–08.

24. Valentine and Feinauer, "Resilience Factors," 220–21.

25. Norman Garmezy, "Resilience in Children's Adaptation to Negative Life Events and Stressed Environments," *Pediatric Annals* 20, no. 9 (1991): 459–66.

4. MOTHERING

1. Victoria L. Banyard, Linda M. Williams, Jane A. Siegel, and Carolyn M. West, "Childhood Sexual Abuse in the Lives of Black Women: Risk and Resilience in a Longitudinal Study," *Women and Therapy* 25, no. 3–4 (2002), 45–58.

2. Anne R. Douglas, "Reported Anxieties Concerning Intimate Parenting in Women Sexually Abused as Children," *Child Abuse & Neglect* 23, no. 3 (2000), 432.

3. Mary W. Armsworth and Karin Stronck, "Intergenerational Effects on Incest Parenting: Skills, Abilities and Attitudes," *Journal of Counseling and Development* 77, no. 3 (1999), 307.

4. Tamar Cohen, "Motherhood among Incest Survivors," *Child Abuse & Neglect* 19, no. 12 (1999), 1427–28.

5. Pamela C. Alexander, Laureen Teti, and Catherine L. Anderson, "Childhood Sexual Abuse History and Role Reversal in Parenting," *Child Abuse and Neglect* 24, no. 6 (2000), 831.

6. Marjorie Saltzberg, "Parenting Challenges for Women with Abuse Histories," *Journal of Feminist Family Therapy* 12, no. 1 (2000), 45–48.

7. Susan C. Mapp, "The Effects of Sexual Abuse as a Child on the Risk of Mothers Physically Abusing Their Children: A Path Analysis Using System Theory," *Child Abuse & Neglect* 30, no. 11 (2006), 1303.

8. Pamela Schuetze and Rina Das Eiden, "The Relationship between Sexual Abuse during Childhood and Parenting Outcomes: Modeling Direct and Indirect Pathways," *Child Abuse & Neglect* 29, no. 6 (2005), 655–56.

9. Ayelet Meron Ruscio, "Predicting the Child-Rearing Practices of Mothers Sexually Abused in Childhood," *Child Abuse & Neglect* 25, no. 3 (2001), 381.

10. Wendi Cross, "A Personal History of Childhood Sexual Abuse: Parenting Patterns and Problems," *Clinical Child Psychology and Psychiatry* 6, no. 4 (2001), 563–74.

11. Armsworth and Stronck, "Intergenerational Effects," 303–14.

12. Christine M. Kreklewe and Caroline C. Piotrowski, "Incest Survivor Mothers: Protecting the Next Generation," *Child Abuse & Neglect* 22, no. 12 (1998), 1305–12.

13. David DiLillo, "Interpersonal Functioning among Women Reporting a History of Childhood Sexual Abuse: Empirical Findings and Methodological Issues," *Clinical Psychology Review* 21, (2001), 566.

14. Norman Garmezy, "Resiliency and Vulnerability to Adverse Developmental Outcomes Associated with Poverty," *American Behavioral Scientist* 34, no. 4 (1991), 416–30.

5. MOTHERING

1. Mary W. Armsworth and Karin Stronck, "Intergenerational Effects on Incest Parenting: Skills, Abilities and Attitudes," *Journal of Counseling and Development* 77, no. 3 (1999), 309.

2. Emmy Werner and Ruth S. Smith, *Overcoming the Odds: High-Risk Children from Birth to Adulthood* (New York: Cornell University Press, 1992), 13.

3. Judith B. Bachay and Pamela A. Cingel, "Restructuring Resilience: Emerging Voices," *Affilia* 14, no. 2 (1999), 162–75.

4. Victoria L. Banyard, Linda M. Williams, Jane A. Siegel, and Carolyn M. West, "Childhood Sexual Abuse in the Lives of Black Women: Risk and Resilience in a Longitudinal Study," *Women and Therapy* 25, no. 3–4 (2002), 45–58.

5. Wendi Cross, "A Personal History of Childhood Sexual Abuse: Parenting Patterns and Problems," *Clinical Child Psychology and Psychiatry* 6, no. 4 (2001), 563–74.

6. Lanae Valentine and Leslie L. Feinauer, "Resilience Factors Associated with Female Survivors of Childhood Sexual Abuse," *The American Journal of Family Therapy* 21, no. 3 (1993), 220–21.

7. Valentine and Feinauer, "Resilience Factors Associated with Female Survivors," 220–21.

6. THE THERAPEUTIC RELATIONSHIP
AND ITS IMPORTANCE TO
RESILIENCY AND HEALING

1. J. Christopher Muran and Jacques P. Barber, *The Therapeutic Alliance: An Evidence-Based Guide to Practice* (New York: Guilford Press, 2010), 11–12.

2. Carl R. Rogers, *A Way of Being* (New York: Houghton Mifflin Company, 1980), 160.

3. Paula B. Poorman, "Perceptions of Thriving by Women Who Have Experienced Abuse or Status-Related Oppression," *Psychology of Women Quarterly* 26, no. 1 (2002), 58.

4. Steven J. Ackerman and Mark J. Hilsenroth, "A Review of Therapist Characteristics and Techniques Positively Impacting Therapeutic Alliance," *Clinical Psychological Review* 23, no. 1 (2003), 1.

5. Charles J. Gelso and Ayelet Silberberg, "Strengthening the Real Relationship: What Is a Psychotherapist to Do?" *Practice Innovations* 1, no. 3 (2016), 154–63.

6. Ackerman, and Hilsenroth, "A Review of Therapist Characteristics," 7.

7. Nancy A. Ridges, "Therapist's Self-Disclosure: Expanding the Comfort Zone," *Psychotherapy: Theory, Research, Practice, Training* 38, no.1 (2001), 22.

8. Cristelle T. Audet, "Client Perspectives of Therapist Self-Disclosure: Violating Boundaries or Removing Barriers," *Counseling Psychology Quarterly* 24, no. 2 (2011), 89.

9. Sarah Knox and Clara E. Hill, "Therapist Self-Disclosure: Research-Based Suggestions for Practitioners," *Journal of Clinical Psychology* 59, no. 5 (2003), 529–39.

10. Leslie S. Greenberg and Shari M. Geller, "Congruence and Therapeutic Presence," *The Person-Centered Journal* 7, no. 2 (2000), 159.

11. Carl R. Rogers, *On Becoming a Person: A Therapist's View of Psychotherapy* (New York: Houghton Mifflin, 1980), 201.

12. Christine A. Courtois and Julian D. Ford, *Treatment of Complex Trauma: A Sequenced, Relationship-Based Approach* (New York: Guilford Press, 2013), 65–68.

7. A LEGACY OF TRAUMA

1. Monica McGoldrick, Randy Gerson, and Sueli Petry, *Genograms: Assessment and Intervention.* 3rd ed. (New York: Norton & Company, 2008), 4–7.

2. Selma Fraiberg, Edna Adelson, and Vivian Shapiro, "Ghosts in the Nursery: A Psychoanalytic Approach to the Problems of Impaired Infant–Mother Relationships," *Journal of the American Academy of Child Psychiatry* 14, no. 3 (1975), 395.

3. Fraiberg et al., "Ghosts in the Nursery," 395–96.

4. Alicia F. Lieberman and Patricia Van Horn, *Psychotherapy with Infants and Young Children: Repairing the Effects of Stress and Trauma on Early Attachment* (New York: Guilford Press, 2008), 13.

5. Lanae Valentine and Leslie L. Feinauer, "Resilience Factors Associated with Female Survivors of Childhood Sexual Abuse," *American Journal of Family Therapy* 21, no. 3 (1993), 218.

6. Paul Farmer, "On Suffering and Structural Violence: A View from Below," *Daedalus* 125, no. 1 (1996), 280.

7. Sebastian L. Lipnia, "The Biological Side of Social Determinants: Neural Costs of Childhood Poverty," *Quarterly Review of Comparative Education* 46, no. 2 (2016), 267–69.

8. Jessica L. Semega, Kayal R. Fontenot, and Melissa A. Kollar, "US Census Bureau, Current Population Reports, P60-259, Income and Poverty in the United States: 2016," (Washington, DC: US Government Printing Office, 2017).

9. David S. Zielinski, "Child Maltreatment and Adult Socioeconomic Well-Being," *Child Abuse & Neglect* 33, no. 10 (2009), 672.

10. Ujunwa Anakwenze and Daniyal Zuberi, "Mental Health and Poverty in the Inner City," *Health and Social Work* 38, no. 3 (2013), 149.

11. Howard Steele, Jordan Bate, Miriam Steele, Kerri Danskin, Hannah Knafo, Adella Nikitiades, Shanata Rishi Dube, Karen Bonuck, Paul Meissner, and Anne Murphy, "Adverse Childhood Experiences, Poverty, and Parenting Stress," *Canadian Journal of Behavioural Science* 48, no. 1 (2016), 32–38.

12. Bridget Klest, "Childhood Trauma, Poverty, and Adult Victimization," *Psychological Trauma, Research, Practice, and Policy* 4, no. 3 (2012), 245.

13. Henrietta H. Filipas and Sarah E. Ullman, "Child Sexual Abuse, Coping, Reponses, Self-Blame, Post-Traumatic Stress Disorder, and Adult Sexual Revictimization," *Journal of Interpersonal Violence* 21, no. 5 (2006), 665–69.

14. Liz Grauerholz, "An Ecological Approach to Understanding Sexual Revictimization: Linking Personal, Interpersonal, and Sociocultural Factors and Processes," *Child Maltreatment* 5, no. 3 (2000), 9–11.

15. Grauerholz, "An Ecological Approach to Understanding," 7–14.

16. Heather J. Risser, Melanie D. Hetzel-Riggin, Cynthia J. Thomsen, and Thomas R. McCane, "PTSD as a Mediator of Sexual Revictimization: The Role of Reexperiencing, Avoidance, and Arousal Symptoms," *Journal of Traumatic Stress* 19, no. 5 (2006), 688.

17. Michelle A. Fortier, David DiLillo, Terri Messman-Moore, James Peugh, Kathleen A.DeNardi, and Kathryn J. Gaffey, "Severity of Child Sexual Abuse and Revictimization: The Mediating Role of Coping and Trauma Symptoms," *Psychology of Women Quarterly* 33, no. 3 (2009), 316.

18. Grauerholz, "An Ecological Approach to Understanding," 8.

19. Fortier et al., "Severity of Child Sexual Abuse," 317.

20. Anakwenze and Zuberi, "Mental Health and Poverty," 149.

21. Sarah B. Johnson, Jenna L. Riis, and Kimberly G. Noble, "State of the Art Review: Poverty and the Developing Brain," *Journal of Pediatrics* 137, no. 4 (2016), 7.

22. Vincent J. Felitti, "Adverse Childhood Experiences and Adult Health," *Academic Pediatrics* 9, no. 3 (2009), 131.

8. IMPLICATIONS FOR TREATMENT AND POLICY

1. Babette Rothschild, *The Body Remembers: The Psychophysiology of Trauma and Trauma Treatment* (New York: W. W. Norton, 2000), 82–83.

2. Stephen W. Porges, "Neuroception: A Subconscious System for Detecting Threats and Safety," *Zero to Three Journal* 24, no. 5 (2004), 19–24.

3. Alicia F. Lieberman and Patricia Van Horn, *Psychotherapy with Infants and Young Children: Repairing the Effects of Stress and Trauma on Early Attachment* (New York: Guilford Press, 2008), 3.

4. Leila Beckwith, "Prevention, Science, and Prevention Programs," in *Handbook of Infant Mental Health*, 2nd ed., ed. Charles H. Zeanah Jr. (New York: Guilford Press, 2005), 441.

5. Lieberman and Van Horn, *Psychotherapy with Infants and Young Children*, 6–25.

6. Lieberman and Van Horn, *Psychotherapy with Infants and Young Children*, 8.

7. Gabriela Martorell, Diane E. Papalia, and Ruth Duskin Feldman, *A Child's World: Infancy through Adolescence* (New York: McGraw-Hill, 2014), 237–38.

8. Martorell et al., *A Child's World*, 472–74.

9. Judith V. Jordan, Maureen Walker, and Linda M. Hartling, *The Complexity of Connection* (New York: Guilford Press, 2004), 38.

10. Melissa J. Himelein and Jo Ann V. McElrath, "Resilient Child Sexual Abuse Survivors: Cognitive Coping and Illusion," *Child Abuse & Neglect* 20, no. 8 (1996), 754–55.

11. Lanae Valentine and Leslie L. Feinauer, "Resilience Factors Associated with Female Survivors of Childhood Sexual Abuse," *American Journal of Family Therapy* 21, no. 3 (1993), 216–24.

12. Alice Miller, AZQuotes.com, Wind and Fly LTD, 2017, http://www.azquotes.com/author/10094-Alice_Miller (accessed September 26, 2017).

13. Stephen W. Porges, "The Polyvagal Perspective," *Biological Psychology Journal* 74, no. 2 (2007), 120.

14. Porges, "Neuroception," 19–24.

15. Stephen W. Porges, "The Polyvagal Theory: New Insights into Adaptive Reactions of the Autonomic Nervous System," *Cleveland Clinical Journal of Medicine* 76, no. 2 (2009), 1–7.

16. Peter A. Levine, *In an Unspoken Voice: How the Body Releases Trauma and Restores Goodness* (Berkeley, CA: North Atlantic Books, 2010), 102.

17. Bessel van der Kolk, *The Body Keeps the Score* (New York: Penguin Group, 2014), 205.

18. Levine, *In an Unspoken Voice*, 109–12.

19. Levine, *In an Unspoken Voice*, 104–05.

20. van der Kolk, *The Body Keeps the Score*, 217–18, 249–53, 264–65, 269–71, 314–15.

21. Donnel B. Stern, *Partners in Thought: Working with Unformulated Experience, Disassociation, and Enactment* (New York: Routledge, 2010), 23.

22. Joy K. Rice, "Poverty, Welfare, and Patriarchy: How Macro-Level Changes in Social Policy Can Help Low-Income Women," *Journal of Social Issues* 57, no. 2 (2004), 359–60.

23. R. P. Mills, J. C. Stevens, B. Shay, and R. Purga, *Meeting the Needs of Public Assistance Recipients Under Welfare Reform in New York State* (Potsdam, NY: New York State Welfare to Work Technical Assistance Team, 2001).

24. Bruce Fuller, Sharon L. Kagen, Gretchen L. Caspary, and Christiane A. Gauthier, "Welfare Reform and Childcare Options for Low-Income Families," *Child Welfare and Reform* 12, no. 1 (2001), 104.

25. Martorell et al., *A Child's World*, 182–84.

26. Aletha C. Huston, "Reforms and Child Development," *Child Welfare and Reform* 12, no. 1 (2001), 63.

27. Barbara B. Blum, "Five Commentaries: Looking to the Future," *The Future of Children* 12, no. 1 (2002), 206.

28. Fuller et al., "Welfare Reform and Childcare Options," 106–08.

29. Rice, "Poverty, Welfare, and Patriarchy," 365.

30. Michael R. Sosin, "Negotiating Case Decisions in Substance Abuse Managed Care," *Journal of Health and Social Behavior* 43, no. 3 (2002), 277.

31. Norma C. Ware, William S. Lachicotte, Suzanne R. Kirschner, Dharma E. Cortes, and Byron J. Good, "Clinician Experiences of Managed Mental Health Care: A Rereading of the Threat," *Medical Anthropology Quarterly* 14, no. 1 (2000), 6.

32. Sosin, "Negotiating Case Decisions," 280–84.

33. van der Kolk, *The Body Keeps the Score*, 210.

34. John Bowlby, "Maternal Care and Mental Health," *World Health Organization Monograph*, Serial 5 (1951), 84.

35. Xiangming Fang, Derek S. Brown, Curtis Florence, and James A. Mercy, "The Economic Burden of Child Maltreatment in the United States and Implications for Prevention," *Child Abuse & Neglect* 36, no. 2 (2011), 161.

BIBLIOGRAPHY

Abraham, Suzanne. *Eating Disorders: The Facts*. New York: Oxford University Press, 2008.

Ackerman, Steven J., and Mark J. Hilsenroth. "A Review of Therapist Characteristics and Techniques Positively Impacting Therapeutic Alliance." *Clinical Psychological Review* 23, no. 1 (2003): 1–33.

Alexander, Pamela C., Laureen Teti, and Catherine L. Anderson, "Childhood Sexual Abuse History and Role Reversal in Parenting." *Child Abuse & Neglect* 24, no. 6 (2000): 829–38.

American Psychiatric Association. *Diagnostic and Statistical Manual of Mental Disorders: DSM-5*. Washington, DC: American Psychiatric Publishing, 2013.

Anakwenze, Ujunwa, and Daniyal Zuberi. "Mental Health and Poverty in the Inner City." *Health and Social Work* 38, no. 3 (2013): 147–57.

Anda, Robert F., Maxia Dong, David W. Brown, Vincent J. Felitti, Wayne H. Giles, Geraldine S. Perry, Edwards J. Valerie, and Shanta R. Dube. "The Relationship of Adverse Childhood Experiences to a History of Premature Death of Family Members." *BMC Public Health* 9, no. 106 (2009): 1–10.

Anderson, Kim M. *Enhancing Resilience in Survivors of Family Violence*. New York: Spring Publishing, 2010.

Armsworth, Mary W., and Karin Stronck. "Intergenerational Effects on Incest Parenting: Skills, Abilities and Attitudes." *Journal of Counseling and Development* 77, no. 3 (1999): 303–14.

Audet, Cristelle T. "Client Perspectives of Therapist Self-Disclosure: Violating Boundaries or Removing Barriers." *Counseling Psychology Quarterly* 24, no. 2 (2011): 85–100.

Bachay, Judith B., and Pamela A. Cingel. "Restructuring Resilience: Emerging Voices." *Affilia* 14, no. 2 (1999): 162–75.

Banyard, Victoria, L., Linda M. Williams, Jane A. Siegel, and Carolyn M. West. "Childhood Sexual Abuse in the Lives of Black Women: Risk and Resilience in a Longitudinal Study." *Women and Therapy* 25, no. 3–4 (2002): 45–58.

Beckwith, Leila. "Prevention, Science, and Prevention Programs." In *Handbook of Infant Mental Health*, 2nd ed., ed. Charles H. Zeanah Jr. (New York: Guilford Press, 2005).

Beitchman, Joseph H., Kenneth J. Zucker, Jane E. Hood, Granville A. DaCosta, Donna Akman, and Erika Cassavia. "A Review of the Long-Term Effects of Child Sexual Abuse." *Child Abuse & Neglect* 16 (1992): 101–18.

Blum, Barbara B. "Five Commentaries: Looking to the Future." *The Future of Children* 12, no. 1 (2002): 187–207.

Bowlby, John. "Maternal Care and Mental Health." *World Health Organization Monograph*. Serial 5, 1951.

Boyd, Reiko K. "Psychological Theories and Low-Wage Work." *Journal of Human Behavior in the Social Environment* 24, no. 1 (2014): 16–25.

Bridges, Nancy A. "Therapist's Self-Disclosure: Expanding the Comfort Zone." *Psychotherapy: Theory, Research, Practice, Training* 38, no. 1 (2001): 21–30.

Bryant-Davis, Thema, Sarah E. Ullman, Yuying Tsong, Shaquita Tillman, and Kimberly Smith. "Struggling to Survive: Sexual Assault, Poverty, and Mental Health Outcomes of African American Women." *American Journal of Orthopsychiatry* 80, no. 1 (2010): 61–70.

Buist, Anne, and Helen Janson. "Childhood Sexual Abuse, Parenting, and Postpartum Depression: A Three-Year Follow-Up Study." *Child Abuse & Neglect* 25, no. 7 (2001): 909–21.

Burkett, Linda P. "Parenting Behaviors of Women Who Were Sexually Abused as Children in their Families of Origin." *Family Process* 30 no. 4 (1991): 421–34.

Bywaters, Paul, Lisa Bunting, Gavin Davison, Jennifer Hanratty, Will Mason, Claire McCartan, and Nicole Steils. "The Relationship Between Poverty, Child Abuse and Neglect: An Evidence Overview." *Joseph Rowntree Foundation*, 2016: 1–74.

Clarke-Stewart, Alison, and Cornelia Brentano. *Divorce: Causes and Consequences.* New Haven: Yale University Press, 2006.

Coates, Susan W., Jane L. Rosenthal, and Daniel S. Schechter. *September 11: Trauma and Human Bonds.* Hillsdale, NJ: The Analytic Press, 2003.

Cohen, Tamar. "Motherhood among Incest Survivors." *Child Abuse & Neglect* 19, no. 12 (1995): 1423–29.

Courtois, Christine A. *It's Not You, It's What Happened to You: Complex Trauma and Treatment.* Longboat Key, FL: Telemachus Press, 2014.

Courtois, Christine A., and Julian D. Ford. *Treatment of Complex Trauma: A Sequenced, Relationship-Based Approach.* New York: Guilford Press, 2013.

Covell, Katherine, and R. Brian Howe. *Children, Families and Violence: Challenges for Children's Rights.* London, England: Jessica Kingsley Publishers, 2008.

Cowen, Emory, and W. Work. "Resilient Children, Psychological Wellness, and Primary Prevention." *American Journal of Community Psychology* 16, no. 4 (1988): 591–607.

Cross, Wendi. "A Personal History of Childhood Sexual Abuse: Parenting Patterns and Problems." *Clinical Child Psychology and Psychiatry* 6, no. 4 (2001): 563–74.

DiLillo, David. "Interpersonal Functioning among Women Reporting a History of Childhood Sexual Abuse: Empirical Findings and Methodological Issues." *Clinical Psychology Review* 21, (2001): 553–76.

DiLillo, David, George C. Tremblay, and Lizette Peterson. "Linking Childhood Sexual Abuse and Abusive Parenting: The Immediate Role of Maternal Anger." *Childhood Abuse and Neglect* 24, no. 6 (2000): 829–38.

Douglas, Anne. R. "Reported Anxieties Concerning Intimate Parenting in Women Sexually Abused as Children." *Child Abuse & Neglect* 23, no. 3 (2000): 425–34.

Fang, Xiangming, Derek S. Brown, Curtis Florence, and James A. Mercy. "The Economic Burden of Child Maltreatment in the United States and Implications for Prevention." *In Child Abuse & Neglect* 36, no. 2 (2011): 156–65.

Farmer, Paul. "On Suffering and Structural Violence: A View from Below." *Daedalus* 125, no. 1 (1996): 261–83.

Feinauer, Leslie L., and Daniel A. Stuart. "Blame and Resilience in Women Sexually Abused as Children." *American Journal of Family Therapy* 24, no. 1 (1996): 31–40.

Felitti, Vincent J. "Adverse Childhood Experiences and Adult Health." *Academic Pediatrics* 9, no. 3 (2009): 131–32.

———. "The Origins of Addiction: Evidence from the Childhood Experiences Study." Department of Preventive Medicine, Kaiser Permanente Medical Care Program, San Diego, CA (2003): 1–8. Published in German as: Felitti, V. J. Ursprünge des Suchtverhaltens— Evidenzen aus einer Studie zu belastenden Kindheitserfahrungen. Praxis der Kinderpsychologie und Kinderpsychiatrie, 2003; 52: 547–59.

———. "The Lifelong Effects of Adverse Childhood Experiences." In *Chadwick's Child Maltreatment: Sexual Abuse and Psychological Maltreatment,* ed. David Chadwick. St. Louis, MO: STM Learning, 2014.

Felitti, Vincent J., Robert F. Anda, Dale Nordenberg, David F. Williamson, Alison M. Spitz, Valerie Edwards, Mary P. Koss, and James S. Marks. "Relationship of Child Abuse and Household Dysfunction to Many of the Leading Causes of Death in Adults." *American Journal of Preventive Medicine* 14, no. 4 (1998): 245–58.

Filipas, Henrietta H., and Sarah E. Ullman. "Child Sexual Abuse, Coping, Reponses, Self-Blame, Post-Traumatic Stress Disorder, and Adult Sexual Revictimization." *Journal of Interpersonal Violence* 21, no. 5 (2006): 652–72.

Fine, Susan B. "Resilience and Adaptability: Who Rises Above Adversity?" *Journal of Occupational Therapy* 45, no. 6 (1991): 494–501.

Finkelhor, David. *A Sourcebook on Child Sexual Abuse.* Beverly Hills, CA: Sage Publications, 1986.

Forgatch, Marion S., and David S. DeGarmo. "Accelerating Recovery from Poverty: Prevention Effects for Recently Separated Mothers. *Journal of Early & Intensive Behavior Interventions* 4, no. 4 (2007): 681–702.

Fortier, Michelle A., David DiLillo, Terri Messman-Moore, James Peugh, Kathleen A. De-Nardi, and Kathryn J. Gaffey. "Severity of Child Sexual Abuse and Revictimization: The Mediating Role of Coping and Trauma Symptoms." *Psychology of Women Quarterly* 33, no. 3 (2009): 308–20.

Fraiberg, Selma, Edna Adelson, and Vivian Shapiro. "Ghosts in the Nursery: A Psychoanalytic Approach to the Problems of Impaired Infant-Mother Relationships." *Journal of the American Academy of Child Psychiatry* 14, no. 3 (1975): 387–421.

Fuller, Bruce, Sharon L. Kagen, Gretchen L. Caspary, and Christiane A. Gauthier. "Welfare Reform and Childcare Options for Low-Income Families." *Child Welfare and Reform* 12, no. 1 (2001): 97–119.

Garmezy, Norman. "Resiliency and Vulnerability to Adverse Developmental Outcomes Associated with Poverty." *American Behavioral Scientist* 34, no. 4 (1991): 416–30.

———. "Resilience in Children's Adaptation to Negative Life Events and Stressed Environments." *Pediatric Annals* 20, no. 9 (1991): 459–66.

Gelso, Charles J. and Ayelet Silberberg. "Strengthening the Real Relationship: What is a Psychotherapist to do? *Practice Innovations* 1, no. 3 (2016): 154–63.

Goodyear-Brown, Paris, Abbe Fath, and Lori Myers. *Handbook of Child Sexual Abuse: Identification, Assessment, and Treatment*, ed. Paris Goodyear-Brown. Hoboken, NJ: John Wiley & Sons, 2012.

Grauerholz, Liz. "An Ecological Approach to Understanding Sexual Revictimization: Linking Personal, Interpersonal, and Sociocultural Factors and Processes." *Child Maltreatment* 5, no. 3 (2000): 5–16.

Greco, Donna, and Sarah Dawgert. "Poverty and Sexual Violence: Building Prevention and Intervention Responses." *Prevention Coalition Against Rape* (2007): 1–110.

Greenberg, Leslie S., and Shari M. Geller. "Congruence and Therapeutic Presence." *The Person-Centered Journal* 7, no. 2 (2000): 148–66.

Hannan, Susan M., Holly K. Orcutt, Lynsey R. Miron, and Kristen L. Thompson. "Childhood Sexual Abuse and Later Alcohol-Related Problems: Investigating the Roles of Revictimization, and Drinking Motivations among College Women." *Journal of Interpersonal Violence* 32, no. 14 (2015): 2118–38.

Hartley, Sarah, Carly Johnco, Marthinus Hofmeyr, and Alexis Berry. "The Nature of Posttraumatic Growth in Adult Survivors of Child Sexual Abuse." *Journal of Child Sexual Abuse* 25, no. 2 (2015): 201–20.

Himelein, Melissa J., and Jo Ann V. McElrath. "Resilient Child Sexual Abuse Survivors: Cognitive Coping and Illusion." *Child Abuse & Neglect* 20, no. 8 (1996): 747–58.

Huston, Aletha C. "Reforms and Child Development." *Child Welfare and Reform* 12, no. 1 (2001): 59–77.

Johnson, Sarah B., Jenna L. Riis, and Kimberly G. Noble. "State of the Art Review: Poverty and the Developing Brain." *Journal of Pediatrics* 137, no. 4 (2016): 1–16.

Jordan, Judith V., Maureen Walker, and Linda M. Hartling. *The Complexity of Connection.* New York: Guilford Press, 2004.

Karr-Morse, Robin, and Meredith S. Wiley. *Scared Sick: The Role of Childhood Trauma in Adult Disease*. New York: Basic Books, 2012.

Katz, Mark. "Overcoming Childhood Adversities: Lessons Learned from Those Who Have Beat the Odds." *Intervention in School and Clinic* 32, no. 4 (1997): 205–15.

Klest, Bridget. "Childhood Trauma, Poverty, and Adult Victimization." *Psychological Trauma, Research, Practice, and Policy* 4, no. 3 (2012): 245–51.

Knox, Sarah, and Clara E. Hill. "Therapist Self-Disclosure: Research-Based Suggestion for Practitioners." *Journal of Clinical Psychology* 59, no. 5 (2003): 529–39.

Kreklewe, Christine M., and Caroline C. Piotrowski. "Incest Survivor Mothers: Protecting the Next Generation." *Child Abuse & Neglect* 22, no. 12 (1998): 1305–12.

Levine, Peter A. *In an Unspoken Voice: How the Body Releases Trauma and Restores Goodness*. Berkeley, CA: North Atlantic Books, 2010.

Lieberman, Alicia F., and Patricia Van Horn. *Psychotherapy with Infants and Young Children: Repairing the Effects of Stress and Trauma on Early Attachment*. New York: Guilford Press, 2008.

Lipnia, Sebastian L. "The Biological Side of Social Determinants: Neural Costs of Childhood Poverty." *Quarterly Review of Comparative Education* 46, no. 2 (2016): 265–80.

Mapp, Susan C. "The Effects of Sexual Abuse as a Child on the Risk of Mothers Physically Abusing Their Children: A Path Analysis Using System Theory." *Child Abuse & Neglect* 30, no. 11 (2006): 1293–1310.

Martorell, Gabriela, Diane E. Papalia, and Ruth Duskin Feldman. *A Child's World: Infancy through Adolescence*. New York: McGraw-Hill, 2014.

McGoldrick, Monica, Randy Gerson, and Sueli Petry. *Genograms: Assessment and Intervention*. 3rd ed. New York: W. W. Norton & Company, 2008.

McNally, Richard J. *Remembering Trauma*. Cambridge, MA: Belknap Press, 2003.

Miller, Alice. AZQuotes.com, Wind and Fly LTD, 2017. http://www.azquotes.com/author/10094-Alice_Miller, accessed September 26, 2017.

Mills, R. P., J. C. Stevens, B. Shay, and R. Purga. *Meeting the Needs of Public Assistance Recipients Under Welfare Reform in New York State*. Potsdam, NY: New York State Welfare to Work Technical Assistance Team, 2001.

Muran, J. Christopher, and Jacques P. Barber. *The Therapeutic Alliance: An Evidence-Based Guide to Practice*. New York: Guilford Press, 2010.

Poorman, Paula B. "Perceptions of Thriving by Women Who Have Experienced Abuse or Status-Related Oppression." *Psychology of Women Quarterly* 26, no. 1 (2002): 51–62.

Porges, Stephen W. "Neuroception: A Subconscious System for Detecting Threats and Safety." *Zero to Three Journal* 24, no. 5 (2004): 19–24.

———. "The Polyvagal Perspective." *Biological Psychology Journal* 74, no. 2 (2007): 116–43.

———. *The Polyvagal Theory: Neurophysiological Foundations of Emotions, Attachment, Communication, Self-Regulation*. New York: W. W. Norton & Company, 2011.

———. "The Polyvagal Theory: New Insights into Adaptive Reactions of the Autonomic Nervous System." *Cleveland Clinical Journal Med* 76, no. 2 (2009): 1–7.

Rando, Therese A. *Treatment of Complicated Mourning*. Champaign, IL: Research Press, 1993.

Rice, Joy K. "Poverty, Welfare, and Patriarchy: How Macro-Level Changes in Social Policy Can Help Low Income Women." *Journal of Social Issues* 57, no. 2 (2004): 355–74.

Ridges, Nancy A. "Therapist's Self-Disclosure: Expanding the Comfort Zone." *Psychotherapy: Theory, Research, Practice, Training* 38, no. 1 (2001): 21–30.

Risser, Heather J., Melanie D. Hetzel-Riggin, Cynthia J. Thomsen, and Thomas R. McCane. "PTSD as a Mediator of Sexual Revictimization: The Role of Reexperiencing, Avoidance and Arousal Symptoms." *Journal of Traumatic Stress* 19, no. 5 (2006): 687–98.

Rogers, Carl R. *A Way of Being*. New York: Houghton Mifflin, 1980.

———. *On Becoming a Person: A Therapist's View of Psychotherapy*. New York: Houghton Mifflin, 1994.

Rothschild, Babette. *The Body Remembers: The Psychophysiology of Trauma and Trauma Treatment*. New York: W. W. Norton & Company, 2000.

Ruscio, Ayelet Meron. "Predicting the Child-Rearing Practices of Mothers Sexually Abused in Childhood." *Child Abuse & Neglect* 25, no. 3 (2001): 369–87.

Saltzberg, Marjorie. "Parenting Challenges for Women with Abuse Histories." *Journal of Feminist Family Therapy* 12, no. 1 (2000): 45–48.

Schuetze, Pamela, and Rina Das Eiden. "The Relationship between Sexual Abuse during Childhood and Parenting Outcomes: Modeling Direct and Indirect Pathways." *Child Abuse & Neglect* 29, no. 6 (2005): 645–59.

Semega, Jessica L., Kayal R. Fontenot, and Melissa A. Kollar. "US Census Bureau, Current Population Reports, P60-259, Income and Poverty in the United States: 2016." Washington, DC: US Government Printing Office, 2017.

Sosin, Michael. R. "Negotiating Case Decisions in Substance Abuse Managed Care." *Journal of Health and Social Behavior* 43, no. 3 (2002): 277–95.

Steele, Howard, Jordan Bate, Miriam Steele, Kerri Danskin, Hannah Knafo, Adella Nikitiades, Shanta Rishi Dube, Karen Bonuck, Paul Meissner, and Anne Murphy. "Adverse Childhood Experiences, Poverty, and Parenting Stress." *Canadian Journal of Behavioural Science* 48, no. 1 (2016): 32–38.

Stern, Donnel B. *Partners in Thought: Working with Unformulated Experience, Disassociation, and Enactment.* New York: Routledge, 2010.

Summit, Ronald C. "The Child Abuse Accommodation Syndrome." *Child Abuse & Neglect* 7, (1983): 177–93.

US Census Bureau News. *Profile America Facts for Features.* Washington, DC: US Department of Commerce, 2012.

Valentine, Lanae, and Leslie L. Feinauer. "Resilience Factors Associated with Female Survivors of Childhood Sexual Abuse." *American Journal of Family Therapy* 21, no. 3 (1993): 216–24.

van der Kolk, Bessel A. *The Body Keeps the Score.* New York: Penguin Group, 2014.

van der Kolk, Bessel A., Alexander McFarlane, and Lars Weisaeth. *Traumatic Stress: The Effects of Overwhelming Experience on Mind, Body, and Society.* New York: Guilford Press, 1996.

Ware, Norma C., William S. Lachicotte, Suzanne R. Kirschner, Dharma E. Cortes, and Byron J. Good. "Clinician Experiences of Managed Mental Health Care: A Re-reading of the Threat." *Medical Anthropology Quarterly* 14, no. 1 (2000): 3–14.

Werner, Emmy, and Ruth S. Smith. *Overcoming the Odds: High-Risk Children from Birth to Adulthood.* New York: Cornell University Press, 1992.

Wright, Margaret O'Dougherty, Joan Fopma-Loy, and Stephanie Fischer. "Multidimensional Assessment of Resilience in Mothers Who are Child Sexual Abuse Survivors." *Child Abuse & Neglect* 29, no. 10 (2005): 1173–93.

Zielinski, David S. "Child Maltreatment and Adult Socioeconomic Well-Being." *Child Abuse & Neglect* 33, no. 10 (2009): 666–78.

INDEX

adverse childhood experiences (ACEs), 42–43; child abuse, 42; child neglect, 42; cigarette smoking, 43; health-risk-taking behaviors, 42–43; health outcomes, 41, 43; household challenges, 42; life expectancy, 42; obesity, 42–43; scores, 42

Alicia's story, 34–35

anorexia nervosa, 34

anxiety disorders, 31–32; fear, 31; anxiety, 31, 74–75; panic attacks, 32; agoraphobia, 33

assessing resiliency, 68, 69

attachment, 18, 52, 61, 69, 147–148, 161–162, 164, 170, 180; attunement, 76, 114, 115, 126, 148, 162, 167. *See* insecure attachment

autonomic nervous system (ANS), 167

betrayal, 14, 15, 17, 21, 113, 117

blame, 12, 17; internalized, 12; externalized, 12, 13

borderline personality disorder, 40–41; anger, 40; emptiness, 40; impulsivity, 41; self-injury, 41; splitting, 40; suicide, 41; terror, 40; worthlessness, 40

Bowlby, John, 180

bulimia nervosa, 35; binging, 35; purging, 35

child care, 91, 176–177; after-school care, 176; day care, 176; protective factor, 176–177

child sexual abuse, 9; definition, 9; overt, 9; covert, 10; legal, 10; prevalence, 10

Chloe's story, 115–117

Claire's story, 56–60

Clara's story, 134–145

client as object, 127, 128

collaboration, 124–125, 130; egalitarian, 124; personal power, 124–125

complex trauma, 21

complicated grief, 43–44

compulsive and emotional eating, 36

congruency in communication, 126–128; body language, 126–127; tone of voice, 126–127

defensive behaviors, 31, 91, 150, 151–152, 170

defense mechanisms, 6, 146; denial, 6, 21; dissociation, 6, 21–22, 150; numbing, 6, 22, 27, 38, 76, 150, 152; repression, 6, 21, 22, 146, 172, 173; fantasy, 21, 22

depression, 26–27, 73–75, 77; suicide ideation, 27; sleep, 27; weight, 27

discipline, 77–80; following through on consequences, 79–80, 91; harsh discipline, 77, 79; overprotective, 78, 79, 91; permissive, 77–79; setting boundaries, 78–79

domestic violence, 77, 87, 150, 160

early intervention, 162
economic costs of maltreatment, 181
empathy, 114, 115, 123, 146
Emily's story, 68–69
employment and training, 177

Fatima's story, 62–63
fears associated with mothering, 80–82;
    children will be sexually abused,
    80–81, 82; lack of trust, 80, 81, 91
feelings, 172–174; connecting with, 173;
    erroneous beliefs about, 173;
    expression of, 172; fears of, 172;
    identifying, 174; regulation, 171
Fellitti, Victor, 42, 43, 156. *See* adverse
    childhood experiences
feminization of poverty, 157, 175, 177
fight/flight/freeze, 170–171. *See* polyvagal
    theory
financial instability, 89–90, 92, 175–176;
    low-wage work, 175; pink collar jobs,
    175; policy, 176; stress, 89
Fraiberg, Selma, 146
functional adequacy, 69

generalized anxiety, 33
grief and bereavement, 21, 43, 44, 44–45,
    54, 148
group therapy, 22, 121–122, 161, 165;
    child rearing skills, 161;
    communication skills, 161; de-
    escalating conflict, 165; mutual
    support, 122; personal power, 122;
    reciprocal relationships, 122;
    regulating emotions, 165; resiliency,
    121, 122; social support, 121, 130;
    sustaining relationships, 165

health outcomes and disease, 41, 42–43,
    149, 169; auto-immune disease, 43, 47;
    cancer, 43; diabetes, 43; obesity,
    42–43; substance use, 39–40, 42, 55,
    152, 159, 160
hypothalamus-pituitary-adrenal cortex
    (HPA), 168–169

impoverished communities, 148,
    149–150, 157, 169; lack of supportive
    services, 149; mental health concerns,
    149; violence, 149
insecure attachment, 53, 157;
    consequences, 147–148; prolonged
    stress, 147–148
intergenerational transmission process,
    146, 147, 156; intergenerational cycle
    of abuse, 120; intrapsychic dynamics,
    146–148; poverty, 148–153; risk
    factors, 153–156
interview process, 128; questions, 128;
    objectification of clients, 127–128
intimacy, 29

Katz, Mark, 66

lack of external supports, 84; absent
    fathers, 86, 92; limited family contacts,
    84–85; single mothering, 80; strained
    relationships, 84–85, 92
Laura's story, 29–30, 44, 45
learned helplessness, 150
long-term mental health consequences of
    abuse, 21, 23, 160; anxiety disorders,
    31–32, 33; borderline personality
    disorder, 40–41; depression, 26–27;
    eating disorders, 34, 35–36; post-
    traumatic stress disorder, 28–29, 31;
    shame and isolation, 23; substance use
    disorders, 39–40

Madison's story, 10–11
Maggie's story, 36–38
Mary's story, 32–33
mental health and treatment time limits,
    178–179; long-term treatment, 178,
    179; managed care, 178, 179; short-
    term treatment, 178–179. *See* long-
    term consequences of abuse
Miller, Alice, 166
mind/body/feeling connection, 166, 167
mind/body therapies, 170–171; working
    with fight/flight/freeze responses,
    170–171
mothering and resilience, 93; Alcoholics
    Anonymous (AA), 103–104; education,
    101–102, 111; extended family, 93,

96–99, 110; friends, 94, 99–101, 110; protective factors, 93, 110; spirituality and religion, 94, 103–106, 110

mothering risks, 71–72; difficulties, 5, 6; flashbacks, 75; lack of emotional connection, 76, 77; mental health concerns, 73–75, 91; negative perceptions of self, 72–73; physical and emotional caregiving, 75–76, 91; role reversal, 76. *See* poverty

multiple responsibilities, 88–89, 92; limited energy, 88, 89, 90; stress, 88, 89, 89–90

non-offending parent, 18

Nora's story, 7–8

parenting education, 161–164; developmental stages, 161, 163

parasympathetic nervous system (PNS), 167, 167–168

perpetrators, 10, 12, 14–15, 17, 18, 53, 84, 113, 125, 127, 151, 167–168, 172

persistent depression, 27

polyvagal theory, 167–169; autonomic nervous system (ANS), 167; dorsal vagal complex (DVC), 167; fight/flight response, 167, 170–171; freeze-immobile response, 168, 170–171; hypothalamus-pituitary-adrenal cortex (HPA), 168–169; neuroception, 167; parasympathetic nervous system (PNS), 167, 167–168; social engagement system (SES), 167; sympatho-adrenomedullary (SAM), 168–169; sympathetic nervous system (SNS), 167, 168–169, 170; vagal brake, 58; ventral vagal complex (VVC), 58, 168

Porges, Stephen, 167. *See* polyvagal theory

posttraumatic stress disorder, 28–29; avoidance, 28; flashbacks, 28; flooding, 29; hypersensitivity, 31; intimacy, 29; sleep problems, 28; startle responses, 28

poverty, 51, 53, 58, 69, 89, 133, 146; chronic poverty, 148, 153; federal poverty level, 148; homelessness, 150;

learned helplessness, 150; maternal stressors, 148, 152–153; mental health and, 149; physical health and, 169; poverty-related trauma, 148–153, 175; re-victimization and, 150; self-appraisal and, 72, 148; sexual abuse and, 148, 149, 152, 157

prevention services, 134

protective factors, 8, 159; definition, 49; public policies, 180–181; relationship building, 180; social supports, 180; strategies, 179

protective factors/community and school, 65; religion/spirituality, 67; school, 66–67; teachers, 66

protective factors/family, 61; caring relationships, 61, 64–65; parental involvement, 61; predictability, 62; secure attachment, 61

protective factors/individual, 60–61; intelligence, 60, 61; social competence, 61; talent, 61; temperament, 60

reciprocal relationships, 122, 130, 165; resiliency, 122; self-confidence, 122

religious and spiritual supports, 166. *See* protective factors/community and school

repetition of abuse, 146; unresolved trauma, 146–147, 148. *See* intergenerational transmission process

resiliency, 49–50, 159; definition, 49–50, 69

re-victimization, 13, 15, 55, 148, 150, 152; dissociation, 150; hyper-arousal, 152; hypo-arousal, 150; mental health, 157; passivity, 151; poverty, 157; substance use, 152

risk factors, 50–51; defined, 49

risk factors/community school, 55; lack of structure, 55; peer, 55; school, 55; substance use, 55

risk factors/family, 52–55; abuse, 52; authoritarian, 53; divorce, 52, 54–55; grooming by perpetrator, 53; isolation, 53; neglect, 52; permissive, 52; poverty, 53, 153; single parenting, 53; substance abuse, 52; victimization, 53

risk factors/individual, 51; disability, 51, 52; individual, 51; poverty, 51; temperament, 51–52
Rogers, Carl, 114, 127

secrets, 15, 25; impact of disclosure, 17
self-disclosure as a clinical tool, 125–126; conditions for use, 126; definition, 125; humanize relationships, 126
self-harm, 45–46; flashbacks, 45; traumatic memories, 46
self-perception, 22, 26, 36, 174; in mothering, 72
shame, 18, 23
significant relationships, 164–165; extended family, 162; friends, 166; grandparents, 164; husbands and life partners, 164–165; protective factors, 162. *See* protective factors/family
social services, 154–156; inadequate practices, 154, 156; limited funding, 154, 156; time-limits, 154, 155, 156
somatic therapy, 171
Sonja's story, 24–26
Sophia's story, 16
strategies used to protect children, 83–84, 91; educate children about body, 83–84; open communication, 84
stress and the body, 41–43, 169. *See* polyvagal theory
substance use, 39–40, 152; alcohol, 39; coping strategy, 39; impaired control, 39; social impairment, 39; tolerance, 39; treatment with survivors, 40; withdrawal, 39

sympatho-adrenomedullary (SAM), 168–169
sympathetic nervous system (SNS), 167, 168–169, 170
Summit, Roland, 14
supporting therapeutic alliance, 123–128; consistency, 124; rapport, 123; techniques, 123

therapeutic relationship and alliance, 113–115, 160; active process, 115; attunement, 114, 118; characteristics, 160; empathy, 115; impact, 160; modeling, 118–119, 119–120, 160; trust, 115
therapeutic role, 114, 118; corrective experience, 118, 120, 130; healthy relationships, 118, 119–120; low self-esteem, 121; resiliency and, 114, 118, 130; skill training, 119, 120
training and supervision, 128–129; increase effectiveness, 128–129; supervision, 129
trauma and the nervous system, 167–169. *See* polyvagal theory
traumatic factors, 11–12; age of child, 12; frequency and severity, 13–14; relationship to perpetrator, 14–15; reactions after disclosure, 17–18
trust concerns and relationships, 14, 15, 23, 62, 65, 80–82, 84, 115, 165, 170

vigilant mothering, 82–83, 91; close monitoring, 82–83; overprotection, 82

ABOUT THE AUTHOR

Teresa Gil, PhD, is a full professor and teaches courses in psychology and social work. She has also worked as a psychotherapist and trainer for more than twenty-five years. Her practice and clinical focus has been working with women with histories of child abuse and trauma. She is also a trainer and consultant in human service settings, and has developed and facilitated workshops at conferences designed to provide helping professionals and child welfare staff with the knowledge and skills necessary to help assess and respond to families in crisis.